A CIRCLE OF LOVE

A CIRCLE OF LOVE

DAILY DEVOTIONS FOR PARENTS

Laura Brown, Guy Chandler, Jane Swindell

A JANET THOMA BOOK

THOMAS NELSON PUBLISHERS
Nashville

Published in Nashville, Tennessee, by Thomas Nelson, Inc.,
and distributed in Canada by Lawson Falle, Ltd., Cambridge,
Ontario.

Scripture quotations are from the NEW KING JAMES
VERSION of the Bible. Copyright © 1979, 1980, 1982,
Thomas Nelson, Inc., Publishers.

Library of Congress Cataloging-in-Publication Data

92–50833
ISBN: 0-8407-4561-3

Printed in the United States of America
1 2 3 4 5 — 97 96 95 94 93

Introduction

*T*here is no doubt in our minds that the family is the single most important entity that exists in our society today. It is the bloodline that sustains the body of our nation, and indeed our world. As the family goes, so goes our world. We also recognize that the childhood and teenage years are the most important, and yet the most difficult, years to live. Full of changes, pressures, and complexities, these years are often harsh and unforgiving. During these years our children need and deserve our protection, guidance, and understanding for they truly are precious gifts from our heavenly Father.

It is with these presumptions that we began this endeavor to in part address your needs as parents as you undertake perhaps the most crucial task possible—to teach, correct, love, and relate to your children. We hope to focus *daily* on the importance of proper parenting based on Truth that will not return void (see Isa. 55:11).

May we together grow in our understanding of God's truths, His character, and how He relates to us to find insight into principles of godly parenting. And may these daily devotions inspire and encourage us to train up our children in the way they should go, so that when they are old they will not depart from it (see Prov. 22:6).

In His Love,

Guy, Jane, and Laura

THE PAIN OF CHILDBEARING

To the woman He said:
"I will greatly multiply
your sorrow and your conception;
In pain you shall bring forth children."
—GEN. 3:16

*T*he mother of eight children was asked about her toil as a parent. She replied in a beautiful southern drawl, "I'm always tard 'cause I'm workin' hard!"

To say parenthood is difficult is an understatement. It's hard work! A partial job description reads: to nurture, provide, sacrifice, listen, discipline, teach, protect, bandage, understand, transport, forgive, guide, and separate from our children. And we must do so with no pay, no appreciation, and no complaining!

Many have said the pain of childbearing includes the entire process of parenting. It is one of the most difficult and challenging adventures we'll ever undertake. Even when our children are grown, we may continue the adventure being exalted to the position of "grand" parent. But we have a mighty Resource to help us with the hard work of parenting. Jesus said if we ask for help we will receive it. "Come to Me, all you who labor and are heavy laden, and I will give you rest. . . . For My yoke is easy" (Matt. 11:28,30). We still have a yoke to bear on our journey, but it will be easier with God's help.

▼ *Thank You, Lord, for Your perfect provision. I trust that You are always with me on my journey.*

GC

OPTIONS

*And He said to them, "Follow Me, and I will
make you fishers of men."*
—MATT. 4:19

*W*hat are you going to be when you grow up? People
begin asking that question when a child is still in elementary school. The answer changes as quickly as the
weather. Toward the end of high school, there is a big
push to come up with the final decision.

I once knew a man who was in his thirties. He was a
very successful architect. He also was an amateur pilot,
but flying was what he enjoyed most. Secretly he toyed
with the idea of making a career of flying and giving up
architecture. A friend asked him when he had decided
to be an architect. He said that he had made the decision when he was seventeen and a senior in high school.
His friend replied, "You mean you are going to let a
seventeen-year-old boy tell you what to do with the rest
of your life?"

Healthy people are willing to keep all their options
open and to give themselves the freedom to move in any
direction. Remember Peter started a fisherman and
ended up an apostle. He never could have done that
without his willingness to consider the options.

▼ *Dear Father, make my child aware of his strengths
and his weaknesses.*

JS

ENDURANCE

Praying always with all prayer and
supplication in the Spirit, being watchful to
this end with all perseverance and
supplication for all the saints.

—EPH. 6:18

*W*ow! As fathers and mothers do we need endurance! Whether at home or at a job, we *are* working. Help! Being single with kids. Help! Sometimes just being a parent. Help! All you moms or dads with young ones who kept you up late last night or woke you up four to six times raise your hand. I bet a lot of you did.

Last night my five-month-old decided to have a party at 4 A.M. For the next three hours he was wide awake, laughing, cooing, and eager to do anything but sleep. Then at 7:30 A.M. when he was finally ready to go back to sleep, guess who was up and ready for the day—his big two-year-old brother.

Parents really need to learn how to persevere. When we lack the strength and energy we need, we can always ask God to give us an extra boost. It reminds me of my old long distance running days when I learned to run eight miles. How? By pacing myself and praying a lot! Unlike running, parenting is a full-time job. But whether it be part-time running or full-time parenting, pacing myself and praying—a lot—are still the keys.

▼ *God, please give me the strength and endurance I*
need, one step at a time, to keep up with my kids.

LB

GET ALL THE FACTS

*"And when he flees to one of those cities, . . .
and declares his case in the hearing of the
elders of that city, they shall take him into
the city as one of them, and give him a
place, that he may dwell among them."*
—JOSH. 20:4

*W*hat was your reaction when your child broke that beautiful vase that used to sit on the mantle, or when your teenager had an accident with your car?

Feelings of disappointment, anger, or fear would be common. But it's what you do with those emotions that is critical. You might feel the urge to lash out in anger. Maybe dole out a good hearty punishment to fit the crime. Or, as today's Scripture suggests, you might choose to hear your child's story and get all the facts.

There is a difference between how intentional and unintentional infractions should be handled. It was important even in Joshua's day to have the rights of the accused protected. The Lord told Joshua to appoint cities of refuge where the accused could flee to avoid anyone who might take vengeance before the case came before the congregation.

In our own families, we must always consider the facts surrounding the infraction. Was the vase broken because of a clumsy hand, or was it broken by a game of football in the house?

▼ *Dear God, teach me Your wisdom in handling difficulties in my own household.*

GC

THE CART BEFORE THE HORSE

*Now the body is not for sexual immorality but
for the Lord, and the Lord for the body.*
—1 COR. 6:13

For years, I thought the reason sex before marriage
was a sin was because God said so. Then one day I
realized the reason God said it was a sin was because it
doesn't work.

Reese was in counseling because she and her husband were having serious marital problems. She had a
history of numerous sexual relationships prior to marriage. This was her second marriage, and she was concerned that he was drifting away. She was lonely.

As she talked about the relationship, Reese told me
there was no intimacy and very little trust. I explained
that was because they got the cart before the horse.
They began their relationship with sex rather than with
commitment (marriage) followed by sex. They left out
the important part of building trust and sharing intimacy.

Sex is the most intimate act possible, but only if the
groundwork of trust and sharing are achieved first. The
natural next step in intimacy is the commitment to protect and cherish each other. Then sex can be the beautiful act God intended.

▼ *Dear Lord, enhance my intimacy with You and with
my mate.*

JS

TRUST

*Trust in the LORD with all your heart,
And lean not on your own
understanding.* —PROV. 3:5

*T*rust—it's one of the hardest things we do. Trusting ourselves, trusting our mates, trusting our kids, hopefully learning how to trust God.

Our faith was tested when our first child was eight months old. He seemed to choke trying to swallow a mushed up bean. When he had difficulty breathing, we rushed him to the hospital where he ended up in emergency surgery. He seemed okay when he came home from his hospital stay, but soon he again had a tough time breathing. My husband had to trust my judgment as we brought him back to the hospital. I had to trust God to heal my child of pneumonia and croup.

We made it through those two weeks but it wasn't easy. Stress was high, especially when my husband at first questioned if it was really necessary to go back to the hospital.

Husbands and wives don't always agree. We often come from different families with different backgrounds. No wonder there is tension. How do *we* discipline? What should *we* do? The answers are not simple. The most important thing is that *we* talk to each other and God. We will find the answers, and our trust in one another and the Lord will grow.

 God, help me to trust You to take care of us.

LB

WAR

*On the seventh day ... they rose early, ...
and marched around the city seven times in
the same manner. ... And the seventh time
it was so, when the priests blew the trumpets,
that Joshua said to the people: "Shout, for
the LORD has given you the city!"*
—JOSH. 6:15–16

𝒰nfortunately, many families consider their household a battleground. A battle of the wills. A conflict of personalities. Skirmishes between two opposing opinions. Conflict is common in any household; but all too often it becomes frequent, long lasting, and intense. Passive aggressive actions become not so passive behavior. Attacking, hurtful comments become attacking, hurtful blows. "War" is declared.

It's interesting that when God promised to give Jericho to the sons of Israel, He did not ask them to take the city by force. He told them to march around the city for six days, and on the seventh day to march around the city seven times. What a test of faith and perseverance.

When we give our family battles to the Lord, we shouldn't be surprised if He asks us to do something other than fight back.

▼ *Help me, God, to do all I can to resolve conflicts in my home. Help me to shout praises to You rather than shout at my children!*

GC

CURFEWS

*"Honor your father and your mother, that
your days may be long upon the land which
the LORD your God is giving you."*
—EX. 20:12

*C*inderella returned to poverty at midnight. Many times that is the curfew set for teens. It's never late enough. Ten minutes later is much better.

In our household there were never curfews. Each time our teens went out, we set a reasonable time for them to return home. They knew they were expected to be home by then or to call. Sometimes they were expected home by ten. Other times, depending on the activity, it was later. Very few times did they disappoint our trust in them.

We also functioned under the same guidelines and made every effort to return at the promised time. Our point was made abundantly clear one evening when we arrived home an hour later than the designated time. Our teens were frantic that something happened to us. After that they were more considerate. Curfews, like other responsibilities, are directly dependent on maturity. As our children are able to handle less restrictions, then it makes sense to ease up on the rules.

▼ *Dear Father, help me prepare my child for adult responsibilities.*

JS

SACRIFICE

*For to this you were called, because Christ
also suffered for us, leaving us an example,
that you should follow His steps.*
—1 PETER 2:21

 $\mathcal{O}$ ne thing we hear over and over again is, "Kids are such a sacrifice." Sometimes we hear added, "But they're worth it." I think we add this so we won't feel guilty about what we first said. But saying it doesn't make it any easier. Raising children is a tough job.

Remember the days you used to hop in the car and just go? I barely do. Now with kids, we don't just run to the car and hop in. What about those car seats? And don't forget the diaper bag and, oh yes, the stroller, bottles, snacks, and a towel for the spills. After awhile you feel like a walking baby store.

And sleep? I remember when sleep was no big deal, but now if I get four to six hours straight, I feel I've just been given a great luxury and a time of missed peace.

When I'm having a difficult day, it helps me to remember how much God sacrificed for us. I suspect I have only a small idea of how much it cost Him when Jesus went to the cross. God and Jesus thought we were worth the sacrifice. May we understand how much our children are worth the sacrifices we may need to make.

▼ *God, thank You for sacrificing Jesus. Jesus, thank
You for suffering for me. Help me to be willing to
sacrifice for my children.*

LB

REWARDS

*Whatever you do, do it heartily, as to the
Lord and not to men, knowing that from the
Lord you will receive the reward of the
inheritance; for you serve the Lord Christ.*
                    —COL. 3:23–24

A young lady leaving for college wrote the following
to her parents: "Thanks, Mom and Dad, for all that
you've done for me. You have done so much, and I can
honestly say that both of you have been my inspiration
and my comfort through so many trials. . . ."

It would be nice if we could feel appreciated by our
children every day, or at least once a year or so! It would
be nice to receive a thank you for the sacrifices we make
and the inconveniences we experience. Maybe someday they will write us a letter of thanks, but better yet
will be the reward of seeing them grow up to be fine,
upstanding citizens.

But if we are normal, we need encouragement frequently. That's why it's important to know where to turn.
We can't expect to be affirmed by our children. Rather,
we need to look to our spouse, friends, books, or support groups. Most importantly, we need to look to God.
He knows all the missed naps, aching muscles, and
Christmas Eves we stayed up half the night putting not
so simple toys together! And He will reward us.

▼ *Lord, I want to do all things for You. Give me the
strength and encouragement I need.*

                                                    GC

ABANDONING THE FAITH?

Work out your own salvation with fear and trembling.
                                    —PHIL. 2:12

"*J*esus Loves Me" is probably the first Christian song children learn. They are ready to believe the words just because their parents say so. They don't think a whole lot about the theology. But as they reach adolescence, it's time for them to re-examine their faith to determine if their parents are correct.

A preacher once said there are no second generation Christians. Everyone has to accept Christ for themselves. That's why adolescents have lots of questions. The secular world encourages them to ask even more questions when new theories and ideas are introduced. The first several years of college present the final challenges. After that, they begin to incorporate their faith into the proper place in their world.

Parents get upset over this process feeling their children are abandoning the faith. But it is necessary for them to develop a lasting faith of their own. The religious training and background we give our children will greatly influence their mature faith. This is part of letting them grow up to be their own person. We have a valuable tool to help the process. It's called intercessory prayer.

▼ *Dear Father, mold my children into the mature Christians You want them to be and perpetuate the faith within them.*

JS

ANGER IS A FEELING

*"Be angry, and do not sin": do not let the
sun go down on your wrath.*

—EPH. 4:26

*F*or some reason our society seems to say, "Anger is not okay. Don't feel it. Just blow it off or stuff it away." Although we may try, we just can't slough off our emotions. They are a gift of God's creation that we need to learn to handle in healthy ways.

My son has entered the terrible twos. One of the toughest things a two-year-old needs to learn is how to express anger. And guess who is teaching our children? Monkey-see, monkey-do. Do you want to know how you express your anger? Watch your children. They have a way of mirroring back our behavior in ways that may make us uncomfortable.

One day my two-year-old was playing with his toys when he dropped several. Frustrated, he blurted out a word that might be considered cussing. But the way he said it was odd, as if it was his phrase for dropping things. After explaining to him a better word, I asked myself, *Where did he learn how to say that?* The next day I dropped a glass. It broke on the floor. Guess what came out of my mouth? Since our children learn from us in so many ways, we need to learn how to be angry but not sin.

▼ *Lord, help me not to let the sun go down on my anger.*

LB

CONTROL

*And when they ran out of wine, the mother of
Jesus said to Him, "They have no wine."
Jesus said to her, "Woman, what does your
concern have to do with Me? My hour has not
yet come." His mother said to the servants,
"Whatever He says to you, do it."*
—JOHN 2:3–5

*E*very young person journeys through "rites of passages" en route to adulthood. If we try to control their lives, the process may be interrupted or hindered.

Intensely angry feelings result when teenagers feel controlled, even in small ways. When they don't know how to express their feelings, they may begin to act out, usually in a disrespectful or harmful manner.

In today's passage it appears Jesus' mother wants Him to do something about the wine, but she is subtly and indirectly attempting to control Him. Jesus knows He has reached that point in His ministry where no one can tell Him what to do. His mother has overstepped her boundary. She acknowledges this by giving *Him* the control when she says, "Whatever He says to you, do it."

Acknowledging the control (or choices) our children have can begin at a very early age. How are we helping our children be in control of their own lives? How are we helping them feel respected?

▼ *Thank You, Lord, for helping me to instill feelings of respect in my children by giving them choices.*

GC

NAME BRANDS

Now Israel loved Joseph more than all his children, because he was the son of his old age. Also he made him a tunic of many colors.

—GEN. 37:3

Guess what? *Guess* was the name in clothing—at least for a brief moment. It appeared on the waist bands of jeans and demanded a higher price tag. While it was *in*, it had a lot of clout. However, as soon as it was gone, another name was on the horizon.

Jan is an example of how these name brand clothes impact a teen's life. She insisted that her social standing would suffer greatly without some black, stone washed *Guess* jeans with an impressive price tag. Her parents, needing to make every dollar count, had problems justifying the price when there were other suitable jeans in their price range. They finally relented. Their daughter was immensely happy for several days. Then, as quickly as those jeans were a necessity, they were out of style.

Parent's need to teach their teens that if self-esteem is based on name brand clothes, it will be fleeting and short lived. More lasting qualities are responsible for their sense of importance and their acceptance by their peers. Friendliness, contentment with their lives, and involvement in other's lives will wear better than *Guess* jeans.

▼ *Dear Lord, enhance my children's self-esteem. Help them to realize that You created them and are well pleased.*

JS

TANTRUMS

See that no one renders evil for evil to
anyone, but always pursue what is good both
for yourselves and for all.

—1 THESS. 5:15

*M*y two-year-old used to bite. Whenever he and his best friend got together, my son would bite his friend. I'd feel about two inches tall when I got reports of the teeth marks. The message was clear. My son was angry about something, but for him—and me—to have good friends, I needed to help him learn how to get his anger out without hurting others.

It's not easy for a child who has just begun to learn to speak to use words instead of his teeth. That's why I think we need to show them more effective ways of expressing emotions. I've tried to show my child how to vent his anger on things he can't really hurt. Hitting a pillow or a doll is a safe way to show how you feel. After demonstrating this to him a few times, he finally got the idea. "I'm angry at you. No, don't do that," he says (sometimes yells) as he takes whatever he has and hits the chair or sofa.

As long as a child is not getting hurt, or hurting others, it's amazing how quickly a tantrum comes and goes, often shorter each time.

▼ *Dear Lord, help me to model my feelings in healthy ways. Teach me not only for my sake, but for my children's sake as well.*

LB

GOOD APPLES

For the unbelieving husband is sanctified by the wife, and the unbelieving wife is sanctified by the husband; otherwise your children would be unclean, but now they are holy.
　　　　　　　　　　　　　　—1 COR. 7:14

The adage "it only takes one bad apple to ruin the barrel" is certainly true. Just the fragrance of a rotten apple can infiltrate otherwise good tasting apples and ruin the entire bunch. What a miracle it would be if we could place just one delectably ripe apple into a barrel of bad ones and improve the whole barrel.

God places great importance on families and relationships. Although you may be the only believer in your family, you do not need to be overwhelmed in your role as the one who champions the cause of Christ. God will give you strength to influence your spouse and children in a positive way.

During the short time Jesus was here on earth, He had only a few close friends. But as He walked among the multitudes, many experienced the sweet fragrance of His truth. Many miracles were performed. Just as Jesus influenced others, so can you. Don't be a rotten apple. Be the apple of God's eye! Know that as a believer you can be the vessel through which miracles can occur.

▼ *Thank You, Lord, for the assurance that You will give me the strength I need to be Your witness to my family.*

　　　　　　　　　　　　　　　　　　　　　　　GC

REBELLION

"When I was a child, I spoke as a child, I understood as a child, I thought as a child; but when I became a man, I put away childish things." —1 COR. 13:11

The major job in a child's development is to learn to be completely dependent on his parents. This develops the basic trust needed to build relationships for the rest of his life. As soon as this dependency is complete, the next developmental goal is to become independent from his parents and to become self-sufficient.

Going to school is one of the first moves toward independence. The final thrust begins at junior high age when he questions everything he hears and challenges his parent's opinions and authority. He begins to think for himself.

The tool to gaining separateness is rebellion. Every teen has to rebel to break the dependency that binds him to his parents. Some families are more difficult to break out of than others, so the rebellion must be more dramatic like doing drugs or running away. Other families are less difficult and require only an unmade bed, a smart mouth, or a curfew violation.

Rebellion breaks up the family system enough to allow the teen to become a separate individual with thoughts, feelings, and opinions different from his parents. It's a painful but necessary process.

▼ *Dear heavenly Father, I want to let my child grow up into a healthy adult. Help me to stay out of the way.*

JS

JUDGMENT

*"Judge not, and you shall not be judged.
Condemn not, and you shall not be
condemned. Forgive, and you will be
forgiven."*
—LUKE 6:37

Last Sunday I saw a skit in church that helped me focus on how to be a good parent. It presented a typical scene of a frustrated mother versus a stubborn, disobedient teen. After their argument, the discouraged mother finally decided to talk to God. God replied with a strange question, "Who are you really following?"

The mother was baffled. "Lord, I don't mean to be rude," she said, "but my daughter is the problem—not me."

God asked again, "What about Me? Have you forgotten whom you follow? Do you do as I ask, or are you ignoring Me?"

Confused, she shouted out, "What about my rebellious daughter?"

It was quiet at first and then God spoke, "You can decide whether or not to stay on My path. Your daughter will look and eventually see."

▼ *Dear God, please open my eyes to see where I need to grow. Help me not to judge or condemn my children, but instead to love and forgive them as You love and forgive me.*

LB

ARE YOU FEELING NEGLECTED?

Love suffers long and is kind; love does not envy.
—1 COR. 13:4

*O*ftentimes our love for our spouses can become unfocused and entangled in selfish desires. This can be especially true when the first child in a family is born.

A newborn has special needs. Except for a few moments each day, they must have our constant undivided attention. This means the time we used to spend with our spouse is now spent with our baby. For some families this can be a ready gateway through which jealousy may enter.

Do you feel neglected by your husband or wife? If so, you need to talk openly about your feelings. Almost always the specific message underneath the feeling is, "I miss you and I love you." This message needs to be brought to the surface, discussed, and even nurtured.

Make time to ask one another some important questions: How have I expressed my love for you in the past? How can I show my love for you now? Are the ways I'm trying to show my love meeting your needs?

But remember, although it is healthy to get our needs met, it is not healthy to do so at the cost of someone else—especially the baby God gave to you. Selfishness leads to jealousy. Jealousy leads to resentment. And resentment will keep you from loving your spouse and your newborn in the way they need.

▼ *Please help me to be sensitive to each member's specific needs.*

GC

TEDDY BEARS

"It is to your advantage that I go away; for if I do not go away, the Helper will not come to you; but if I depart, I will send Him to you."
—JOHN 16:7

*T*eddy bears are wonderful creatures. They are meant for adults as well as children. They are nurturing and comforting. They fill up the spot that is feeling empty. Of course they have to be cuddly or they don't do the trick.

While working with adults who are in therapy because they were abused as children, sometimes I recommend buying a large cuddly teddy bear to carry and hold. This touches the childlike part of their personality. I have been surprised at how accessible this makes them. In order to understand better (and because I really like teddy bears), I bought one. I was surprised at how good it felt to hold it while watching TV. It has a magic of its own.

Parents have to give a lot to their children. They need to find ways to refill themselves. A little self-indulgence in the shape of a teddy bear might be just what is needed. See if a teddy bear makes a difference for you, especially when you are feeling vulnerable. How fortunate we are that teddy bears are fashionable. Someone knows we need something special.

▼ *Dear Lord, at times I feel childlike and vulnerable. That is when I need special care from You.*

JS

TAKING CARE OF YOURSELF

Jesus said to him, "'You shall love the LORD your God with all your heart, with all your soul, and with all your mind.' This is the first and great commandment. And the second is like it: 'You shall love your neighbor as yourself.'"

—MATT. 22:37–39

*I*n my profession there is a major theme I talk about all the time: "You have to take care of yourself first." Yet we as Christians are often taught to take care of others before we take care of ourselves. Should we really give and give and give?

When we study the Gospels, we see how the God-Man, Jesus, took care of Himself first. Even though hundreds were pawing at His clothes, Jesus took time to be alone with the Father. He took care of Himself first!

As a wife and mother, some days I have three boys tugging at my shirt-tails: a two-year-old, a three-month-old, and a thirty-six-year-old man! What time do I have to give to myself? I'm learning to make time every day to take a hot bath. As often as possible, I give myself some quiet time or go on a shopping spree. And when I don't do everything society expects me to do—clean the house, work, cook, look beautiful all the time—I try not to beat myself up.

▼ *Help me, Lord, to take good care of myself so I will have the strength I need to take care of those You have given to me.*

LB

ZEAL

For I bear them witness that they have a zeal for God, but not according to knowledge. For they being ignorant of God's righteousness, and seeking to establish their own righteousness, have not submitted to the righteousness of God. —ROM. 10:2-3

$\mathcal{I}$t's been said that practice makes perfect. More correctly it should be said that perfect practice makes perfect! In some things it is futility to put forth effort if we're not doing it right in the first place. The car we drive will not go faster if we are putting pressure on the clutch. Practicing our tennis stroke for hours with a baseball bat will not improve our tennis game.

To have zeal for God is a great thing. To desire for our children to know God is also a great thing. However, just wanting it does not necessarily mean it will happen even if we want it badly with a zeal that is unmatched. In fact, a misdirected zeal may do more harm than good.

The process by which our children come to know the Lord and learn about Him is as important as our zeal to see this happen. Pushing or forcing our rules and beliefs on our children can push them away, especially if they do not see us walking our talk. We need to pursue righteousness and persistently pray for our children. Remember that the prayers of the righteous will accomplish much.

▼ *Dear God, may my relationship with You be a real and meaningful example to my children.*

GC

MEMORIES

*For in that He Himself has suffered, being
tempted, He is able to aid those who are
tempted.*
                                    —HEB. 2:18

I understand. I've been there before." It's the kiss of
death in a conversation with any teenager. At that point
the conversation is over, punctuated by, "No you don't."
They're right. They want to talk about their problem
and their pain—not yours.

When my children were in junior high, it brought
back floods of memories from my youth. Suddenly I
remembered the insecurities, hurt feelings, and pain of
being thirteen. When they complained about problems
in school, I could feel the pain from years ago. I was
perplexed that my familiarity with their pain didn't improve our communication at all. My children were very
possessive of their pain. They had to work it out themselves, but I believe being in touch with my youthful
issues did give me a better perspective.

It's easy for parents to get so absorbed in adult problems that things like missing a phone call or not being
chosen to be a cheerleader seem insignificant. If we
take time to remember how important those issues were
to us when we were thirteen, it will help keep us in
touch with our teen. Probably the most reassuring
thought is that we survived and so will our teen.

▼ *Dear Lord, keep memories of my past fresh so I
don't get so bogged down in my responsibilities that
I lose perspective.*

                                                      JS

SOLOMON'S WISDOM

And God gave Solomon wisdom and exceedingly great understanding, and largeness of heart like the sand on the seashore.
—1 KINGS 4:29

$\mathcal{H}$ow many times as a parent have you said to yourself, *Okay, what do I do? Where's the book that tells me how to handle this?* Or you might ask, *Okay God, I need an answer and I need it in writing via express mail.*

Sometimes a song comes to my mind. One of the lines says, "God works in mysterious ways." Maybe that's why *I* can't figure it out! Oh, how I wish I had the gift of Solomon. I wish I had His knowledge and wisdom.

When I went back to work as a counselor, I had to ask myself, *Who can I trust to care for my three-month-old?* Since I work a lot with abuse victims, that was a hard question. I knew I needed God's wisdom. But God doesn't always send the answer via express mail. I sure wish He did. Life would be a lot easier, wouldn't it! I finally did get an answer in an unexpected way that only God could have arranged.

Like Solomon, we will be given wisdom if we ask for it. We just need to be open to the surprising ways God may be leading and patient to wait on His perfect timing.

 God, open my eyes to see where You are leading me.
LB

LETTING GO

"And I spoke to you at that time, saying: 'I alone am not able to bear you.'"

—DEUT. 1:9

*F*or most of us, being in charge or in control feels good. We may feel our way is best (and it may be), but like Moses, being in charge of everything is overwhelming, if not logistically impossible.

To construct and control our own small world would be an ingenious feat. Ingenious but alas impossible! Yet truth be known, many of us struggle with this very issue all of our lives. The serenity prayer is based upon this theme. Changing (controlling) that which we can, accepting that which we cannot, and having the wisdom to know the difference.

Some parents might argue that we must be in control of everything that happens in our families. But a wise parent knows it is better to make *final* decisions, not *first* decisions. We need to delegate responsibility to our children—to allow them to handle some things without our involvement or intrusion. Not only does it build trust, it gives us time to relax and enjoy our children, parenting, and life in general.

▼ *Lord help me to remember that when I try to catch every ball that is thrown, especially when they are thrown all at once, I may miss all of them.*

GC

INDIVIDUALITY

But solid food belongs to those who are of full age, that is, those who by reason of use have their senses exercised to discern both good and evil.
—HEB. 5:14

*I*ndividuality is a gift possessed by everyone equally. Each person has his own style of approaching life. At the same time, there is the law of human nature called conformity that urges everyone to be the same. Parenthood is the same. Some parents are easygoing and laid back. Others do it by the book. Just as in other areas of life, people are more successful when they embrace their individuality.

In therapy I saw a woman who had read every book, including the Bible, to learn how to parent her child. She took everyone's advice even though some was not very good. She tried everything to be the perfect parent except the one tool no one could give her. That was her ability to think and reason for herself—to be the unique parent she was equipped to be especially when she was empowered by God. When she began to depend on her own judgment, her decisions were more in line with what her children needed and they thrived.

We have to rely on our own judgment. That's how God enables us to parent in our own individual way and to help our children grow up to be the unique individuals they were meant to be.

▼ *Dear Lord, empower me to do the job of parenting in my own individual style.*

JS

WHO'S IN CHARGE HERE?

*"God resists the proud,
But gives grace to the humble."*
—JAMES 4:6

*W*ho is in control? You? God? Your kids? It's an important question to figure out. If we're the one in control, or worse yet our kids are in control, we are in for a roller coaster of a ride—so hold on!

The control issue really begins at birth. It becomes very obvious in the toddler and teenage years. My preschooler, for instance, attempts to be in control when he wants candy before dinner. He knows how to manipulate me. At times, to my chagrin, he succeeds.

Children are good at testing our limits. Sometimes we clearly have to stand firm for their own good. The world can be a very unsafe place for both a toddler and a teen. Other times we may need to bend some, recognizing that our child is growing up. We increasingly need to give him more freedom to prepare him for adult life.

Whether we stand firm or bend, we need to remember there is a fine line between being overly dominating parents, and being parents that let kids run things the way they see fit. The real key lies in letting God be in control of every part of our lives, every rise and fall. Then we can relax. With God in control the roller coaster is not nearly as bumpy.

▼ *Father, I humbly admit my need for You to be in control. Thank You for being such a good parent.*

LB

SEPARATING

*When they saw Him, they were amazed; and
His mother said to Him, "Son, why have You
done this to us? Look, Your father and I have
sought You anxiously."* —LUKE 2:48

*J*esus and His parents have gone up to Jerusalem for
the Feast of the Passover. His parents start home, and
Jesus stays behind without their knowledge. After a
day's travel, they realize He is not in the caravan. They
return to Jerusalem and anxiously search for Him. We
can almost hear the anger and fear in Mary's voice
when she finally finds Him. Likewise, we can almost
anticipate a somewhat defiant reply from Jesus. "Why
is it that you sought Me? Did you not know that I must
be about My Father's business?" (Luke 2:49).

Jesus is growing up. He is taking care of His Father's
business and separating from His family. Rather than a
passage about a mother and son arguing, this is a passage that reveals the importance of a mother letting go
and a son becoming more responsible.

Of course, to imply certain emotions within this his-
torically recorded mother-son dialogue may be pre-
sumptuous. Yet emotions such as fear and anger are
commonplace in scenarios involving our own families.
Every child will go through a separation process as they
grow older. Expect it. Learn from Mary's example. She
did not fight it. She, in fact, treasured it in her heart.

▼ *Help me to allow my children to grow up and to trust
that Your protection is sufficient.*

GC

LEARNING TO PLAY

*And Sarah said, "God has made me laugh,
so that all who hear will laugh with me."*
—GEN. 21:6

*I*n the day hospital where I work, one of the groups I lead is a play therapy group. For mentally ill adults, it is an effective treatment tool because many of them never learned to play. Others left play behind to go on to more important things. If they do play, it is with the attitude that they must break par on every round of golf. Blowing bubbles, jumping rope, and popping balloons bring on belly laughs from people mired down in their problems.

Parents need to relax and enjoy themselves first so they can enjoy their children. The child in you can meet your child and create a bond that will grow through the years. When children are little, they love to be teased and wrestled. When they grow into teens, they like to share jokes or play them on each other. Laughter is a precious commodity. Memories of laughing together help us through the tough times. Have fun with your children. Playfulness need not pass with youth. And it does wonders for life's stress.

▼ *Dear Lord, please don't let me forget how to laugh and have fun.*

JS

TIME-OUT

*Now no chastening seems to be joyful for the
present, but grievous; nevertheless, afterward
it yields the peaceable fruit of righteousness
to those who have been trained by it.*
—HEB. 12:11

The other day my two-year-old got into my lipstick. He
got it everywhere. His face, his hands, his clothes, his
hair, and the furniture. He and the house were all
"made-up." I had no sooner cleaned him up, than I
caught him up on the kitchen table "playing" in the
sugar bowl. Sugar crunched under my feet as I cleaned
up yet another mess. Suddenly the baby began to wail.
My frustrated and frustrating two-year-old had decided
to shake the baby. You ask yourself who is in control?

Children need to learn what is safe and what is not.
It is our job to help them by setting limits. So after talking with God and my husband, I set some limits for my
son. Getting down to his eye level I said, "Pushing your
brother is not okay. You will get time-out." I explained
time-out meant he would have to sit in a chair for three
minutes. Three minutes seems like an eternity to him
and seconds to me. But it's enough time for me to cool
down, and for him to know he's crossed the boundary
line. Discipline needs to begin as soon as our children
start testing the limits. It won't feel pleasant to them or
to us, but the results are worth the effort.

▼ *God, please give me wisdom to know how to discipline my child. Help me to understand his tests as a
search for safety as he explores his world.*

LB

VALIDATING

*Rejoice with those who rejoice, and weep
with those who weep.*   —ROM. 12:15

*C*an you remember a time when you were sad or depressed and you looked to someone for consolation? Whom did you seek out? Someone gleefully energetic or somberly understanding? Chances are you found someone who could relate to your circumstances and feelings.

We constantly need and strive for security in our lives. Part of that security is an attempt to attain "validation of experience." Knowing that what we feel and experience is normal. Counselors understand the importance of this. Most parents also know the importance of validating their children's emotions. How many times have you said to your child, "When I was your age, I felt the same way"?

Communicating to our children that we understand how they feel can be a powerful tool. It can build trust and confidence and bring us closer to our children. It can also, if we are not sensitive, close down communication with our children—especially with our teens. *I'm different,* they think. *Why can't they see that?* It is important to first share in their emotions and circumstances. Then the door may be wide open to share the wisdom of our own experience.

▼ *Dear God, help me to understand and validate my children's feelings. I pray that I might always give them permission to feel any emotion.*

GC

EXPECTATIONS

"A new commandment I give to you, that you love one another; as I have loved you, that you also love one another."
—JOHN 13:34

*A*mber was sixteen, a straight A student, a cheerleader, and a beauty queen—all to her mother's delight. She was compliant and never made waves. She was always smiling and cheerful, but never told anyone what she thought or felt. She was five foot six and weighed ninety-six pounds. This puzzled her parents because she had a healthy appetite. Soon it became apparent she was bulimic.

Sixteen-year-old girls are bundles of feelings. They have some ideas of their own about what they want. If they never dared to challenge their parents and express their thoughts and feelings, they may have never learned to accept themselves. When they feel critical of themselves, their bodies are the first thing to come under scrutiny.

Accepting your child unconditionally with a minimum of expectations enables them to accept themselves just the way they are. That's the way Jesus accepts us.

▼ *Dear Lord, keep my expectations to a minimum and help me to love my children as Christ loves me.*

JS

LONELINESS

Do not hide Your face from me in
the day of my trouble;
Incline Your ear to me;
In the day that I call, answer me
speedily. —PS. 102:2

One of the toughest parts of being a stay-at-home parent is loneliness. We may have plenty of kids and company, but still feel lonely. Whether we have one child or six running around, crying, and carrying on, we may feel exhausted and depressed. We may need to take a break, but that's not easy with infants and toddlers.

When my newborn finally arrived, I was flying high in the beginning. But after all of the grandparents left and friends stopped calling, the excitement wore off. I couldn't wait until my husband got home at night. You might call it postpartum depression. I call it loneliness and pain. My adult life felt like a lost world. I needed to find some time and people for myself. So I began to pray and to call old friends expressing my needs. I invited neighbors over. I took the baby to the park and made friends with parents of children the same age.

God does answer prayer. The system of self-care He led me to establish did help me to avoid further depression and loneliness. I was able to take better care of my baby as my own needs were met.

▼ *Thank You, God, for always being there when I'm feeling lonely and down. Help me to work through my feelings and to find Your answers.*

LB

IMPARTING WISDOM

Now Joshua the son of Nun was full of the spirit of wisdom, for Moses had laid his hands on him.   —DEUT. 34:9

$\mathcal{A}$ man walking down a country road came to a general store. There were two older gentlemen and a young boy sitting on the front walk. The passerby stopped and asked for directions to a faraway town. The first gentleman said the best way to go was by train. "It leaves in about one hour, and will take you direct to that town." The second gentleman disagreed. "Take the bus. It leaves in thirty minutes. You'll have to make two stops along the way but it's cheaper." Then the young boy spoke up. "My advice to you, mister, is to buy a soda pop and wait just a minute. My daddy is the owner of this store, and I know that every day about this time he drives to that town in our pickup truck. You can come along if you want." The youngster had the wisest counsel because, unlike the other two, he knew his father's routine. It was his relationship with his daddy that made him "wise" in this situation.

Joshua had the spirit of wisdom because of his relationship with Moses. So, too, it is by an ongoing, involved relationship that our children will acquire wisdom from us. Relate to your child. Impart wisdom.

▼ *Dear God, please show me how to have a deeper relationship with my children.*

GC

DATING

To everything there is a season,
A time for every purpose under heaven.
—ECCL. 3:1

*W*hen Shirley was in high school she had many friends, boys and girls alike, but she felt very unpopular because she didn't have a boyfriend. She missed out on the proms and special events. Shirley felt like a real failure—that she was the only one in high school with her problem. Twenty years later, she was surprised when her bright, appealing daughter showed little interest in high school dating. Not only that, but several of her daughter's friends also were not interested in dating. Shirley realized that high school dating does not necessarily have much to do with success or failure. The teens she observed were successful and productive. They just hadn't reached the point where dating was that important.

High school and dating go together. This is an accepted fact. Cheerleaders and football heros are classic folklore on every high school campus. But not all high school students date. Parents need to discard their preconceived ideas and accept their high schooler where they are. Dating will come whenever their teen is ready for it, and there is no need to rush things.

▼ *Dear Lord, give me patience to wait on my teens'*
timing as they develop and mature.

JS

FEAR NOT

"I, the LORD your God,
will hold your right hand,
Saying to you, 'Fear not,
I will help you.'"
—ISA. 41:13

*H*ave you made it a habit to bury Scripture in your heart? The above verse is an especially good one to memorize when you're pregnant. You may find yourself going back to it again and again.

When we are first expecting, we may have a lot of different fears—miscarriage, stillbirth, deformity, the impending pain of childbirth. But we don't have to stay bound to our worries and fears because God cares. He will always be with us. He will strengthen and help us.

You might worry about the medication or cold tablets you took before you realized you were pregnant. Did they hurt your baby? You might wonder and worry about how your child is developing in your womb. You want him to be born perfect, but there's so much you can't control. Yes, it helps to follow all of your doctor's advice. And it's important to eat well and to take care of yourself. But most of all you need to leave all your worrying to God. He is the One who is in control of shaping your baby from the moment of conception. Rest in His care and rejoice in being part of His miracle of creation.

▼ *Help me, Lord, to trust You and Your Word.*

LB

ALWAYS THERE

*"No man shall be able to stand before you all
the days of your life; as I was with Moses, so
I will be with you. I will not leave you nor
forsake you."*
　　　　　　　　　　　　　　—JOSH. 1:5

𝒜 high school football coach came to his team before their big game against the formidable crosstown
rival. After mustering up a few inspirational cliches, he
sent them onto the field. At halftime they were losing
24–0. "You worked hard during the first half," he told
them. "Now it's time for me to work hard with you."

Friday night the Fighting Gophers played their hearts
out and came back to win a last second thriller, 28–27.
The coach, in the post game interview, said to a city
reporter, "I told our young men they were losing because they had been outcoached. I studied the other
team and figured out their weakness. Then I made a
few changes in our game plan. I didn't give up and
neither did they. When we lose we are outcoached.
When we win it's because we have outplayed the other
team. Whatever the outcome, I always want them to
know I'm in there fighting with them." To have the confidence to achieve in life, our children need to know we
will always be there. We can't promise we'll always be
what they want us to be, but we can promise always to
try to do what is in their best interest.

▼ *Just as You never forsake me, help me always be
there for my children, fighting with them in their
battles.*

GC

QUIET RESTING PLACES

*My people will dwell in a peaceful
   habitation,
In secure dwellings,
   and in quiet resting places.*
          —ISA. 32:18

*C*hildren need security and tranquility. They need a safe place to grow and develop. If their home and family are not like that, many times they will look elsewhere. Safety from physical harm and emotional abuse are important in developing trust with people.

In a group therapy session, I asked people to envision the home in which they grew up. I asked them to think of the safest place in their home. I was surprised at the unexpected answers. Several people named a place outside their home—like a tree house or the garage. Others named secluded hiding places like a closet or a bathroom with the door closed and locked. I guess I expected they would name their bed or cuddling with their mother in a rocking chair.

What a shame! The one thing a child needs is safety, and they find it by hiding or avoiding their parents. Parents should be the "quiet resting place" who embrace their children and act as a shield to the world. Children need rest in their parents' arms knowing they are safe and loved no matter what happens.

▼ *Dear Lord, let me be a resting place for my children just as You are my resting place.*

JS

FATIGUE

*For I consider that the sufferings of this
present time are not worthy to be compared
with the glory which shall be revealed in us.*
—ROM. 8:18

*H*ow tired can a person become? In the first three
months of pregnancy you drag yourself around. Morning sickness may last all day and into the night. Maybe
you're not really sick. You just don't feel really good.
You don't feel like yourself.

By the second trimester you finally may be starting to
feel better. Then wham, the third trimester hits! You
can't sleep and yet you're exhausted. Perhaps it's because you can't get comfortable no matter which way
you roll. Or perhaps you and your child-to-be already
have your days and nights reversed. He may decide to
tumble and turn just as you collapse into bed and turn
off the light.

How well I remember my own pregnancies and can
empathize with all you pregnant moms out there. Again
I know the answer lies in turning our eyes on the Lord.
When insomnia sets in, pray. If you still can't sleep,
pray some more. Pray for the child growing within you.
Pray for the energy you need to get through each day.
Know that your struggles will seem like nothing compared to the wonder you'll experience as you hold your
newborn in your arms.

▼ *Dear Father, when I'm feeling exhausted, help me to
remember the glory soon to be revealed in the birthing of my child.*

LB

FAMILY DEVOTIONS

*"Again I say to you that if two of you agree
on earth concerning anything that they ask, it
will be done for them by My Father in
heaven."*
　　　　　　　　　　　　—MATT. 18:19

*O*ne of the most commonly asked questions is,
"Should I require my children to attend a family devotional time?" This is a difficult question. There is no greater opportunity to create a sense of belonging and closeness than coming before God as a family in Scripture reading, study, and prayer. But we know the usual outcome when we require a child to do something against his or her will.

How can we hold family devotions that are pleasant experiences and appealing to our children? Today's Scripture contains a beautiful truth. The purpose of gathering, in this case, was to pray and to lift petitions to God. Instead of using family devotional times to teach our children, why not try involving them in prayer. This puts everyone on an equal level. Listen to their prayers. You'll discover things you may not have known about them or about the simplicity of prayer.

Finally, when you do teach, be relational and practical, not religious and theological. Use illustrations that are easily understood and relevant to their lives. And don't do all the talking. You may be surprised how much you can learn from them.

▼ *Dear God, as I gather with my family, help me
always to respect my children and glorify You.*

　　　　　　　　　　　　　　　　　　　GC

THE FAMILY PHOTO ALBUM

"Remember the days of old,
Consider the years of many generations.
Ask your father, and he will show you;
Your elders, and they will tell you."
—DEUT. 32:7

$\mathcal{A}$t a baby shower, a mother with older children said how disappointed her third child was in looking through the family album and never finding any pictures of him alone. All the pictures were of the three children together. The mother realized her zeal of capturing the whole family left that child feeling less important than his brothers.

Pictures are important to children and their parents. They offer continuity and document history. Pictures record a child's growth and changing interests as well as their friends and family members. Some of the events, like winning second place in the Pinewood Derby, will be lost from the child's memory. But if Mom and Dad thought those events were important enough to photograph, they must have been important. Most of all, a pictorial history of each child says to them that they are important and loved.

▼ *Dear Lord, the Bible is full of recorded family history. Remind me to preserve my family's history with pictures.*

JS

RUNNING THE RACE

Let us lay aside every weight, and the sin which so easily ensnares us, and let us run with endurance the race that is set before us.
—HEB. 12:1

Strength doesn't come with only having a little sleep. Stay home with a two-year-old and a three-month-old and you'll be feeling lucky if you have enough energy and time to get your face washed.

Picture this. You hit the floor at 6 A.M., dress the kids, drop them off at the sitters, and make it to work—just on time. The pace doesn't slow down at work. Before you know it, it's time to pick up the kids, make dinner, survive bath and homework time, and finally crawl into bed.

It's the dailiness of the race that's what often gets to me. But when I choose to stay close to the Lord and to confess the sins that may be tripping me up, He does renew my strength. He gives me the endurance I need to run the race set before me.

▼ *Thank You, Lord, for all those mothers who have run the race before me who serve as godly role models. Help me to draw on the strength of their example and on You.*

LB

SIBLING RIVALRY

And it came to pass, when they were in the field, that Cain rose against Abel his brother and killed him.
—GEN. 4:8

*T*here are certain things that are inevitable—death, taxes, and jealousy among siblings! And just like death and taxes, jealousy and rivalry among siblings can be a very unpleasant experience for parents.

How does sibling rivalry become such a nightmare? All too easily we can be lured to handle jealousy by making futile attempts to balance the scales between siblings. When children sense what we're trying to do, they may become manipulative. They may easily learn, "If I cry 'Unfair!' loud enough, Mom and Dad will give me what I want." Suddenly, we are thrust into a position where our power and control are put to the test. Actually, it is our child that should be put to the test.

We need to listen to appropriately expressed feelings and focus on their behavior. Resist making quick concessions or compromising to ease feelings of jealousy. Allow them to deal with their own feelings and consider positive actions they can take. In today's Scripture, we see Cain's jealousy toward Abel. But God did not focus on Abel. His focus was on Cain. God put the responsibility back on Cain for his feelings and behavior. "If you do well, will you not be accepted? And if you do not do well, sin lies at the door" (Gen. 4:7).

▼ *Help me, Lord, not to ignore sibling rivalry. Show me how to be a fair and wise parent.*

GC

WE ALL MAKE MISTAKES

"I dwell in the high and holy place,
With him who has a contrite and humble spirit,
To revive the spirit of the humble,
And to revive the heart of the contrite ones."
—ISA. 57:15

*T*om's dad was quick to make decisions without getting all the facts. Often Tom would be grounded because of something his brother did or because his mom didn't tell him he was expected home early. His dad never changed his position even when all the facts came to light. Tom was extremely angry, especially at his father.

Jim's dad was different. He attempted to learn the facts and waited until he had time to think about it. Still there were times his judgment was faulty. When he recognized that he had made a mistake, he apologized. Because of his father's attitude, Jim could go to him when he made mistakes.

Parents don't need to be on pedestals. God is the only One who belongs there. We need to be just what we are—human beings who make mistakes and live to make still more mistakes. That's why we can understand when our children make mistakes. We can still love them, and they can still love us despite the mistakes we all will make.

▼ *Dear Lord, help me to say I'm sorry when I make a mistake.*

JS

PATIENCE

"Hear, O LORD, and have mercy on me;
LORD, be my helper!" —PS. 30:10

A mother of two sons, a two-year-old and an eight-month-old, said to me, "I wish I had more patience—right now!" Then she added, "Oh no, I really didn't mean that, because when you ask God for something, you usually get more than what you ask for."

With her droopy eyes, no makeup, and sloppy clothes, she didn't have to convince me her kids were getting to her. "It's so hard," she cried. "I'm always tired, and always wishing I had more patience with my children. They drive me crazy. They're always whining and wanting something. I never get to sit down. I'm constantly doing for one or the other. And they're always getting into something. What I really need is endurance . . . and a long vacation."

Raising children isn't easy. Good parenting requires a great deal of patience, strength, and energy. But it's important to remember that God is on our side. He is always there to help us. Don't be afraid to pray for patience and endurance. He will have mercy and help us. God knows our needs. All we have to do is ask.

▼ *Dear God, You know I want to be a good parent. Please give me the patience and endurance that I need.*

LB

GET SPECIFIC

*"Has the LORD as great delight
  in burnt offerings and sacrifices,
As in obeying the voice of the LORD?
Behold to obey is better than
  sacrifice,
And to heed than the fat of rams."*
—1 SAM. 15:22

*W*hen Steven's parents told him he could not go outside to play, his heart sank. His best friend had just bought the latest video game. He desperately wanted to play it. Suddenly he thought to himself, *They didn't say I couldn't go over to Jimmy's house and play inside.*

When it serves their purpose, children can be critical thinkers. Their little minds are scrutinizing what we say, just like we look for tax loopholes each year!

Today's Scripture contains a not so obvious truth that is just as poignant as the emphasis on the importance of obedience over sacrifice. Burnt offerings might have been pleasing to God, except that He made it clear what He wanted. He told Saul to destroy all the Amalekites owned and to "kill both man and woman, infant and nursing child, ox and sheep, camel and donkey" (1 Sam. 15:3). He left no room for misunderstanding.

We also need to make our expectations perfectly clear to our children. This doesn't mean we robotize them or leave no room for their own thinking. But we do need to get specific.

▼ *Lord, I want to communicate clearly and effectively. Please help me.*

GC

UNIQUE

And he [Jacob] blessed them; he blessed each one according to his own blessing.
—GEN. 49:28

*M*y children are so different you wouldn't believe they came from the same family. They didn't!

Each child is born into a uniquely different family from the others even if they have the same mother and father. When the oldest is born, there are three people in the family. The next child not only has a mother and father, but a sibling with which to have a relationship. By the time you get to number four, maybe eight years have passed. Dad is making more money, but traveling. Mom is running a car pool. Life is very different from the tranquility number one enjoyed. Add a few problems along the way like illness, the death of grandparents, and a move to a new city, and you have a vastly different family.

There is nothing good or bad about this scenario. It's just different for each child. Each child will be impacted differently and will develop his own special personality.

Aren't we lucky to have so many unique relationships within one family? No two are alike. There is no room for comparison or competition. Each family member has a special place in the world and makes a special contribution to the family.

▼ *Dear Lord, thank You for our family. Let us appreciate each person and his unique personality.*

JS

RESPONSIBILITY

How can a young man cleanse his way?
By taking heed according to Your word.
—PS. 119:9

$\mathcal{I}$ counsel children. Lots of times they are brought to me because they refuse to do what their parents want them to do. A stand off between the child and his parents often results. Everyone becomes angry and tries to push the other away.

Digging in one's heels and not budging starts at a very young age. We can all remember our children looking at us and saying, "No!" Remember how you felt at the end of the day after hearing your child say no more times than you had the energy to count? Sometimes you may have wanted to pull your hair out!

There is a solution. We need to start early by learning how to set rules. We also consistently need to reinforce the consequences when our children disobey. It helps to make this a joint effort with your spouse. It also helps to make the rules clear. If your children are old enough to understand, allow them to be part of drawing up a contract. When children are part of deciding the consequences when a rule is broken, they gain a healthy sense of responsibility and control.

▼ *God, give me the wisdom I need to guide my children in Your way. Help me to heed Your rules.*

LB

STAND FIRM

> *"Do not fear the reproach of*
> *men,*
> *Nor be afraid of their revilings."*
> —ISA. 51:7

A young mother brought her child to the grocery store. Her face revealed her anxiety.

Supermarkets are not fun places. There are too many aisles, too many packages for little hands to pull off shelves. Our gentle but firm requests to "put that back" are often ignored. Frantically we search our repertoire of tricks to divert attention. Should we avoid a scene by simply ignoring our child's behavior?

This particular young mother had successfully maneuvered through the supermarket aisles. She relaxed with a sigh as she stood in line to check out. Then it happened.

"Mommy! I want bubble gum!"

The mother became instantly aware of the eyes upon her. *What will others think if I give in? But what will they think if I don't give in and my child throws a tantrum?*

It's not easy to do what we know is best for our child when people are staring at us. But we need to stand firm even when it makes us feel uncomfortable.

▼ *Dear God, help me not to be afraid of what others think. Give me Your strength that I might be strong in the midst of pressure.*

GC

PROM NIGHT

> *"Now therefore, please be careful not to*
> *drink wine or similar drink."*
> —JUDG. 13:4

$\mathscr{P}$roms are the most important event in a school career. To some teens it is the measure of a successful high school career. It also is one of the most expensive and dangerous events in a student's life.

What happened to the high school gym decorated with balloons and crepe paper? Now a grand ballroom in a fancy hotel, a rented limousine, and formal wear are only the beginning. Dinner, breakfast, and a rented hotel suite are part of the picture. Punch laced with alcohol and after prom parties only add to the danger. Drunken drivers are the biggest hazard. This is followed by the frightening statistics that more girls lose their virginity on prom night than on any other night. So much for wholesome school sponsored activities!

What can a parent do to stem the tide of peer pressure? One possibility is to offer alternative plans before and after the prom that don't include liquor or sex. We know that fun and pleasure are not contingent on sex or alcohol. It's our job to make sure our teens learn that first hand. It could be fun for us too.

▼ *Dear Lord, help me be creative in solutions to problems.*

JS

INTIMACY

Do not deprive one another except with consent for a time. —1 COR. 7:5

If you have a young child, and especially if you are still nursing, you'll understand the following conversation.

Husband: "I miss you. You never touch me, or cuddle anymore. Is something wrong? Don't you care?" Wife: "I care, I'm just tired. Please don't push me right now."

Husband, perplexed, says to himself: *I haven't touched her in weeks.*

Woman says to herself: *I need a break. I've had enough of being touched by anybody today.*

There are times when mothers and wives are physically overstimulated. There are times her children may touch her constantly. They may want to be held, nursed, and carried constantly. Sometimes a woman may have very little time with no one in her lap! Her disinterest in intimacy with her husband may be hard for him to understand and accept, but it is common and understandable.

When our children are young, it's a good idea to try to spend some time alone each week with your spouse and take time for yourself. It can be a necessary and precious time of getting to know each other again.

▼ *Lord, help us to understand and respond to one another's needs.*

LB

DISCIPLINE

Now no chastening seems to be joyful for the present, but grievous; nevertheless, afterward it yields the peaceable fruit of righteousness to those who have been trained by it.
—HEB. 12:11

The young boy sat in the counselor's office and said, "If my parents say this is going to hurt us more than it's going to hurt them one more time, I'll barf!"

Many parents have a difficult time emotionally when it comes to disciplining their children. It hurts to see a child hurt. It especially hurts to see our own child feel uncomfortable. Problems begin when we avoid the necessary discipline in order to avoid our own emotional hurt. It becomes all too easy to ignore behavior or to allow for special circumstances to negate any meaningful consequences.

The culprit is our natural tendency to rationalize. We rationalize that our children are basically good, or that they know what they did was wrong. Therefore, we tell ourselves, there is no need to follow through with the consequences. But as the young man in the counselor's office might say, "Wrongo, dude!"

Even if it is unpleasant for us as parents, it is important to be consistent and to follow through when our children need to be disciplined. Administered in love, discipline will plant seeds of peace and righteousness.

▼ *Lord, help me to love my children enough to give them the discipline they need.*

GC

WHEN SCHOOL GRADES SLIP

If any of you lacks wisdom, let him ask of God, who gives to all liberally and without reproach, and it will be given to him.
—JAMES 1:5

$\mathcal{T}$ was working with a second grade student whose school work started slipping. He was depressed. He said he hated himself. His teacher reported a change in attitude. The more I learned about him, the more obvious it became that his school work was the problem causing his low self-esteem. Testing pinpointed a learning problem, and there were specific ways to handle the problem. Within a month, he was back on track. He now feels success instead of failure.

Grades can draw the battle lines between parents and children. They can become the measure of success and self-worth. But most children really want to make good grades. They usually strive in that direction until something interferes. Acceptable grades (A, B, and C) are expected performance. If the grades begin to slip, it is an indication that the child is having a problem that needs to be addressed.

Parents know their children and need to intervene whenever things aren't working. They are their children's best advocate because they are the ones who know and love them best.

▼ *Dear Lord, help me to look beyond the obvious and ascertain the underlying problems.*

JS

PUNISHMENT

*"For whom the LORD loves He chastens,
And scourges every son whom He
receives."*
—HEB. 12:6

A young mother threatened to "crack her child's bottom" when her daughter did something she didn't want her to do. Her ten-year-old daughter had been coming to me for therapy because she was extremely angry at her mom. And do we wonder why?

"Please don't spank your child this way anymore," I said to the mother. I proceeded to try to teach her healthy ways to discipline her daughter. God knows our inner thoughts and feelings. He understands our anger and frustration. However, God does not want us to take out our own anger on our children. God does want a person who cannot control her anger to seek help. Through counseling and prayer the vicious cycle of child abuse can be stopped.

Taking out anger on a child is not discipline, it is abuse. And it can be very unhealthy for the child who is forced to endure such abuse.

Does God abuse His kids? No! Neither should we.

▼ *Please help me, Lord, always to discipline my children in love.*

LB

RESPECT

*The fear of the LORD is the beginning of
knowledge,
But fools despise wisdom and instruction.*
—PROV. 1:7

*I*t is interesting that most surveys show the one thing fathers want most from their children is respect. I remember my father talking about the importance of respect in relationships. When Mom and Dad had their "discussions," Dad would later comfort me by saying, "It's all right to talk about anything as long as you respect each other." I grew to respect my father as I understood more about his character. He always respected those around him.

Even at an early age I learned that "the fear of the Lord" was not a cowardly or intimidating fear. It meant a healthy respect and reverence for God. What I learned much later was that as I studied and meditated on God's character, the more I revered Him. Of course, the more I respected my heavenly Father, the more I was drawn to Him. Godly wisdom followed.

We all desire our children to acquire wisdom. As they grow they will learn much from us. Do your children fear you or do they respect you? Begin the process of obtaining knowledge for your children. Allow them to relate to you and respect you. Let your character be known to them. Treat your children with respect.

▼ *Dear God, help me by my example to show my children what it means to fear You.*

GC

THEIR FIRST CAR

To give prudence to the simple,
To the young man knowledge and discretion.
—PROV. 1:4

*O*wning a car is an awesome responsibility. I especially feel that way when it won't start. I haven't the vaguest idea what to do. Immediately owning a car is no longer a convenience but a crisis.

When Bill's son turned fifteen, Bill decided he was going to prepare his son for owning and operating a car. He went to a used car lot and bought a fixable but poorly running car. The next year his son's job was to get the car in running order. They worked together repairing the car and learning how to maintain it. Of course his son had a vested interest because it would be his very own car. Pride exuded from both father and son when he took his driver's test in the car and passed. Their relationship was running smoothly.

This is not only a male rite of passage. It needs to become a female one also. Women spend as much time in cars as men. We need to know what to do when the car stops running. Cars are an exciting experience for teens. Therefore, that's the perfect time to capitalize on their interest by teaching them things that will serve them well the rest of their lives. Besides, they may be able to keep our inconvenience from becoming a crisis.

▼ *Dear Lord, show me creative ways to teach my teen about life and its responsibilities.*

JS

COMMUNICATION

. . . bearing with one another, and forgiving one another, if anyone has a complaint against another; even as Christ forgave you, so you also must do. But above all these things put on love. —COL. 3:13–14

*E*xhausted from the day at the office, I headed straight upstairs to change. Looking through the window, I saw my two-year-old playing out front by the street. Angrily I called to my husband, "Where's our child?"

"He's next door at the neighbors," he replied. "They're watching him."

"No dear," I shouted, "he's out front by himself!" I quickly ran outside and grabbed him, marching over to our usually dependable neighbors to complain.

"We thought your husband was with him," they said.

A lack of communication could have had some bad results. And so we talked. Couple communication and neighbor communication is so important, especially when we need to depend upon others to care for our children when we can't be there.

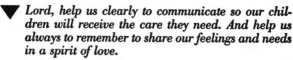 *Lord, help us clearly to communicate so our children will receive the care they need. And help us always to remember to share our feelings and needs in a spirit of love.*

LB

MAKE IT SIMPLE

*For God has not given us a spirit of fear, but
of power and of love and of a sound mind.*
—2 TIM. 1:7

*I*f ever there was a specific request parents have had through the years, it is to make parenting a more simple process. How many times have we said to our own children, "You didn't come from the hospital with a manual."

Today's Scripture holds within it some simple truths about parenting.

First, never operate in fear as a parent. Don't be afraid to listen to your kids. To ask questions or talk about anything. Don't be afraid of being rejected by your children when you need to discipline them or make difficult decisions.

Second, remember the power you have as a parent. You have control over certain consequences that occur in your child's life. You have power over your own emotional reactions. You also have power over the quality and quantity of time you spend with your child.

Third, always love your children. Love them with your words. Love them with your actions. Forgive them and accept them. Love your children unconditionally.

Finally, always be committed to your child's best interest. Make sound decisions for your children. Be a positive example. Seek wise counsel.

▼ *Dear God, teach me by Your example and Your
Word how to be a better parent.*

GC

TEENS AND THE TELEPHONE

> *Let them do good, that they be rich in good*
> *works, ready to give, willing to share, storing*
> *up for themselves a good foundation for the*
> *time to come, that they may lay hold on*
> *eternal life.* —1 TIM. 6:18–19

*T*ammy was having some serious rebellion problems with her parents. She was reasonably compliant in most ways. However, her telephone habits were out of control. She received phone calls all hours of the night. This interfered with her and her parents' sleep. Any restriction placed on her use of the telephone was met with her wrath.

The telephone is the one invention of this century that quickens every teenager's heart. Since peer relationships are so important, the phone is a way to extend past school hours. Life would be unbearable without its existence. It also can cause endless strife between teens and their parents. Call-waiting has served to decrease some of the difficulties, but the essence of the problem lies in the generation gap and the parents' inability to remember their own cauliflower ears from hours on the telephone. To preserve the parents' sanity, realistic limitations must be set and enforced.

▼ *Dear Lord, walking the thin line between balance*
and excess is, at best, hard. Please guide me in the
right balance.

JS

POWER STRUGGLES

Every wise woman builds her house,
But the foolish pulls it down with
her hands. —PROV. 14:1

*T*welve-year-old Emily was brought to me because she was very angry. She wouldn't do anything her parents said—especially her mother. Emily wasn't depressed but she was frustrated. "Mom nags me all the time and never leaves me alone," she said.

All parents have a difficult time letting go of their children. There are times we try to control their every move. We fear what they will become if we don't enforce certain behavior. But as children grow older, they need to have space to make their own choices. Of course it's a different situation when they make a decision that might be dangerous. But let's look at Emily's situation.

Emily's mother is frustrated because Emily won't practice her violin at least thirty minutes a day. Emily says her mother's nagging that she practice and keep repeating a piece over and over makes her not want to play the violin.

Emily and her mother are in a power struggle. Neither is likely to win. The best thing her mother can do is to let Emily know the consequences if she does not practice. Then she needs to leave it up to her.

▼ *Father God, help me to know when and how to let go—to let my children assume responsibility for their own decisions.*

LB

CAMPING

For since the creation of the world His invisible attributes are clearly seen, being understood by the things that are made, even His eternal power and Godhead, so that they are without excuse. —ROM. 1:20

*T*here is something special about camping even if it is in the backyard. Sleeping in sleeping bags in the old pup tent with a friend. Telling stories and giggling for no particular reason. I can remember as a young boy looking up at the stars and for the first time thinking about the vastness of God.

Camping with the family or with a son or daughter can be a powerful spiritual experience. There is something about listening to a hoot owl in the dark night, hearing the crackle of a midnight campfire, and smelling the scent of dew freshened pines. It brings us closer to the Creator and farther away from worrisome distractions and pressures. It allows our sons and daughters to see, hear, and feel the majesty of God's creation.

Provide your children opportunities to experience God in nature through family camp-outs, church camps, and retreats. Being away from the norm of everyday life can lead them to see the true value of relationships—with others and with God.

▼ *Dear God, I am reminded that You walked with Adam and Eve in a garden, not in some shopping mall!*

GC

ONE STEP AT A TIME

He who has begun a good work in you will complete it until the day of Jesus Christ.
—PHIL. 1:6

*W*hen my child was two, I could never imagine her being able to do anything without me. The idea that someday she would be grown up enough to cross the street to go to school was beyond my comprehension. Then one day she did, and she didn't get run over by a car.

Her first overnight also was hard to imagine. I expected her to stay awake all night missing me, but I was the one who didn't sleep. Then came a whole week away at summer camp, church choir tours, and college.

Her first playmate was the little boy next door followed by the boys chasing her on the playground. In third grade they were pulling her pigtails. Then the boys she liked always liked her best friend. Finally Mr. Right came along and she was going steady.

That's the way with children. Slowly, one step at a time, they grow into the person they are going to be. Isn't it magnificent that God planned for it to be a gradual process? I think He knew that is the only way we could ever give them up.

▼ *Dear Lord, Your wisdom astounds me!*

JS

WORKING THROUGH PROBLEMS

Even a child is known by his deeds.
—PROV. 20:11

*I*t's amazing how quickly children will forgive their parents. But forgiving is not forgetting. It's not working through the problems and then letting them go.

A mother told me a story about her four-year-old son. He was a very angry little boy. Of course he denied being angry when his mother asked him what was wrong, but his behavior showed otherwise. When he didn't get what he wanted, he would hit his mother. When she asked him a question, he would ignore her.

After getting to know more about what was happening in this home, it became clear why this little boy was so angry. His mother often had to travel. Underneath his anger he was really feeling hurt about all the times she went away and left him.

When his mother realized what was going on, she helped him work through his frustration. She started talking about her own feelings when she had to leave. She told him why she didn't have a choice. She told him how much she would miss him. And she took the time to sit down and play with him before each trip.

Shortly it got out his irritation about missing his mom. After he got it out, he was ready to forgive her.

▼ *God, help me to learn how to forgive by working through the problem and finally letting it go.*

LB

MORE THAN MEETS THE EYE

"There is a lad here who has five barley loaves and two small fish, but what are they among so many?"
—JOHN 6:9

$\mathscr{A}$t a special Thanksgiving dinner, a young boy told us of the difficulties he had experienced. He had been physically abused and taken from his parents at an early age. When he was taken from his biological parents, he also was separated from his older sister. He moved from foster home to foster home with little emotional nurturing before finally being adopted. So much had been taken away from this young child, much of his dignity as well as his trust in adults. In many ways he lost his childhood years, not to mention his older sister.

What was striking about this young man was his positive attitude and sensitivity to others. "I'm thankful for my new family," he told me. "When I grow up I want to help people somehow."

This young child seemed to have so little to give, but he gave me more than I could have ever imagined. He was a reminder to me that God truly can take what little we have and use it to bless those around us.

How have your children blessed your life? Be thankful for your children. Do not discount what little they may seem to have. God can use them greatly, even as young children.

▼ *Dear God, I thank You for the big blessings that my little ones are to me.*

GC

PERCEPTIONS

And so terrifying was the sight that Moses said, "I am exceedingly afraid and trembling."
—HEB. 12:21

*P*erception influences our experiences. It varies greatly between children and parents. Many times the only difference may be understanding.

Imagine that you received a present in a very large box with a big red ribbon. Immediately you are excited. When you open the box, a floppy object pops out at you. It has stripes on its arms, wild looking red hair, a ghoulish grin, and two glassy eyes. I imagine you would scream and run for cover.

That was exactly the experience of a one-year-old little friend of mine named Kathy. Her grandmother bought her the special gift described above. When Kathy opened the gift, it fell out into her face. She shrieked and withdrew in horror. Her parents and grandparents had a problem understanding. After all, it was only a Raggedy Ann doll. Every little girl loves Raggedy Ann.

A child's behavior is sometimes easier to understand if you put yourself in his or her shoes. Adults have a lot more knowledge and experience. They know Raggedy Ann is only a doll and won't hurt you. A child does not have the same perceptions.

▼ *Dear Lord, help me see the world my children see as I try to help them understand.*

JS

DIVORCE

"You shall know the truth, and the truth shall make you free." —JOHN 8:32

A nine-year-old boy was brought to me because his grades were failing and he was acting out at school. The parents, who were now split up, knew why. They separately told me their side of the story.

There had been an angry divorce with several custody battles. Their son was torn apart as he saw what was happening to his parents. Not only was he torn apart, he was learning to tear apart his relationships with others.

Coping with life by being manipulative was a way for this child to survive. For this boy it was tough for him to do anything but be in the middle of his parents' battle, for that is where they put him over and over again. He tried turning each parent against the other by saying, "Mom did this and Dad did that." It took time and therapy for him to work through his feelings and to learn healthier ways to cope with his parents' divorce. Through God's healing hands, this child got down to his pain and worked through it. He stopped playing his manipulative games. He became free to be honest again even though his parents continued to deny the truth.

▼ *God, help us to be honest with each other so our children can be honest with us.*

LB

TEARS

Jesus wept.
—JOHN 11:35

*W*hen was the last time you cried? I mean really cried. At the end of a sad movie? When grieving the loss of a friend or relative? Maybe a tender moment with your child?

Crying is a very normal response to a multitude of feelings. Sadness, abandonment, grief, even joy. To cry is to be human. While Jesus walked on earth He was fully God and fully man at the same time. He cried when He grieved the loss of His friend Lazarus.

With Christ as our example, we learn that crying is a normal part of life. We should give the same example to our children. Especially to our young sons. There are already too many messages our society gives that teach men to "stuff" or deny their feelings. We should teach our children just the opposite. Permission should be given to feel feelings. To be fully human! When sad feelings are not expressed, it creates an unhealthy independence, anger, depression, or even many physical problems.

I remember the respect I felt when seeing my own father cry. It takes much courage to feel feelings. Teach your children to be courageous by your example, and allow them also to cry openly.

▼ *Lord, please provide me with the courage to be real—to experience and express all my feelings honestly.*

GC

PROMISES

Hope deferred makes the heart sick.
—PROV. 13:12

$\mathcal{I}$ once had a patient whose father was a minister of the largest church in town. Many times he and his father would plan to go fishing or camping. Invariably someone in the congregation would call with an emergency and the trip would be canceled. The patient realized that the congregation was much more important than he was. He quit believing his dad's promises and stopped asking to do anything with him.

Promises are important to keep. They increase trust and let your children know that they can count on your word. When promises are broken, not only do your children conclude that they cannot count on you, they also conclude that other things or people are more important.

One solution is to avoid making promises to your children. But the real issue is to make sure your children are important enough to follow through on the promised act. We are extremely important to them. Probably more important to them than anyone else in the world. A fishing trip would probably catch a lot more than fish.

▼ *Dear Lord, let me be faithful to my promises and realize how important my word is.*

JS

WORKING MOMS

. . . casting all your care upon Him, for He cares for you. —1 PETER 5:7

*N*ow that I've started back to work, I worry that my children don't get as much care and attention as they used to get. Many of us feel guilty if we have to go back to work, yet we feel like we have no choice when our spouse has been laid off of work.

Hurt creeps in when I'm not with my kids all the time like I used to be. Those feelings really hit me one day when I was in a counseling session with a mother and her child. Suddenly I heard one of my boys screaming and crying for me. He was in the lobby with his dad waiting for me to come to say hello to him. I wanted to get up and get my son, but I had a job to do.

Quickly I asked God to help me keep listening so I could help this mother. God was faithful. He calmed my spirit and helped me refocus so I could finish our session. As soon as the mother left with her child, I ran into the lobby and gave my son a big hug. I dried his tears and told him how much I loved him. The guilt still comes and goes, but when it does come, I'm learning to give it to God. Sometimes we cannot be there for our kids, but He will be there always. Let's start giving our children to God.

▼ *God, these are Your children. Help us to love and care for them as best we can without feeling guilty for those things we cannot do.*

LB

AWAY WITH CHILDISH THINGS

When I was a child, I spoke as a child, I understood as a child, I thought as a child; but when I became a man, I put away childish things. For now we see in a mirror, dimly, but then face to face. Now I know in part, but then I shall know just as I also am known. And now abide faith, hope, love, these three; but the greatest of these is love.
—1 COR. 13:11–13

*M*any young couples expecting their first born are awakened to the fact that they need to grow up. They no longer can spend money like they want to, eat what they want to, or stay out as late. They have new responsibilities that come with expecting a child.

Parenting can be a very uncertain process. There are no easy steps. We are never certain of all the right answers. I often wonder if the decisions I make are the best for all those involved. Someday, when I meet my Lord Jesus, I believe I'll no longer see through a mirror dimly. Instead I will see and understand His perfect way.

Until then, I know that I am to abide in faith, hope, and love. But the greatest of these, in all the decisions I make as a parent, is love.

▼ *Dear God, I will place my faith in You as I put away childish things and take on the responsibilities of parenting.*

GC

FAMILY FOLKLORE

These days should be remembered and kept throughout every generation, . . . that the memory of them should not perish among their descendants. —EST. 9:28

*G*irls seem to be better at getting family stories straight and at seeing that they are perpetuated. Most girls want to know the details about their birth and how much they weighed. They want to hear about the cute things they said and did. They want to know where they lived and why.

Boys sometimes are not as quick to ask those questions, but this is information that they need to know. It gives a dimension to their personality by filling in memories that otherwise they may never know. Like the time they fell asleep in the playhouse and had the neighborhood in a panic looking for them. Besides being an interesting story, it shows they were important and someone cared for them.

My patients are usually short on fun loving family stories. Many times it is not because they didn't happen, it's because no one shared these stories with them.

Family stories are folklore. They give a distinct flavor to your family that makes it different from other families. Those stories will live on forever.

▼ *Dear Lord, help me to remember fun and funny stories about my family and to pass them on.*

JS

STRENGTH TO GO ON

For you have need of endurance, so that after you have done the will of God, you may receive the promise. —HEB. 10:36

*D*o you wonder some days where you're going to get the strength to go on? Do you feel tired, rushed, frazzled? Do you find yourself forgetting where you've placed things? Are people becoming a nuisance?

If your answer is "yes," relax. You're normal—especially if you're also a parent.

If you are a stay-at-home parent or one who also works outside your home, the stress of day-to-day living may be really getting to you. Is there hope? Yes! Every day is not going to be like today. Furthermore you're not alone. Other parents are experiencing what you're facing and feeling. There are an increasing number of support groups available with people who understand. Use them. Find out if there's a Mother's Day Out group in your area. Trade off your children with family or friends. Get the time you need to renew your energy and perspective.

God has a plan for your life. Parenting the children He has given you is one of His greatest plans. You can do it with His help.

▼ *God, help me to get through the tough days that seem unbearable. I want to do Your will.*

LB

FAIR BEHAVIOR

*The curse of the LORD is on the house
of the wicked,
But He blesses the habitation of the just.*
—PROV. 3:33

*T*he father told his son, "No one ever said life was fair!" The son angrily murmured, as tears began to flow, "I'm not talking about life, I'm talking about you!"

We all want to be fair with our children. For many of us, being fair means to be perfect. *Au contraire!* For that to be our role as parents, would be unfair to us! We are not to be perfect. Rather we are to model, among many things, fair behavior toward our fellowman and to treat our children fairly. How are we to be fair to our children? Here are some hints:

Always be involved with our children. It's unfair to ignore them. Recognize their accomplishments. It's unfair to focus only on their failures. Acknowledge their feelings. It's unfair to deny them the right to feel. Share our lives with them. It's unfair to hold ourselves aloof.

Allow our children to grow. Do not dominate or overprotect them. It is unfair to hinder a child's development in any way. We need to encourage them to think and express themselves. We need to recognize their agendas and give them the freedom to fail.

We will experience God's rich blessings as we create a just and fair household for our family.

▼ *Dear God, help me to know Your character. You are a just and fair God.*

GC

BROKEN LEGS

> *Likewise the Spirit also helps in our*
> *weaknesses. For we do not know what we*
> *should pray for as we ought, but the Spirit*
> *Himself makes intercession for us with*
> *groanings which cannot be uttered.*
> —ROM. 8:26

Ted had a severely broken leg. His mother immediately took him to the doctor who put him in the hospital for a month in traction. His mother had to work and was busy with other family problems. She rarely visited. Of course it didn't take Ted long to become severely depressed. Besides the loss of his mobility and the pain he suffered, he felt completely abandoned by his family. At the time he needed them the most, he got the least from his parents.

Times of injury or illness offer unique opportunities to show your children how much you care. It's a time when unconditional love can be demonstrated to your child. It's a time when special attention is needed and readily accepted from even the most independent child. They need to know that you are taking care of them and protecting them because they feel so vulnerable. They may not always understand what is happening, but they will understand that you care. Times of injury or illness can become special times your children will always remember.

▼ *Dear Lord, increase my sensitivity when my children are ill or injured and need special care.*

JS

EAR INFECTIONS

*. . . looking unto Jesus, the author and
finisher of our faith, who for the joy that was
set before Him endured the cross, despising
the shame, and has sat down at the right
hand of the throne of God.* —HEB. 12:2

$\mathscr{B}$oth my children have chronic ear infections. By the
time my oldest was six months old, he needed to have
surgical tubes inserted in his ears. I can't begin to count
the number of nights we've gone without sleep. I also
can't begin to count how many doses of antibiotics
we've given them—or how much we've spent on medicine and doctor visits. Sometimes I've wondered what
good it's doing.

Caring for a sick child is an incredibly tiring and difficult task. We may feel so helpless, so discouraged by
an illness we cannot prevent or cure. How can we get
through the stress of watching them suffer?

It helps to find a friend who understands. Talking to
another parent can alleviate some of our worries and
fears. There's also the comfort of knowing we're not
alone. But for me the greatest comfort, as well as the
strength to keep on, has come from looking to Jesus.

He willingly chose to endure the pain of the cross for
my sin. Keeping my eyes on Him, my faith is renewed.

▼ *Help me, Lord, to get through those days when my
children are sick. Give me the energy to care for
their needs and the faith to trust You for their healing.*

LB

SEEKING HELP

A wise man will hear and increase learning,
And a man of understanding will attain
wise counsel.
—PROV. 1:5

*P*eople are reluctant to visit a counselor for many reasons. They fear being blamed. They are afraid therapy may be unduly painful. For many people there exists a very negative stigma in seeing a counselor. "Will someone think I'm crazy?" Others may feel that seeing a counselor means they are weak or are a failure.

To admit needing help in handling emotions, family conflicts, or some crisis can be a difficult process. But it is sometimes crucial. One particular family avoided seeking help for their teenage daughter even when they saw all the warning signs. Isolation, mood swings, refusal to eat. They were afraid to admit their family was less than the all-American family. That they really had serious conflicts that needed to be addressed.

When Jenny rapidly lost weight, her medical problems could not be ignored. Fortunately she was given the best medical help. Over time, with much intensive individual and family counseling, she was able to overcome the anorexia nervosa that threatened her life. For the good of our families, we need to never be afraid to seek wise counsel.

▼ *Lord, help me not to be bound by fear or pride.*
Teach me to seek Your wisdom as well as counsel
from others.

GC

IMAGINATION

*For it is God who works in you both to will
and to do for His good pleasure.*

—PHIL. 2:13

*T*oys are important for children, but not necessary. A piece of string or a cardboard box is enough. Effective toys must require imagination to make them operate. Batteries won't do. Children need to decide which direction the play goes, not the toy.

The most successful toy my children had was a wagon with a long handle to push. It started as a walker toy to steady my toddler's balance. It then became a wagon for blocks, a doll buggy, and transportation for pets or other children. In summertime it was a lawn mower. Six years later, I was contemplating discarding this toy when I looked out the window and saw it perched on my daughter's shoulders and heard her vending popcorn and peanuts like she had seen the night before at the baseball game. My children never did use that toy for exactly what it was designed, but we certainly got our money's worth.

Adults need to tap into imagination too. It is what adds zest to life and takes away the harsh shadows of reality. Try it. You might like it.

▼ *Dear Lord, help me to remember the fun of a day
filled with imagination.*

JS

EMPATHY

For we do not have a High Priest who cannot sympathize with our weaknesses, but was in all points tempted as we are, yet without sin.
—HEB. 4:15

I had just finished a two-hour family session with a father and mother and their younger daughter. By the time the session was finally over I felt like I had made no progress. The father could not empathize with his daughter, not at any level. All he did was intellectualize everything she said. Finally I told him point blank, "You are not hearing her! When you show her you are not with her, she shuts you out."

Empathy is s very important skill to help us connect with anyone, especially with our kids. What is empathy? It is understanding how someone else feels, letting them know you understand.

For instance, how would you respond to your child if he said, "I'm scared of the tiger in my room"? Most parents are likely to answer, "There's no tiger in here. Just go to sleep." But instead of denying their feeling, try identifying by saying, "You sound scared of the tiger." Then you can go on to help by asking, "Do you think we can get him so you'll be safe?"

As we acknowledge our children's feelings, we build their self-confidence and self-esteem. We also grow a stronger trust relationship with them.

▼ *God, help me to have for others, especially my children, the same empathy You have for me.*

LB

TRAINING FOR THE RACE

*Do you not know that those who run in a
race all run, but one receives the prize? Run
in such a way that you may obtain it.*
—1 COR. 9:24

*R*unning in the New York City marathon can be one
of the most exhilarating experiences ever for a runner.
The thousands that participate each year train hard to
prepare for what probably is the most celebrated 26.2
miles in the world!

Preparing for this great race, or any marathon for
that matter, is not easy. It takes months of hard training.
Sacrifices must be made. Real pain experienced. To
think of running such a race without adequately preparing would be ludicrous. No one would ever try.

Likewise no one should ever have to deal with the
difficulties of adult life without proper training and
preparation. That's why it is vital for our children and
teens to deal with difficulties on their own. To shield
them from all emotional hurt and pain is to sabotage the
proper training needed for adult life.

Be a coach for your children. Know what they can
endure. Allow them to run in such a way as to build up
their emotional strength. It's the best preparation you
can give them for the marathons of life.

▼ *Dear God, thank You for Your guidance and for allowing me and my children to grow stronger.*

GC

WHEN OUTSIDE HELP IS NEEDED

The righteous cry out,
and the LORD hears,
And delivers them out of all their troubles.
—PS. 34:17

*T*herapy! When do you need it for your child? When life is out of control and unmanageable, for sure. Or when a problem appears to be persistent and does not respond to changes in your approach.

Cheryl, age thirteen, had always had some school problems and only a few friends. Recently she was having problems adjusting to a new stepfather. Her mother encouraged her to make more friends. She talked with the teachers about Cheryl's grades. One Saturday night Cheryl ran away from home. She returned two days later. This is an example of things becoming unmanageable and out of control. It was definitely a situation that required immediate therapy. However, the fact that Cheryl had long-term school problems and few friends, might have been a previous indication that she was having some problems functioning.

Parents know their children better than anyone. If their behavior suddenly changes or they are constantly in a position that assaults their self-esteem, it's a signal they need some outside help to gain a new perspective, and you need to learn new ways of helping them.

▼ *Father, alert me to warning signs in my teen's behavior and guide me to a therapist for intervention.*

JS

PUTTING OUT FIRES

*"The LORD is longsuffering and abundant in
mercy, forgiving iniquity and transgression."*
—NUM. 14:18

I'd been putting out fires all day. First my two-year-old poured water over his Play-Doh.® He got his hands coated with the mess. By the time I discovered what he was doing, he had his hand prints all over the sofa and recliner. Then he took off his diaper and went in a bowl. At the same time, his younger brother filled his diaper and playsuit.

I turned my back for just a few minutes to hose down the baby in the tub. What did my two-year-old do? As usual he took advantage of the opportunity to get into something else. This time he pulled a chair over to the counter to get into the candy. We thought we had put the sweets out of his reach. Not so, or at least not now. Somehow he managed to reach the bag and dump it all over the floor. By the time Dad came home I needed to get out of the smoke.

What are we supposed to do on those days when our patience wears thin and our temper begins to flare? We can ask the Lord to help us cool down before we lose control. We can remind ourselves of His longsuffering and mercy. And we can determine, in His strength, to keep loving and forgiving our children.

▼ *Help me, Lord, to let my children be children. Help
me to learn to laugh at the things they do and to
keep relying on You to put out the fires.*

LB

ABANDONED

A father of the fatherless,
a defender of widows,
Is God in His holy habitation.
—PS. 68:5

Standing in line at the grocery store you've probably noticed headlines on the tabloids: "Boy Raised by Elephants," "Child Raised by Pack of Wolves." Such tragic accounts are, to say the least, hard to believe. There are few documented accounts. Yet they bring to mind the tragedy of the 100,000 children who are left for adoption or abandoned each year in our country. Equally tragic are the many children who live with their parents and are emotionally abandoned.

Did you live with an absentee mother or father? Do not underemphasize the significance of being emotionally neglected while growing up. Your parenting skills are derived mainly from what you learned from your own parents. It is impossible to give what you don't have. Properly parenting your own children is too important and too difficult not to look at what you've gleaned or haven't gleaned from your own parents.

If memories are difficult to explore, you may seek the help of a counselor or trusted friend. Ask your heavenly Father to parent you. He is the perfect Father and the giver of all good things. He will surely instruct you and help you to raise your own children.

▼ *Thank You, God, for meeting my needs as only a perfect Father could.*

GC

CHAPERONS

"My heart has understood great wisdom and knowledge." —ECCL. 1:16

*C*haperons are necessary, especially at teenagers' parties. Teens can be responsible, dependable people alone, in pairs, or even in small groups. But it takes only one or two teens who are drinking or out of control to turn an enjoyable party into a major fiasco. Where James went to high school, parents would frequently go out of town for the weekend leaving their teens alone. What a great time for a party! James was excited to be invited to one of these unchaperoned parties along with many of his friends. It was fun. There was lots of music and laughter until about 10:00 P.M. when several couples came who had been drinking. Soon it was out of control. Two hours later the police broke up the party, but not before many teens were drunk and the house was a shambles.

You need to know about the parties and activities your teens will attend and what adults are in charge— even if the gathering is at the church. You need to know not because you have a problem trusting your teens, but rather to avoid having them in a situation that is out of their control.

 Dear Lord, teach me the difference between protection and over-protection and help me to achieve the proper balance.

JS

SCATTER-BRAIN

You will keep him in perfect peace,
Whose mind is stayed on You.
—ISA. 26:3

$\mathcal{D}$o you ever feel scattered and disorganized—like you're running into walls? There are times you may feel lucky if you know where you are only half the time! No, this doesn't mean you're going crazy—though it may feel that way. It means you're a parent with ten million things to do and ten million things going through your brain. With that responsibility, no wonder there are times you feel out of it.

When I find myself so scattered that I'm beginning to get teased about it, I go back to God and ask Him for some peace in my life. When my husband comes home from work I jump into a hot bath and relax and say, "Thank You, Lord, I needed this." Resist the temptation to get down on yourself and beat up on yourself for being scattered. It's pretty normal in raising kids. Also resist the temptation to compare yourself to a friend you think has it all together. The truth is they probably don't. Some people are just good at covering up and putting on a show. Other parents are probably as frustrated and torn as you. So relax and take life in stride. Tell yourself, I'm okay. Remember how Jesus took time to be alone with His Father. If He needed this time, don't we need it too?

▼ *God, when I'm feeling tired and scattered, teach me to turn my thoughts toward You.*

LB

*We know that an idol is nothing in the world,
and that there is no other God but one.*
—1 COR. 8:4

*T*een idols have come and gone throughout the years.
If you've ever seen the hysteria of infatuated teenagers,
you know it can be contagious. What is it about the idols
the media has created that make them so enthralling to
young teens?

First, teens feel as if they have a personal relationship
with their idol. They create in their own minds an image
that is the ideal. They see their idol as someone who will
always be there for them—someone who completely
and unconditionally accepts them.

Second, holding close to a well-known heartthrob
provides teens with a sense of identity and belonging.
They share with their peers a common purpose—to be
that star's fan, to know everything about him, to follow
faithfully to the very end.

Fortunately teen idols do come and go; yet, we can
learn something from them. The very things that attract
teens to these idols can be emphasized as we present
Christ to them. Who is more perfect, more faithful than
our Lord Jesus? What provides a stronger sense of belonging or purpose than being a part of His family?

▼ *Dear God, thank You for being who You are. You are
the One I worship.*

GC

TEENAGE PREGNANCIES

God is our refuge and strength,
A very present help in trouble.
—PS. 46:1

*B*ecky became pregnant when she was a junior in high school. She never considered doing anything other than raising her child. There were several years of anguish and concern for her by her parents, but today Becky is married and has made a healthy life for her child.

Then there's Lori. She gave her baby up for adoption. It was a hard thing to do. She will always have a place in her heart for her child. So will her parents.

Debbie made her decision to marry the father of the baby. They have a happy family that began before they were ready, though they missed out on the last part of their youth and the carefree early part of marriage.

Abortion seemed to be the only answer for Carla, who was planning to start college in a month. It was a hard decision for Carla and her parents.

It's not the way God intended and it certainly would have worked better and been easier if these girls and boys had waited until the proper time. But God is a forgiving God, and He has made us resilient. Parents need to remember that and claim some of the resilience for themselves.

▼ *Dear Lord, guide us through these really difficult trials because we can't do it without You.*

JS

IT'S OKAY TO EXPRESS FEELINGS

*He drove them all out of the temple . . . and
poured out the changers' money and
overturned the tables.* —JOHN 2:15

*T*oday I walked out of my counseling office knowing I
had done the right thing, but it was hard to do. I had
pushed an adolescent in therapy to the point where he
was very angry and tearful. Even though he hurt inside,
it was good for this child to express his feelings emotionally and verbally. He had buried them and then built up
a thick armor so no one could get in. The only way to
help him get some of those feelings out was to blast
them out. Anger is a tough feeling. This boy had a hard
time expressing it. Instead he took drugs, got drunk, or
ran away to pacify the million sparks he felt inside.

Please teach your child from an early age *that it's
okay to express how they feel* as long as they don't hurt
others or themselves in the process. Let them know it's
safe to express their feelings to you—that they can be
angry, sad, or fearful and you'll still love and accept
them. Don't make them have to build walls, like this boy
did. It only hurts the child in the end.

Even Jesus became angry and ventilated His feelings
to His Father and to His disciples. May we do the same.
For God has given us feelings that we need to express in
healthy ways.

▼ *God, help us guide our children to a healthy self-
image, and teach them positive ways to express their
emotions.*

LB

OBJECT LESSONS

My son, do not forget my law,
But let your heart keep my commands;
For length of days and long life
And peace they will add to you.
—PROV. 3:1

*F*reckles was a beautiful Dalmatian puppy full of life and curiosity. When Andy's father brought him home from the pet shop, it was clear Andy would be forever committed to his new found friend. If only Freckles had been as committed to Andy.

As time passed and Freckles grew, he began to leap the fence and venture to neighboring yards. Andy frantically searched for Freckles. Each time Andy found him, he scolded him and tugged him back home. But Andy was only postponing the inevitable. One day Freckles got out of the yard and Andy couldn't find him. After a week passed, it was clear Freckles would never be found. Andy was distraught.

As father and son talked about the loss of a good friend, an object lesson emerged. "Freckles may not be so happy now that he doesn't have you to take care of him. He just wouldn't take to heart your commands to stay home." Andy and his father read the above Scripture together. And Andy decided then he would never want to wander far from God's care.

▼ *Lord, I want so much for the Bible to come alive to my children. Show me how to relate its truths first to my own life and then to my children's experiences.*
GC

AN ENDLESS TASK—AND ADVENTURE

And let us not grow weary while doing good, for in due season we shall reap if we do not lose heart.
—GAL. 6:9

*P*arenting is impossible to do unless you take it as it comes rather than anticipate the problems that lie ahead. You think you'll never make it through colic. Then come the terrible two's and their favorite word, "no." Your head spins from thousands of spelling words and math problems, not to mention dance lessons and soccer games. You suffer as much as they do when you have to ground them and take away privileges. You grow weary hearing them say, "You just don't understand." Dating and missed curfews, scholarships and colleges, are all a part of parenthood. And through it all is an endless cash flow. There are times you want to give up, but you won't. You will persevere.

Speaking as one who has made it through, I wouldn't have missed a day of it. It was an exciting adventure for both me and my husband. God was with us and blessed us every step.

Funny thing about parenthood—it never stops. But when your children are grown, then you get the reward. Besides looking at a job well done, you have a wonderful adult person to develop a relationship with as you begin a whole new adventure.

▼ *Dear Lord, thank You for the incredible blessing You gave me in my children.*

JS

UNITED

"Every city or house divided against itself will not stand."
                                        —MATT. 12:25

*C*hildren have a knack for splitting their parents. When one parent tells them "no," they quickly learn to go to the other hoping they can get them to say "yes." All too often they are successful at dividing their parents and getting their own way. It seems to be an instinctive way all children test the limits, and they learn how to do it at a very young age.

My two-year-old, for instance, knows his limits. He knows I won't give him candy in the morning. It's interesting to hear him ask for his daddy just after I tell him "no." It doesn't take long to figure out what he's doing when I later find him with a piece of candy in his mouth. My husband and I try to present a united front by allowing candy, "only after lunch or dinner, and not after 7:00 p.m." We are constantly talking to each other to see what our child is asking the other, and then we decide upon a united answer to our child's questions.

When was the last time you sat down with your spouse to make certain you were giving the same message to your children regarding rules and consequences? Determine to work together, to be consistent. Don't let your children divide you.

▼ *Lord, help me and my spouse to present a united front when our children seek to divide us.*

                                                    LB

THE CLOGGED HOSE

"Be angry, and do not sin": do not let the sun go down on your wrath.

—EPH. 4:26

*J*immy was more than miffed at his father's request to do yard work Saturday mornings. Yet he didn't dare say anything. Dad had to work extra hours because of cutbacks at the factory. Now he had to work Saturdays too. Mom was working part time to help pay the bills. His younger sister was having painful ear infections.

There was little conversation between Jimmy and his parents. No one knew about his recent struggles at school or the fight with his best friend. No one knew how much he missed playing ball with Dad. No one knew how angry he was about all the attention his younger sister received.

That Saturday morning as he turned on the faucet to water the yard, he was too preoccupied to notice the dirt clogging the end of the hose. At first the hose didn't work. The pressure increased until finally, water burst through the hose, twisting it violently.

When our children are not free to express their feelings, pressure also builds up. They may become violent or explode. Because feelings do not disappear, we need to make daily maintenance checks to prevent their feelings from becoming clogged.

▼ *Dear God, help me to understand that being angry is not a sin. Help me to teach my children not to let the sun go down on their anger.*

GC

NO EASY ANSWERS

For the wages of sin is death, but the gift of God is eternal life in Christ Jesus our Lord.
—ROM. 6:23

*J*oan was thirty-five when she came to see me. She had an abortion when she was fifteen because she and her boyfriend felt they could not take care of a child. Twenty years later she sat in my office and wept for her aborted baby. She had been trying to deal with the abortion all this time with little positive results.

We tend to like instant solutions to problems. Abortion seems like an easy answer to an unwanted pregnancy, especially if it involves an unwed teenager. The problem is, it is *not* an instant solution. Women, like Joan, struggle for years after their abortions to process their feelings about their decision.

An unwanted pregnancy must be faced, either now or later. Parents must help their teens face their feelings about their pregnancy no matter how they choose to deal with the problem. As they do, it can provide a step toward maturity for their teen and a closer emotional bond within the family. God is our source as we struggle with life's most difficult decisions.

▼ *Dear Lord, things like these require Your abundance of wisdom and guidance.*

JS

ENCOURAGING CREATIVITY

He who sows sparingly will also reap sparingly, and he who sows bountifully will also reap bountifully. **—2 COR. 9:6**

$\mathcal{V}$alentine's Day—it's a day of love, sweethearts, and lots of chocolate sweets. This year I decided to celebrate it by doing something I've wanted to do for a long time. With my two-year-old son beside me watching my every move, I got out the cookbook, flour and sugar, rolling pin, and the heart-shaped cookie cutter I'd been wanting to use.

With flour on our noses, clothes, and the floor, my son and I began to create. Jesse had a blast rolling dough in a ball, mashing it down, and then rolling it flat. I had fun, too, watching him take his new toy, the heart-shaped cutter, and cut out hearts his own way. Of course we made a huge mess, but it was worth it to see the look on Jesse's face as his cookies came out of the oven. "I made them," he proudly told everyone as he gave them one of his cookies.

I remember when I was young. I wasn't allowed in the kitchen because of the mess my mother said I would make. That is the worst thing a parent can do. Let your child grow and explore. Sure you'll have a mess, but you and your child can clean the mess together, furthering your relationship even more.

▼ *God, help me to encourage my child's creativity, and to enjoy the process.*

LB

ANY IDOLS IN YOUR LIFE?

*These nations feared the LORD, yet served
their carved images; also their children and
their children's children have continued
doing as their fathers did, even to this day.*
—2 KINGS 17:41

*I*t is common for children to learn similar skills and
pursue similar professions as their parents. One family
of eight children has seven practicing chiropractors. Another family has a printing business in which everyone
has made a career. Another family has five generations
of policemen. What is also as common, but sometimes
less obvious, is how families influence the values and
beliefs of future generations.

Of course we want our children to know Christ as
their personal Savior. We can best help this to happen
by the importance we place on our own relationship
with Christ. Is He the center of our lives? What about
our church attendance, our personal devotional time,
our treatment of people? Do we have any idols?

Idols? Yes. In our fast paced, materialistic society it is
easy to develop idols. New cars, sports clothes, and
even work can become an idol. This is not to suggest
these things should not be a part of our lives. But how
important are they? How much time and money do they
consume? Have they become so important to us that
Christ is no longer the center of our lives?

▼ *I want You to be the center of my life, God. Search
my heart and show me any idols in my life.*

GC

WHAT'S IN A NAME?

"You shall call His name JESUS, for He will save His people from their sins."
—MATT. 1:21

The sweetest sound on earth is your name. It was probably the first word that had meaning to you. Your name is intermingled with your identity and self-esteem. It is even more significant if you are named for someone. Children named after their parents or grand-parents sometimes inherit a lot of expectations with the name. They may be expected to be an extension of the person for whom they are named. This can cause them to feel pressured or to feel special and filled with pride that they have been chosen to carry the name.

I was counseling a thirteen-year-old named Mary Suzette. She suffered from a very low self-esteem. In an attempt to improve her feeling of self-worth, she decided her name was Suzette. That was the image she hoped to capture. Of course it left her parents confused. But they were able to let her change her identity at least for a while.

Remember that your child's name is important. Even though they may want to play around with it, parents must always respect it and use it as an extension of their identity.

▼ *Dear Lord, help me to be sensitive to my child's feelings about his identity as expressed in his name.*

JS

MY WEAKNESS, HIS STRENGTH

"My grace is sufficient for you, for My strength is made perfect in weakness."
—2 COR. 12:9

*T*his week I counseled with a single mother. She works twelve hours a day because she has to support her two children and herself. It's tearing her apart. Her children are showing signs of missing her. She feels guilty for leaving them in day care.

Single mothers and mothers who work outside their homes are not the only mothers who struggle with feelings of guilt. Some stay-at-home mothers also feel guilty for not spending enough time with their children. Others may feel guilty for secretly resenting all the time their children consume.

Guilty feelings have a way of attacking every mother, or maybe we're just good at laying guilt trips on ourselves. We have high, often unrealistic, expectations of ourselves. We're painfully aware of our weaknesses. The question is, are we also aware of the One whose strength compensates for our weaknesses? God promises that His grace is sufficient for everything we face—including the challenges of mothering.

▼ *Lord God, thank You for meeting me at my point of weakness, for forgiving me when I do fail, and for making me strong in You.*

LB

For Christ did not send me to baptize, but to preach the gospel, not with wisdom of words, lest the cross of Christ should be made of no effect.
　　　　　　　　　　　　　　　　—1 COR. 1:17

*T*he family was in turmoil. They fought constantly. There seemed to be one crisis after the other. Everyone felt tense and uneasy. Closeness between family members appeared to be an imaginary idea propagated only by fictional characters on television. The father was at wit's end. Feeling responsible as head of the household, he earnestly attempted to restore order but with no success. Try as he may, the divisions within his family ran too deep and too wide.

The same situation existed within the church at Corinth. Paul recognized the urgency of the situation and placed it first on his agenda in the letter he wrote to them. Notice Paul's inspired perspective. If anyone was adept at waxing eloquent or debating to defend the truth, it was Paul. But he chose to do neither. He simply focused on the basics—the gospel of Christ.

When divisions exist in our families, we also need to focus on the basics. We need to remind ourselves that ultimately we are committed to loving each other. In Christian households, we also can focus on our commitment to Christ and the commitment to us that He demonstrated on the Cross.

▼ *Help me to avoid clever attempts to manipulate my children but to focus instead on who they are in You.*

GC

OUT AFTER MIDNIGHT

"And none of you shall go out of the door of his house until morning." —EX. 12:22

*I*n our town, curfews are being imposed. Many teens and parents are up in arms about it. The parents are upset because they will be fined if the teens are not compliant. Everyone has some kind of an opinion, but it's hard to think of some good reason for teens to be out after midnight. Even if your child is trustworthy, other people are not necessarily acting out of innocent motives.

When my son was sixteen, he and three friends went to a baseball game about an hour away. They should have returned at midnight. About that time, we received a telephone call saying they had car trouble. Would we come to pick them up? I hadn't been out at that time at night for quite a while. I was surprised to see so many questionable people out on the streets. I felt relieved when my son and friends were safely home.

Community support might assist in the problems that can develop when teens are out after midnight. But the responsibility really lies with the parents. We are responsible for our children's behavior and for their protection. Sometimes this may not make us popular with our teens.

▼ *Dear Lord, guide me in decisions regarding my child's curfew and protection.*

JS

TEETHING PAIN

"Peace I leave with you, My peace I give to you."
—JOHN 14:27

$\mathscr{D}$o you ever wonder if your child will ever stop teething? It begins only months after birth. They drool, cry, and chew on everything. My five-month-old is beside himself because his mouth is hurting so much. He cries constantly. Nothing I do helps. Sometimes I want to scream with him.

The pediatrician says, "Oh, what swollen gums. Are you ever teething." I feel like shouting, "I know he's teething. Do something!"

Unfortunately there's not much that can be done to ease the pain of teething. But what about our pain? It hurts to hear them cry and cry and cry. We feel so helpless.

I find what helps me the most is to take frequent prayer breaks. I keep asking for God's help—for me and my teething baby. Sometimes the Lord gives my baby, and me, the gift of sleep. Other times He gives me that unexplainable peace in the midst. I know He's with me and my little one. And my hope is renewed that these days of teething will not last forever.

▼ *God, help me to get through the teething years. Help my infant not to hurt so bad, and help us all to get some sleep.*

LB

KNOWING RIGHT FROM WRONG

. . . wage the good warfare, having faith and a good conscience, which some having rejected, concerning the faith have suffered shipwreck. . . .   —1 TIM. 1:18–19

The eyes of the convicted serial murderer seemed lifeless and cold. They reflected no remorse or regret for the horror for which he had been convicted. As the deputies led him from the courtroom for the last time, a devilish smirk crossed his face. He paused for the cameras. It was a chilling scene.

One of the most important aspects of a child's maturation is the development of a conscience. If the right ingredients don't exist, the possibility for poor relationships, criminal behavior, or other atrocities becomes more likely.

When children disobey, it is vital for parents to address their behavior. Consistent, fair consequences are a normal part of every child's development. Explanations of what is right and wrong should be made. Examples of what is right and wrong should be shown.

Children also should be allowed to experience forgiveness. Never hold a grudge. Help your children know that it can be a positive experience to admit that they were wrong. It can build their confidence. It can strengthen their relationships. And it can develop a healthy conscience.

▼ *Dear God, search my heart and lead me to a clear conscience.*

GC

OUR IMAGE OF GOD

*"I am the LORD, exercising
lovingkindness, judgment, and
righteousness in the earth.
For in these I delight," says the LORD.*
—JER. 9:24

Sunday I sat behind a father with his daughter. He had his arm around her and occasionally gave her a little squeeze. I immediately was transported in time to when I was a little girl. I remembered sitting on my daddy's lap. I remembered him putting his arm around me. It was a precious feeling. That is how I envision God's love. I see myself sitting on His lap. I feel His love and care and know I am special to Him.

Working with adults, I have found many times their image of God and His love correspond with the relationship they had with their own father. If their father was like mine, they have a loving picture of God. If their father was abrasive or filled with rage, they see God as vengeful and angry. A preoccupied, unavailable father brings forth the image of an indifferent God.

The Bible describes God as ever present, loving, accepting, and involved in everyone's life. As an adult, we can change our concept of God, but it may be hard to leave behind those old feelings. How much better it will be for our children if we create the appropriate image of God as they are growing up.

▼ *Dear Lord, teach me how to be the kind of father You are, who can impart his tender, loving mercies to all his children.*

JS

PREOCCUPATION

"He who has ears to hear, let him hear!"
—MATT. 13:9

One day seven-year-old Steven asked his mother and father if he could play with his older brother Joey's drum set. The parents were so busy arguing about household issues they didn't really hear Steven and said, "okay, okay." When Joey got home, he wasn't happy. Complaining to his parents, Joey said, "Steven messed up my drums and cymbals, did you tell him it was okay to play with them?" The parents looked at each other and said, "We never told him he could do that." Steven knew that his parents were not listening to him when he asked to play the drums, and he was tired of being called a liar, so he did something clever. Steven had recorded his parents giving him permission and produced his evidence to Joey and his parents. Both Steven's mom and dad turned bright red with embarrassment as they learned a valuable lesson.

Many times we are so caught up with our own world that we do not really hear our children. Our preoccupation could have even worse consequences than in Steven and Joey's family. When busy or preoccupied, we need to take a break to listen to our children and hear their needs, or at the very least let them know that we will listen to them later. God is like that. He always listens to us patiently.

▼ *God, help me to listen to You and to my children. Thank You for always listening to me.*

LB

CONSEQUENCES

I know, O LORD, that Your judgments are
*   right,*
And that in faithfulness You have afflicted me.
—PS. 119:75

*H*arry's son always has been somewhat of a rabble-rouser. Even as an infant he was always active, flailing his arms, and crying loudly. And then there was the terrible twos! Or was it threes and fours?

In high school it was much the same story. One time he cut class. Harry made it clear he disapproved. He told him there would be consequences if he did it again. When the call came from the school counselor, Harry knew he had to follow through with what he had said. Harry talked to his son. He listened to what he had to say. His son's reasons were understandable. It was the last class of the day. They had a substitute teacher and only busy work to do. He had some errands to run before football practice. Nevertheless, Harry took his car away for the rest of the week.

The son was shocked and furious. He stormed off to his room. Sometime later he came back and announced, "I know, Dad, that your judgments are right, and that in faithfulness you have afflicted me." That's when Harry woke up from his nap!

Our children may never say "thanks for the consequences," but we still need to be faithful and consistent in discipline.

▼ *Thank You, God, for Your steadfast character.*

GC

SPORTS AND STRESS

Let us run with endurance the race that is set before us.
—HEB. 12:1

*W*hen my son was eight, he was very excited about playing baseball. Since baseball was his father's favorite sport, we felt it was a good choice. Remembering his father's spontaneous Sunday afternoon games on vacant lots, none of us were prepared for the competitive spirit on his team. The competition, surprisingly, was with the parents, not the kids! Parents would verbally abuse their child and other children if they made an out or missed the ball. They offered monetary rewards for caught balls or home runs. Some parents almost got into fistfights with the coach. My son was so intimidated by the atmosphere, he wouldn't try to hit the ball. He took his chances at a walk.

Sports can be fun for the whole family, or it can be stressful and anything but fun. Children do not need excessive stress because they are subjected to it daily at school and with friends.

Children need to be children. They need to have fun playing whatever they play. They have many years to enter competition and excel. Parents need to watch and enjoy their children's childishness, realizing it's fleeting.

▼ *Dear Lord, being a child is wonderful. Let us enjoy every minute.*

JS

SWITCHING ROLES

Better is a dinner of herbs where love is,
Than a fatted calf with hatred.
—PROV. 15:17

*I*n our society, fathers and mothers are having to switch roles because of the economy. Fathers are becoming house husbands, and mothers are being pushed into the work world. I know from personal experience that it's not easy for parents. Not only is it stressful for the mothers who feel torn in several directions, it's also stressful for the fathers who feel pretty confused and worn out.

Each day when I came home from work my husband said, "I'm ready to go back to work. This is too tiring and too much work for me." I responded, "I wish I were home with my kids. I hate working."

Switching roles is hard on the whole family. It's important to talk to your children about what's going on. Don't just talk about how you feel, but how they feel too. And don't forget your spouse. He is suffering too. Talk to each other and depend on God. He cares for you more than you can know. He will take care of you and your family.

▼ *Dear God, in the midst of changing roles, may our love for You and for one another never change. Thank You for Your unchanging love and Your promise to provide for all our needs.*

LB

COVERINGS

Blessed is he whose transgression is forgiven,
Whose sin is covered.
Blessed is the man to whom
* the LORD does not impute iniquity.*
                    —PS. 32:1–2

*I*t is the covering of the Lamb's blood that allows our heavenly Father to see us as cleansed and righteous. Fortunately there is nothing we can do to change what was done on Calvary. Christ's blood was shed. A sacrificial covering was made once and for all.

A covering needs to exist for our children too.

Many times we may feel they are really undeserving of our love. They may constantly be getting in trouble, fighting with us, or intentionally breaking rules. Yet still they are deserving of our love.

When our children misbehave, we know there are always reasons for their acting out. Kids are never just bad kids. When our children were born, they became our children. It was a done deal. We know to impute their acting out on something else rather than just on who they. Our unconditional love, because they are our own, is the covering that allows us to do so.

▼ *Dear God, thank You for forgiving my sins. Thank You for Your unconditional love.*

                    GC

PEACE AT ANY PRICE?

For to you it has been granted on behalf of Christ, not only to believe in Him, but also to suffer for His sake, having the same conflict which you saw in me and now hear is in me.
—PHIL. 1:29–30

*C*onflict is part of life. Many times it is accompanied by anger, arguments, and harsh words. Sometimes these are mishandled, but conflict in itself is not a bad thing. Through conflict, resolution comes.

Beth grew up in a house where no harsh words were spoken. All disagreements were resolved in private or not at all. Beth was very frightened of conflict. She saw it as something to be avoided at all cost. As a married woman, she avoids disagreements with her husband because she is afraid their whole relationship will fall apart with one harsh word or disagreement.

I tell my patients, "Show me a marriage without conflict, and I will show you a marriage where nothing is resolved." Conflict is not the operative word, resolution is. Resolution comes when people have their conflict; share their thoughts, feelings, and opinions; and come to some solution if only to agree to disagree.

Children need to learn healthy communication tools from their parents. How to argue and resolve conflicts is an important part of their education.

▼ *Dear Lord, remind me that resolution of conflicts will make my family healthy and increase trust and intimacy.*

JS

MOVING TOO FAST

[Jesus] often withdrew into the wilderness and prayed.
—LUKE 5:16

*H*ave you ever felt you were moving too fast? Have you wished the merry-go-round would stop and let you off? With doctors' appointments, swimming lessons, school, homework, clubs, soccer practice, church meetings, and more meetings, we have become too busy. When we stop long enough to look at our children, we see that years have passed. They are growing up too fast.

Children do grow up quickly, and many of us are missing out. We don't have time to smell the roses, much less spend time with our children. We want the clock to slow down, but it seems to be racing ahead out of control.

Jesus packed more into three short years than many of us pack into a lifetime, but He never appeared to be rushed. He always had time for people, and always had time for His Father. Even during those final days when the cross loomed before Him, I suspect His habits didn't change. Jesus knew the importance of taking time for prayer. Do we?

▼ *Lord, You know how busy I get. Help me never to get too busy for You or for my family.*

LB

HE KNOWS

The LORD looks from heaven;
He sees all the sons of men. . . .
He fashions their hearts individually;
He considers all their works.
—PS. 33:13, 15

It's an old holiday favorite. Probably you remember singing it when you were a child. You know, the one about the all-seeing Santa Claus who "knows when you've been bad or good." I remember realizing for the first time all the similarities between what we tell our children about a fictional jolly old fellow in a red suit, and what we tell them about our heavenly Father.

As parents it is impossible for us to know everything about our children. We can't keep our eye on them every minute. If we could, it might be easier to teach and correct them. We would know their feelings and perceptions of what they experienced, and could help them make sense of things. We could lovingly intervene when their motives were less than pure. It would be easier to shape their character.

What a comfort it is to know that our God really is all knowing. He does indeed know when our children are "bad" or "good." More than that, He knows their hearts and motives. Our Father knows them individually. He can fashion their hearts and develop their character as we can never do.

▼ *Dear God, I trust You are shaping the hearts of my children. I shall always pray for them.*

GC

BEING ISOLATED

"And yet I am not alone, because the Father is with Me."
                                        —JOHN 16:32

*B*eing isolated is not a fun place to be. Friends break into our isolation with the warmth of caring and concern. They are a barometer of our feelings of self-worth and our well-being. Children need friends, and usually are very upset if they don't have at least a few. Many time a lack of friends is the first sign that all is not well.

Eight-year-old Julie repeatedly complained that nobody liked her. When her mother checked it out, it was true. Julie had alienated herself from the children in her class. Not only was she left out of their activities, her classmates picked on her and made fun of her. Julie's mother and teacher attempted to help her by involving her in class activities, but to no avail. That's when Julie's mother decided Julie needed counseling.

Parents must make it a point to know how their children are doing with their peers and take whatever steps necessary to correct the situation if there is a problem. Counseling is one way to address the issue and find out the cause of the problem. Parents also may need to involve themselves in counseling with their child because they are the ones who can implement the solution.

▼ *Dear Lord, since You surrounded Yourself with friends and disciples, You understand the importance of friends for my child.*

JS

REBELS

Do not withhold correction from a child.
—PROV. 23:13

*I*n a few weeks Bob will be seventeen. He is quiet and somewhat shy—not the kind of boy you'd picture as rebellious. But Bob usually does whatever he wants. This includes a lot of lying to his parents about sneaking out at night and coming home in the morning. He loves to be with his friends and enjoys drinking. Bob says his only problem is that his parents are too strict. The only time he's unhappy is when he gets caught and punished. Then he's anything but quiet. He yells at his parents and then wishes he were dead.

Bob is hard to reach. He has a big problem with denial and drinking. Soon he will be on his own. I can only hope that a spark will light inside him. I pray that God will lead him back to more healthy ways of coping with pain.

If you have a rebellious child, don't give up and don't beat yourself up. It is very stressful to have a child who is constantly going against you. Seek help—not only for them, but also for your own support. We need all the help we can get, from other parents and especially from God.

 God, help those who don't even know they are heading for disaster.

LB

VENGEANCE IS THE LORD'S

Beloved, do not avenge yourselves, but rather give place to wrath; for it is written, "Vengeance is Mine, I will repay," says the Lord.

—ROM. 12:19

*G*eorge could tell something was bothering his teenage son. He seemed preoccupied and a little irritated. "If you want to talk, I'm available," George said. In years past George would have asked a lot of questions. But he had learned that his questions usually got nothing but avoidance or ridicule for being "too nosy."

This time George's son did come and talk to him. He told him he was angry because of some wrong done to him at school. There were rumors going around about him and a girl he barely knew. As they talked, they focused on his angry feelings. Then they talked about what he wanted to do about the situation. Of course he wanted to get back at the person who started the rumor, but he wasn't sure who was responsible.

As father and son talked some more, he realized he couldn't repay the humiliation he had experienced without feeling bad himself. Finally he came to the conclusion that only God could justly get back at the person who started the rumor. "I'm tired of being angry," he said. "Maybe that's why God said 'Vengeance is Mine.'" George agreed and silently thanked God for helping his son to choose God's way.

▼ *Dear God, thank You for knowing our hurts and allowing us to be free from debilitating anger.*

GC

HOMEWORK HASSLES

But by a man of understanding and knowledge
Right will be prolonged. —PROV. 28:2

*H*omework is for kids! Adults never understand the right way to do it. They may get the right answer, but they never have the right technique. Homework has spoiled more tranquil evenings than anything else. It also has been the demise of more than one relationship.

Homework for Sam was torture, partly because he had an attention problem. As soon as Dad arrived home, the homework assignment began. After thirty minutes, Sam's mind was everywhere except on his work. Dad did the problems the way he was taught. They didn't even resemble the example in the book. Within forty-five minutes, Dad was totally frustrated and calling Sam "Stupid" or "Idiot." Sam dissolved in tears believing what his dad said about him. If you're in one of these classic no win situations, it's time to stop and regroup. What are you trying to accomplish? The main goal is to learn the material, but not at the sake of self-esteem. Remember, children who get the message they are stupid, often live up to that self-fulfilling prophecy. You may need to withdraw from the homework chore. It's better to have a good relationship with your children than to be their tutor or teacher.

▼ *Dear Lord, rescue me and my child from homework conflict.*

JS

ANGER

Let all bitterness, wrath, anger, clamor, and evil speaking be put away from you, with all malice.
—EPH. 4:31

*H*ow do you fight with your spouse? One of my family therapy children complained to her parents, "I don't even know how to fight because you two never do." Other children have said that their parents yell, scream, and even throw things at each other. Still others say that their parents just stop talking. "Well, I just give my husband the silent treatment, and it works," one mother said. "He pays attention."

However you fight with your spouse, know that at least two watching and learning eyes will probably carry that skill into adulthood.

I think God had a good psychological reason for saying, "Do not let the sun go down on your wrath" (Eph. 4:26). If we don't work through our anger with our spouse at the time it occurs, it will become a wedge between the two of us. Later it will grow larger and become a thick, hard wall.

▼ *Dear God, help me to learn healthy ways of fighting and resolving my anger so I can model this to my children.*

LB

COMPASSION

As a father pities his children,
So the LORD pities those who fear Him.
—PS. 103:13

 can just imagine our heavenly Father looking down and seeing the poor sinful state His children were in. We were a lost people. In bondage by our inherent sinfulness and doomed to suffer the consequences of death without the Savior. We also were left to suffer the difficulties of daily life here on earth. Can you imagine working through life's trials without Jesus?

I can imagine God looking down and not only having compassion on our sinful state, but also having pity on our emotional state. We know He was so moved by His love for the world that He sent His only begotten Son. Because of this supreme sacrifice, we can have perfect communion with Him and an easier yoke to bear than what the world offers.

Just as God is aware of our emotional needs, we need to be aware of our children's emotional needs. We need to have compassion on our kids when they are hurting emotionally. We need to do whatever is necessary, regardless of the sacrifice it may require, to make certain we do not emotionally deprive or neglect our children.

▼ *Thank You, God, for Your pity and for knowing when I hurt. Help me to be aware of my children's emotional needs.*

GC

TOUGH SKIN

Beloved, if God so loved us, we also ought to love one another. —1 JOHN 4:11

*T*ough skin is sometimes necessary to survive childhood, especially during the transition time which is usually in the sixth or seventh grade. For some reason, children are especially hard on each other during that age. Survival calls for extreme measures.

When my daughter was in the sixth grade, we had a friend who stayed with us after school. Every afternoon the two girls would climb a tree in the front yard. They would take turns reciting epitaphs. "Why you are so low a snake couldn't crawl under you." "If you were any lower I would have to step off the curb to see you." They would find things about each other to criticize. My first reaction was one of concern for what they were doing to each other. Then one day I went to the school and realized that all of the children were very critical of each other. It appeared to be a stage they were going through. It occurred to me that they had to endure these put downs every day so they could toughen themselves to take whatever happened.

The world is a treacherous place to live. Parents can't rescue their child every time. Parents can provide a safe place for their children when they need to regroup.

▼ *Dear Lord, give me compassion for my children and all the trials they go through.*

JS

*We also are weak in Him, but we shall live
with Him by the power of God toward you.*
—2 COR. 13:4

*M*rs. Johnson was nursing her two-year-old when
her three-month-old woke up out of a deep sleep and
began crying. Later when she was nursing the baby, her
two-year-old began throwing things and hitting her. Still
later, her two-year-old hit the baby on the head.

Of course that made the infant cry again. So Mrs.
Johnson is constantly watching to make sure the two-
year-old won't hurt the baby. She is also helping the
two-year-old work through his anger toward his younger
brother by talking about his jealousy.

Jealousy and resentment happen with every family
so don't feel alone or that your child is different. All
children fight. The important thing is to stop the older
child from hurting the younger child and then to talk
about it. Acting out behavior from one or more children
upon the arrival of a new brother or sister is a common
dilemma for families, but it can be overcome.

Be cautioned, however, when your older child constantly hits, or trips, or bites, or scares your younger
child, not to let your anger get out of control. Calm yourself before addressing your child's behavior, and seek
professional help if it is warranted.

▼ *Father, it is so hard to know how to guide my children. Please help me channel their jealousy of each
other in the right direction.*

LB

PASS IT ON

"The secret things belong to the LORD our God, but those things which are revealed belong to us and to our children forever, that we may do all the words of this law."
—DEUT. 29:29

*M*y grandfather told my father and my father told me. When the time comes I will tell my son. It is a story to be told with great reverence for our Jehovah Jireh. It is a story about answered prayer. Of how God provides for and blesses His children.

I look forward to telling my children about God. There is no greater joy than to share your faith with your children.

When my grandfather was a teenager, he very innocently asked God to do something special in his life. That very evening, God began to use him financially to bless a good friend. A total stranger had given him a sum of money, but he didn't feel God wanted him to have it. He prayed for several days to know what God would have him do with this money. When he met with his friend, God revealed to him her specific need. He gave her the money. They were both overjoyed.

God revealed two things: first, the power of prayer; and second, the blessing of ministering to others.

This is a story I will share with my children. I will tell them it belongs to them forever.

▼ *Dear God, reveal Your truth to me. May I hold it dear and faithfully pass it on to my children.*

GC

PATRIOTISM

"In you [Abram] all the nations shall be blessed."
—GAL. 3:8

*P*atriotism was revived with the Persian Gulf War. It did my heart good to see people get excited at the sight of the American flag. That hadn't been the case since the Vietnam War.

When I was a child, every day we said the Pledge of Allegiance followed by several patriotic songs. The flag was raised in ceremony, and everyone swelled with pride. I always got goose bumps and chills when I heard the "Star-Spangled Banner." I was concerned that my children didn't have the same sense of pride and excitement in being an American I had as a child.

It probably has more to do with respect and authority than nostalgia. The symbolism of the flag represents our President making decisions for us. It says we are behind him and that we will respect him for his position. I feel that translates into respect for the authority of others.

It seems for a time patriotism was passé. Respect for authority in our country was at its lowest. But the Gulf War rekindled pride in our nation. Let's help keep the flame burning bright, especially in our own homes, by showing our children how much our country means to us and by showing respect for our leaders.

▼ *Dear Lord, bless our country and foster respect for the authorities who lead us.*

JS

PASSED DOWN

For I, the LORD your God, am a jealous God,
visiting the iniquity of the fathers on the
children to the third and fourth generations.
—EX. 20:5

$\mathcal{A}$ sixteen-year-old boy, Steve, was admitted to the hospital because his parents feared for his safety. He had been drinking and partying all night. They feared he might run away. In family therapy, Steve's family's habit pattern became evident. Both of Steve's parents were also alcoholics. They stated that they were trying to do everything they could. Yet their child was diagnosed with being dependent on alcohol.

The alcoholic pattern is very real. You can trace it through a family's generations, even though several generations may be "dry" and able to refrain from drinking. The pattern is how the children are raised, and it's hard to break that cycle. One of the core patterns is that feelings are not allowed to be expressed in constructive ways. When feelings are buried, they may come out in unhealthy ways like getting drunk.

Can this pattern of alcoholism stop? Yes! People are in recovery from this disease (and, as doctors say, it is truly a physical disease). God can work in families and individuals, as they learn about this sickness and admit they need God's help.

▼ *God, help me to break any unhealthy behavior patterns in my family. Give me a new understanding of Your grace.*

LB

BY EXAMPLE

> *"Only take heed to yourself, and diligently*
> *keep yourself, lest you forget the things your*
> *eyes have seen, and lest they depart from*
> *your heart all the days of your life. And*
> *teach them to your children and your*
> *grandchildren."*
> —DEUT. 4:9

At fifteen years of age this golf prodigy was playing against professionals—and beating them! How was it that this young man had acquired such athletic skill at an early age? As an infant he would sit in his high chair and watch his father hit hundreds of golf balls day in and day out in the garage. A usually complex action, a golf swing, became simple to perform by repeatedly watching his father practice it.

What a great truth! As parents it is vital for us to teach our children by example. It is literally what our children see that will become second nature to them. What most of us forget is that this process begins at an early age. Even before our children are able to perform a particular behavior they are taking notes.

What are your manners like at the dinner table? How do you handle your anger? How do you treat your husband or wife? The list can go on and on. Don't try to be perfect. In fact, the most important question on the list might be how do you handle your imperfections?

▼ *Dear God, I know that I am first accountable to You. May I live my life according to Your will.*

GC

IT'S FUN TO LAUGH

A merry heart makes a cheerful countenance.
—PROV. 15:13

*L*aughter is good medicine. It also relieves a lot of tension. Sometimes we take ourselves and our children too seriously. We forget how to laugh. But when we find ourselves laughing, the day seems brighter and the load lighter.

As a parent, sometimes I would get so self-absorbed and very impatient for my son to do a requested chore. I would be emphatic that he needed to respond immediately. He would start his diversion techniques, usually accompanied by facial gestures and strange noises. In the face of his absurd approach, I usually laughed. He would burst out giggling joined by his sisters. It never failed to relieve the tension, and I must admit occasionally got him out of the requested chore. The bottom line was that it was a lot of fun.

It is fun to laugh. I really believe that's why the TV show of home videos is so successful. It transports people into laughter and everyone feels better afterward.

Children need to laugh with friends and with their parents. We also need to take time to laugh at ourselves. It keeps us from taking ourselves so seriously.

▼ *Dear Lord, I am so glad You made us so we can laugh and enjoy each other.*

JS

ACCIDENTS HAPPEN

Behold, He who keeps Israel
Shall neither slumber nor sleep.
—PS. 121:4

*A*ccidents happen! From birth on up no child is immune from accidents. Some seem to be especially accident prone. I think every mother and father knows the fastest route to the Emergency Room and knows their pediatrician's phone number by heart.

Does God protect our children from accidents? I believe He does. I can think of several close calls where it was hard to believe the child was okay. The other day a mother told me how her six-month-old infant fell head first onto the kitchen floor while he was still in his infant seat. The child was fine, not even bruised. The pediatrician told her that infants are made with extra protection.

God obviously knew what He was doing when he made children. Not only did He give them an inquisitive spirit that causes them to explore their world, He gave them bodies that bounce a lot better than an adult's. Of course we need to do everything possible to protect them from harm, but we can't put them in straight jackets. We need to trust the Lord will watch over them as they bump into their world. Kids are kids, and God is God. And He neither slumbers nor sleeps.

▼ *Lord, help me not to be consumed with worry about my children's safety. Show me the precautions I need to take, and then help me to know You are also watching over them.*

LB

ADMITTING OUR MISTAKES

*Confess your trespasses to one another, and
pray for one another.* —JAMES 5:16

*M*any parents believe they must be perfect in the
eyes of their children. They think to themselves, *I have
to be a perfect example or they won't respect me.* These
statements could not be farther from the truth. In fact, it
is important for children to understand that their parents are not perfect.

Admitting mistakes will improve communication with
our children. It will make us more accessible by lowering us from any lofty pedestals we or our children have
created. Open and honest sharing will be more frequent. Intimacy with your children will become easier.

Admitting our mistakes also promotes realism. The
truth is we are not perfect people. We are prone to fail,
and that's to be expected. Of course it takes courage to
be vulnerable—to allow our children to see our faults
and weaknesses. That's why we have a forgiving heavenly Father. As we grow in Christ, we experience His
unconditional acceptance. We learn to risk more because He will never reject us.

When was the last time you apologized to your children?

 *Dear God, give me the courage necessary to confess
my wrongs and weaknesses to my children—and to
You.*

GC

DEALING WITH DEPRESSION

*Anxiety in the heart of man causes
depression.* —PROV. 12:25

$\mathscr{D}$epression is a major illness in America today. Many
people suffer this painful and debilitating illness. Sometimes the pain is so bad they commit suicide. Usually
the trigger to the depression is a situation or experience
that feels impossible and generates a lot of anger. Teens
and children also suffer depression.

Amy was sixteen when I first saw her because she
told some of her friends she was having thoughts of suicide. She was a model adolescent and rarely caused
problems with her family or at school. She always wore
a plastered-on smile that she used to cover her feelings.
Her family had noticed that she began to withdraw and
lose interest in her normal activities. There were problems between Amy and her parents that frequently re-
sulted in heated arguments. Amy really had no one to
turn to with her feelings. She was depressed and very
angry at all of them. Rather than expressing her anger,
she turned it inward.

Parents are in the best seat in the house to notice
changes in behavior and the onset of depression. It
needs to be addressed quickly. An evaluation or counseling would be a good place to begin.

 *Dear Lord, help me to be alert to any changes in my
children's behavior that might point to a problem.*

JS

BROKEN HEART

Attend to me, and hear me;
I am restless in my complaint.
—PS. 55:2

If you have to leave your children to go to work, this is for you. I know how you feel.

At the beginning of the month, my husband got laid off at work and I had to work a lot more. The sadness I felt was tough. I kept asking where it was coming from. In searching myself, I found I was mourning the loss of being with my five-month-old and two-year-old. It really hurt and was a form of grief. I went through all the stages of grief—first denial, then anger and sadness, and later acceptance. And then I repeated the cycle. I feel a lot of us do not know how a working mom feels. What she has to do to cope with her feelings.

It's important to talk about how you feel. I bet a lot of other moms will understand. Also the time you do have with your children is so much more special. Tell yourself that it's all right that you have to work. God will help you with the loss.

▼ *God, help the working moms cope with not only the stress of working but also with the pain of leaving their children each day.*

LB

ALWAYS WITH GRACE

Let your speech always be with grace,
seasoned with salt, that you may know how
you ought to answer each one.

—COL. 4:6

*H*ave you ever said something to your son or daughter that you regretted? We all have. In the midst of all the trials and stresses we face as parents, it's easy to slip and make hurtful comments. I still remember hurtful statements my parents made to me when I was a child. I know that I will make hurtful comments to my children, too. It's an unavoidable part of being a parent. It's an unavoidable part of growing up as a child.

Do not underestimate the power and effect of what you say to your children. Parents are very central to a child's life. What we say can impact and shape their very identity. It has been said that for every one negative statement, it takes four positive statements to keep a balance.

Not only do we need to season everything we say with kindness and gentleness, we need to recognize our children are unique. They may respond to us differently. Speaking always with grace provides us the proper foundation to interact with each of our children no matter how diverse they may be and no matter what the situation.

▼ *Dear God, help me to speak with grace upon my lips.*

GC

RAINDROPS OF WISDOM

Let my teaching drop as the rain,
My speech distill as the dew,
As raindrops on the tender herb,
And as showers on the grass.
                    —DEUT. 32:2

*W*hat a lovely picture of the way we should teach and train our children! I wish I could do that, but at times I feel so frustrated and ineffective. But in reality most of the valuable truths are taught just that way.

When my son was six years old, he wanted to ride his bike to the park with some older boys and his friend who was also six. Not convinced of his bike riding prowess, I decided he could not go. He was extremely angry and said I was a "mean" mother. I felt bad, thinking maybe I was being over-protective. Half an hour later, his friend returned. He had not been ready to negotiate one of the hills. As a result he had an accident with a pickup truck. Fortunately he was not badly hurt. My son came running to tell me the story. He added that I was right. He was not ready for the hill either.

We wonder how we are able to make valid decisions especially when most of the time we are frustrated and anxious. But it is my firm belief that these raindrops of wisdom trickle down from God above.

▼ *Dear Lord, what a blessing to have You on our side*
as we seek to parent our children with Your wisdom.
                                                        JS

POWER STRUGGLE

Stir up Yourself,
*   and awake to my vindication,*
To my cause, my God and my Lord.
                    —PS. 35:23

*K*nowing parental guidelines and consequences is important, especially for those of us with kids. But children, as they grow older, need to have their own space to make their own decisions. If they fail, they learn from their own mistakes.

Joanne's mother is extremely frustrated that Joanne won't practice the violin at least 30 minutes a day. Over and over again, she tells Joanne to practice. Joanne says that this nagging pushes her to not want to play or practice anymore. This is a power struggle. The best thing would be to make Joanne responsible for the consequences of not practicing. The consequences might be that the lessons should stop. Her mom can't make her a violin player. It has to be Joanne's own choice.

Doesn't God do this with His kids? His grace and forgiveness are real for our mistakes, and the results are not what we like. Are we willing to learn from our mistakes?

 God, help me to know where and when to let go and when to let my children be responsible. Help me to set things up so that they learn independence in healthy ways.

LB

THOSE INEVITABLE FAILURES

*My little children, these things I write to you,
that you may not sin. And if anyone sins, we
have an Advocate with the Father, Jesus
Christ the righteous.*   —1 JOHN 2:1

$\mathcal{A}$s much as I want my children to be perfect and never fail, I know that will never happen. I have to consider the source. It is simply impossible for something imperfect to beget something perfect!

Today's Scripture has two important truths that hit home for me. First, John encourages Christians in Asia Minor not to sin, but he understands they are likely to do so. As a parent, I never want to cause my children to stumble. Instead I want to provide right teaching, modeling, and encouragement to live righteous lives. Still it is inevitable that my children will fail and sin against the Father. When that happens, I want to be understanding.

Second, John points out that we have an Advocate with the Father. The word *advocate* suggests that we have someone who comes to our aid and stands by our side. My position with my children should be similar. I always want to be available to them and to aid them whenever it is appropriate. I want to be by their side, not covering for their failures, but standing by them to encourage them on their way.

▼ *Dear God, teach me to live a righteous life. Thank You for Your forgiveness through Jesus.*

GC

HEAD LICE

*"Stretch out your rod, and strike the dust of
the land, so that it may become lice
throughout all the land of Egypt."*
—EX. 8:16

*L*ice are gruesome things to think about. But many times head lice is part of childhood even in the most elite of families. Perhaps God still uses lice to get our attention just as He tried to do with the pharaohs.

A friend of mine who was especially careful with her children was appalled to learn they had head lice. This was one problem she was sure she would never have to worry about. She became concerned when both children kept scratching their heads. When she examined their heads, she found lice. Even more distressing, she found innumerable nits on the hairs that had to be removed. She had been told the name of a product and asked a pharmacist for it. The pharmacist asked why she needed it. In a very soft voice, to cover her embarrassment, she said, "to remove lice."

At times, we think we are immune to some of the nitpicking problems of the world. We intend to protect our children so they don't have to experience them. But we are all in this life together and have the same experiences. Perhaps God uses things like lice as the great leveler.

▼ *Dear Lord, keep our focus on You rather than our nitpicking problems.*

JS

BLENDED FAMILIES

*I also labor, striving according to His
working which works in me mightily.*
—COL. 1:29

Susie is a beautiful and intelligent child who is very
depressed. She lacks motivation, doesn't want to go to
school, and cries a lot. Her appetite has dropped, and
she just wants to stay home in her room. Susie used to
have lots of friends. She was on the swim team and did
well in school. Now she has given up.

Susie's parents separated a year ago. She lives with
her mother who just got remarried. She feels guilty that
she isn't supportive of her mother. She misses her father
and the closeness she once had with her mother. They
used to talk about all their adventures and problems.
Now her mother is always busy and doesn't seem to
need her much. Susie feels set aside.

Susie doesn't know how to nurture herself. It's a
common problem. The parent nurtures the child too
much and never lets the child develop the skills to love
themselves. The mother and child become so en-
meshed that they become almost too close. Boundaries
get violated, and the child gets lost.

It's important to remain a parent and not to let your
child parent you. Teach them the skills to love themselves and to care for their own emotional needs.

▼ *Father, help me to teach my children how to love
themselves. And help me to love myself and not to
depend on them to fill this void.*

LB

WHAT IS PRIORITY?

There is one who makes himself rich,
yet has nothing;
And one who makes himself poor,
yet has great riches.

—PROV. 13:7

$\mathcal{O}$ne of the lies Satan and our society has led us to believe is that material gain is necessary for happiness. From the very beginning the Evil One tempted Christ by offering Him all the kingdoms of the world. Even still, for many who understand this untruth, there exists an imbalance of emphasis on providing financially for our children. It is easy to focus on careers and financial gain all in the name of our "spiritual duty" and miss God's true desire for our lives.

What God does desire is for us to build relationships with our children. To teach them and to love them. That can only be accomplished by spending time with them. We won't have time for them if we give priority to making money or furthering our career. Financial and career goals are important, but it's a mistake to pursue them at the expense of our children. Many will rationalize that providing financially is the way they express their love for their children. It is perhaps *one* of the ways we do so, but certainly not the most important way. Evaluate your priorities today. Are you working to invest in your children's lives? How are you doing so?

▼ *Dear God, help me as I evaluate priorities in my life and undertake the hard work of being a parent.*

GC

THE POOR AND NEEDY

Blessed is he who considers the poor.
—PS. 41:1

Some families are so far removed from poverty that their children have a difficult time understanding what it is all about. Of course these parents are thankful they do not have to live in poverty, and many times they are not anxious for their children to know about it. But children need to understand how all people live in order to learn empathy for others.

My children have had firsthand experiences with people who live in poverty. Every Christmas we have several families for whom we buy Christmas presents. Through the church we support these families all year. It was no problem getting people to provide the money to buy for these families, but it was hard to find someone to deliver the baskets. We frequently ended up with the job, and all of the blessings. Over the years we have come to know these families. We have been in their homes and have been invited to their weddings. We have learned they are just the same as us only their problems are a little different. I'm glad my children have come to know these families.

Our lives do not need to be so safe and secure that we do not become involved in the needs of others. We need to know about the problems of others to keep our lives in perspective.

▼ *Dear Lord, give me a heart for the poor and needy.*
JS

SEXUAL ABUSE

He also brought me up out
of a horrible pit,
Out of the miry clay,
And set my feet upon a rock,
And established my steps.
                    —PS. 40:2

*J*ennifer is fifteen years old. She looks and acts twenty. She dates a man a much older than herself, and she fights a lot with her parents over the rules at home. Ten years ago Jennifer was sexually abused by her great-uncle. The abuse continued for several years. She has just realized it. Jennifer now resents her boyfriends and feels dirty and scared inside.

Sexual abuse is rampant in the world today. A lot of children are being destroyed by it. There is hope for Jennifer, and children like her, through therapy. Those doing the abusing also need help so this disease will stop.

If your child is sexually active, seems a lot older than he or she is, and acts out against you, it's time to find out what's going on. Seek professional help. Don't wait, but also don't despair. God is able to bring sexually abused children out of the pit of despair and to establish their steps.

▼ *Dear Father, give me insight into why my children act the way they do. Help me to know if they need professional help. If they do, show me where to turn. Don't allow me to ignore their need.*

LB

SHEPHERDING

*Be diligent to know the state
of your flocks,
And attend to your herds.*
—PROV. 27:23

I am reminded of the traits of a good shepherd as I read today's Scripture. He is always aware of the state of his flock. He knows each sheep individually, and is aware if one is hurt or missing. Being a good shepherd is a full-time job.

Being a parent is also a full-time job. We're always on call. It takes much diligence to be a parent in this day and time. Unfortunately, most of our lives are not unidimensional. We have several jobs or roles to fulfill. We must be good employees or bosses, good friends, and good spouses. The list may get very lengthy.

When we add together the responsibilities of each family member, along with his or her ever expanding list of activities and commitments, the pace may become unbearable. It may become necessary to call a "state of the family" meeting.

As a parent or shepherd of your family, it's not enough just to know everyone's schedule. It's essential also to know the emotional state of each family member and the emotional atmosphere of your household. Planned meetings may feel awkward at first, but they may be vital to the emotional care of your family.

▼ *Help me, God, to attend to my flock today. Thank You for giving me Jesus as my perfect example.*

GC

LOOKING BELOW THE SURFACE

"You have made known to me the ways of life;
You will make me full of joy in Your presence."
                                    —ACTS 2:28

I just returned from seeing the movie, *Beauty and the Beast,* a lovely fairy tale. It had a wonderful message about not being fooled by outward appearances but instead looking below the surface to know someone. The beast, feeling very unlovable, portrayed an angry front so people could not see his pain and loneliness. The beauty was able to see the real character of the beast beneath his mask.

Many times when our children feel unlovable or insecure, their surface behavior becomes angry and unattractive. It is really hard not to stop there—not to accept that as their identity. But if we search below the surface and risk a little, we may again see their loveliness. By accepting their inner beauty, we can begin to help them shed their mask of anger or fear.

Not everyone is willing to look below the surface of unattractive behavior. Children and teens alike need to know that their parents see beneath their masks to their inner beauty. Parents also need to be accepted in the same way for who they are inside. When both teen and parent can connect on that level, the relationship leaps ahead.

▼ *Dear God, help me to see my child or teen the way You see him.*

JS

My God shall supply all your need according to His riches in glory by Christ Jesus.
—PHIL. 4:19

*I*n my weekly family therapy, my clients discussed how stressful it was when the father lost his job one year ago. "I just couldn't trust God," the father said. "I'm still looking for a job. I continue to panic and cause everyone around me to suffer."

As I sat there trying to remain objective, suddenly I thought to myself, *Laura, your husband may be facing the same thing. He just got laid off from his job. How would we handle it?* That Sunday in church God provided a skit on faith that I needed to see. . .

There was a man called Abraham who almost sacrificed his only son, Isaac. He showed such great faith by believing that God had a plan for Abraham's (and Isaac's) life. Though he could not see the reason for the sacrifice, he trusted God, took the risk, and God rewarded his conviction. Though God did not let Abraham sacrifice Isaac, the experience wasn't easy to go through, but God honored Abraham's faith.

It is so important to depend on God knowing that He will take care of us even when we cannot see God's ultimate plan. He will take care of us, but in His own way, and in His own time.

▼ *Father, You know our needs. Please help me to trust You to meet those needs even as You have promised.*
LB

DON'T GROW WEARY

*And let us not grow weary while doing good,
for in due season we shall reap if we do not
lose heart.*
                                    —GAL. 6:9

The young boy was really a handful for his parents. He was more than rambunctious. Always interrupting, always loud, too often destructively clumsy. His conversation rambled, and he just plain forgot things while at home or at school.

At the request of a teacher, his parents had him evaluated by a psychologist. It was determined he had Attention Deficit Disorder. Through much family counseling, his parents learned how to deal with their own emotions and handle their son's behavior. Their son was given a prescription of medicine for a short time, but the real impact came as his family learned to love and encourage him rather than show their impatience and ridicule.

Though tiring at times, they continued to do a good work with their son. Most Attention Deficit children take much effort and patience to be around, let alone to properly parent. Yet all their efforts were later rewarded. With a well developed positive self-image, this young boy went on to become a medical doctor and dedicated his life to helping others.

▼ *Dear God, help me not to lose heart as I deal with the trials and struggles of parenting.*

GC

AUNTS AND UNCLES

"His uncle or his uncle's son may redeem him; or anyone who is near of kin to him in his family may redeem him."
—LEV. 25:49

*R*elationships with aunts and uncles are a wonderful treasure. Children are considered special just because they are a niece or nephew. Many times aunts and uncles, besides being less serious and more fun-loving, offer a means of escape from daily and family stress.

An aunt makes it a point to maintain the role of special confidante with her nieces and nephews. She tailor-makes birthday and Christmas presents. When they are young, she brings articles to make a real doctor's kit. When they get older, she arranges golf and piano lessons. She is there for weekend and summer visits. She makes a good sounding board to express frustrations about the family without being disloyal to the family.

Parents need to encourage these relationships. Aunts and uncles can bring something to your children that perhaps you cannot because you lack the time or energy. For one thing, they can give a fresh perspective outside the daily hassle of laundry or homework. They also can give you a break to regroup and recharge. Relationships with aunts and uncles are special for all involved.

▼ *Dear Lord, thank You for the gift of aunts and uncles. Thank You for their love for my children and the way they are there to help out when needed.*

JS

Be anxious for nothing, but in everything by prayer and supplication, with thanksgiving, let your requests be made known to God.
—PHIL. 4:6

*J*immy has a short attention span. He rarely does as his mother, Janet, asks. Filled with rage, Jimmy has problems not only at home but anywhere he goes. He can't sit still. He constantly interrupts others. And he never stays on a task for more than two minutes.

Jane tries to set limits, but Jimmy doesn't follow them. She took him to a psychiatrist for several months, and he received medication, which helped some. But Jane still feels hopeless. She now homeschools him and is exhausted. Jane wonders if he will ever change or get better.

When all the earthly channels have failed and we have run into closed doors, it's time to take a second look, knock again, and look for the doors God *has* opened. God gives us hope that He will work things out. We may not know how God will work, but we can begin to ask for some answers. Turn to Him and ask Him to open a door.

▼ *God, when I'm feeling anxious about situations that seem hopeless, help me to turn to You.*

LB

PRACTICE WHAT YOU PREACH

"Or how can you say to your brother,
'Brother, let me remove the speck that is in
your eye,' when you yourself do not see the
plank that is in your own eye? Hypocrite!
First remove the plank from your own eye."
—LUKE 6:42

"Do as I say, not as I do." Sometimes, as when the limits of old age set in, this is an appropriate statement. It's not so easy to teach your son how to throw a curve ball when your arm isn't what it used to be.

But when it comes to values, morals, and the behaviors that reflect what character and integrity really constitute, this should never be stated, whispered, or even thought about! To preach one thing and to practice another is more than hypocritical. It can be devastating for your children's development.

Often we desire our children to be better at the things that are most difficult for us. This is especially true with those things we hate most in ourselves. But if improvement is to be made, let it begin with us parents, not our kids.

Do you have any planks in your eye?

▼ *Dear God, always make me aware of the example I set for children. Help me to practice what I preach.*

GC

SUMMER CAMP

*Then Jesus, being filled with the Holy Spirit,
returned from the Jordan and was led by the
Spirit into the wilderness.* —LUKE 4:1

Summer camp may be the first time you and your
child are separated for any length of time. It can be
traumatic to pack up your child and send him off for a
whole week to live with strangers in somewhat sub-
standard housing. Your anxiety heightens when you realize that you aren't sure if he can find his toothbrush or
remember how to make change.

Summer camp can also be traumatic for your child.

Tina was an active member of her Camp Fire troop.
In March, when it was time to sign up for summer
camp, she was very excited. She could hardly wait for
swimming and horseback riding, not to mention being
able to play with her friends all day and night. In June,
as she started packing her clothes, she began to get a
little anxious.

Tina's mother was teary eyed as the bus pulled out.
Five days away seemed like such a long time. She wondered if the leaders really understood that Tina did not
swim well. The first tearful phone call upset everyone. It
wasn't until Saturday when Tina bounded off the bus
bubbling over with all her adventures, that any of them
were convinced that camp was a good idea.

▼ *Dear Lord, I am not sure whether experiences like
camp are harder on parents or children. We sure
need You to watch over all of us.*

JS

LOVING OURSELVES

Finally, all of you be of one mind, having compassion for one another; love as brothers, be tenderhearted, be courteous; not returning evil for evil. **—1 PETER 3:8–9**

*A*my has lots of emotional problems. When she was five, her mother and father bragged about her to everyone. She was talented, intelligent, and cute. She received lots of praise for what she did and how she looked. Now she is sixteen and very depressed. Her parents are confused because she seems to have everything—good looks, smarts, and lots of talent. Yet she hates herself and wishes she were dead. Amy has low self-esteem. She feels good only when she can do things perfectly. It may be that her family's standards have been too high.

Amy is like many girls her age who have a difficult time loving themselves. Even if they are complimented by others, they reject those compliments because they do not know how to compliment themselves.

God does care for the Amys in our world. He longs to show them how special they are. He will help them work through their problems, but they need to reach for help. We can take them to a professional counselor, but we can't force them to open up. We can be compassionate, loving, and tenderhearted. And we can trust that God loves them even more than we do.

▼ *Dear Father, help me to know how I should respond when my children are depressed.*

LB

PERMISSION TO GRIEVE

*She conceived again and bore a son, and
said, "Now I will praise the LORD."
Therefore she called his name Judah. Then
she stopped bearing.* **—GEN. 29:35**

*M*ost everything in Julie's life had gone as she had
dreamed. She often said how richly God had blessed
her, how she had grown up in fairy-tale fashion. I'm
sure that's why it was particularly troublesome for her
when she had difficulty becoming pregnant with a second child.

Julie came from a large family and wanted to parent
a large family of her own. It was part of her dream.
Surely God would bless her with children. But when the
doctors told her it was medically impossible to conceive
again, she was devastated.

Suddenly both Julie and her husband were thrust
into the grieving process. They went through denial and
experienced bouts with depression. They were angry.
They attempted to bargain with God in order to have a
second child. Acceptance was difficult and took several
years.

As I talked with Julie long after we first met, she
shared with me how she and her husband made it
through those tough times. First, they gave themselves
permission to grieve. Second, she told me they never
forgot to praise God for their first child.

▼ *Help me, God, to give myself permission to grieve
and to know that You are sovereign in my life.*

GC

MORE THAN ABC'S

He who gets wisdom loves his own soul;
He who keeps understanding will find good.
　　　　　　　　　　　　　—PROV. 19:8

School serves an important function for children. Besides the obvious like reading, writing, and arithmetic, it serves as a way to learn other important developmental tasks. It offers the opportunity to learn structure, to be adaptable to different ways to do things outside of the family. And school helps them to learn to respect other authority figures besides their parents.

Before Erin started school, her mother was the authority on everything. Soon, however, her wisdom diminished. The first time they blew winter smoke rings with their breath, Erin was quick to point out that her teacher told her it was condensation. The implication was that her teacher was smarter than her mother.

That is as it should be. Children need to learn to get along with a variety of people, some of whom are vastly different from them. Toying around with new ideas and seeing what they think about them lets them learn to think for themselves.

To develop and be all that God wants us to be, we need to learn to think and discern for ourselves. School is the beginning of that adventure.

▼ *Dear Lord, help me provide for my child the best education that is possible.*

JS

REJOICE

*Rejoice always, pray without ceasing, in
everything give thanks; for this is the will of
God in Christ Jesus for you.*
—1 THESS. 5:16–18

*P*regnant! For some men and women a pink (positive) test tube is cause for great excitement. For many
other women and men, however, this news is unexpected and traumatic. Decisions must be made, not
only about your actions toward this pregnancy, but also
decisions about your feelings for this pregnancy.

Even if you are unsure about becoming a parent,
look to God. God says to rejoice, for a child's birth is a
miracle. We can praise God that it was not us, but Him,
who created that infant. God chose to entrust us with a
child, to raise it according to His teachings, and love it
will all our being.

One of my favorite songs is, "Rejoice in the Lord
Always, Again I Say Rejoice." I think it is important to
always praise God for the blessings He has given us,
even when they may not, at first, appear to be a blessing. Pray to Him for strength and guidance as you em-
bark upon the path toward parenthood. Pray that He
will reveal His plan to you, the reasons for you to become a parent, and trust that He is in control even in
difficult circumstances. And remember, rejoice, for indeed, God has blessed you!

▼ *God, please help me to rejoice. Thank You for new
life.*

LB

FAMILY PATTERNS

"I, the LORD your God, am a jealous God, visiting the iniquity of the fathers on the children to the third and fourth generations of those who hate Me." —EX. 20:5

*M*any parents do not realize it, but they not only are sinning against God but against their children as well. How could this be true?

In counseling it is not unusual to address the problems a child has by looking at family patterns that have their roots in past generations. It is easy to see family patterns of physical abuse or alcoholism. But there are other "sins" that can be just as significant.

An important area we parents need to constantly evaluate is what things we place value on. Do an inventory of how much time or money you spend, or how much knowledge you have about the things in your life. Do your children rank high on your list, or is there an imbalance? Are you worshipping idols? We need to be careful. Not only may we pass these idols on to our children, we may end up neglecting them in the process.

You can know your children and enjoy them. And you can help your children and their children to avoid the punishment of missing out on the joy of real intimacy with their families.

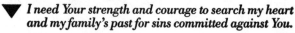 *I need Your strength and courage to search my heart and my family's past for sins committed against You.*

GC

ATTITUDE CHECKS

Be renewed in the spirit of your mind.
—EPH. 4:23

*A*ttitude plays a big part in a teen's ability to make adjustments in his or her life. Every day a teen will encounter frustrations at home and in school. Both teens and adults tend to get angry when they are frustrated. The way anger is expressed can cause problems for the teen or the adults in association with them.

Frequently our church youth group goes on outings. Things don't always go as planned. Sometimes the teens are too close together for too long. They end up a little irritable. Whenever our youth leader notices tension building, he stops and says it is time for an "attitude" check. That's a signal to the teens to take a deep breath and regroup. A prayer helps ease the tension.

We all need attitude checks when things get tense. Parents are no exception. Usually they are rushing ahead without any thought there might be another way that will decrease tension for them and their teen. An attitude check can give time to regroup. Take time for a smile and a prayer. And then make a fresh start.

▼ *Dear Lord, help me to have a positive attitude in dealing with my family.*

JS

TOILET TRAINING

Love suffers long and is kind.
—1 COR. 13:4

$\mathcal{A}$n embarrassed mother admitted to me that she felt as if she was house-breaking a dog rather than trying to toilet train her two-year-old son. "I've had it," she said. She told me how one day her son, grinning ear to ear, proudly presented her a cereal bowl exclaiming "Mommy, look, doo-doo I had!" Several weeks later she heard him playing the piano. She smiled. He wasn't even banging. Then he came running to her. "Mommy, Mommy, doo-doo." His "doo-doo," she discovered, was all over the keyboard! You can guess how she reacted and how perplexed she felt. He had been going in his potty without any problems. What was he trying to prove? Wasn't she doing anything right?

All the books and magazines I've read say not to push toilet training but to wait until the child is ready. Even when you think he is, he can go backwards. This mom wasn't doing anything wrong. The child was either in the process of learning where to go, and he was a little confused, or he was doing this out of anger. If your child's actions are from anger then you must talk to him to try and find the source of the anger. No matter what the circumstance, it all goes back to having lots of patience. And patience is a gift from God.

▼ *God, help me to be patient with my children even as You are patient with me.*

LB

FILL THE VOID

Do you not know that your body is the temple of the Holy Spirit who is in you, whom you have from God, and you are not your own?
—1 COR. 6:19

Someone once said that teaching our sons and daughters to abstain from sexual activity is easy, it's making sure they abstain that is the impossible task! Even in today's age with the heightened awareness of AIDS, sexual activity among teenagers is still on the rise. In fact, most studies show that an understanding of the risks has done little to decrease teen sexual activity.

Most teens become sexually active to fill a void in their lives. Carol was no exception. She lacked real intimacy with her parents—especially her father. Although he was a strong Christian man, he knew little about nurturing his daughter. Not finding love from her father, she sought the shallow short-lived "love" boyfriends and sometimes acquaintances offered her.

As you might expect, Carol developed a reputation. She no longer respected herself, nor could she deny the abuse to which she subjected herself. Where did this process begin? It's hard to tell exactly. There are usually many factors, although I'll never forget the tears in her eyes as she told of feeling unloved by her father. We can best help our sons and daughters respect their bodies by giving them the love and respect they need.

▼ *Lord, I want to nurture my relationships with my children. Please help me.*

GC

CORRECTION VS. CRITICISM

Let no corrupt communication proceed out of your mouth, but what is good for necessary edification, that it may impart grace to the hearers.
—EPH. 4:29

It is easy to cross the line between making legitimate correction and being critical of a child's behavior. Correction has more to do with changing a child's behavior. Criticism tends to be an assault on their character. Self-esteem is at stake in criticism. Children get a lot of criticism from their peers and others. From their parents, they need messages that will build up their self-esteem. Positive input does a lot to inflate a child's confidence.

A second grade teacher that I know is interested in correcting behavior in her class to enable the children to function better as a group. She uses positive reinforcement for incentives to behave well. On Friday, the children who are well behaved get a reward. These rewards, plus noticing the child's good behavior, result in fewer behavior problems.

Children respond well to positive comments. They usually want to behave in a positive way. Encouraging them by noticing their good behavior is important.

▼ *Dear Lord, it is my goal to edify my children. Please help me to notice their good behavior.*

JS

BABY-SITTING

Therefore comfort each other and edify one another, just as you also are doing.
—1 THESS. 5:11

*E*very Tuesday I take care of my friend's child, Tammy. Tammy is the same age as my two-year-old. They have been together since birth and act as if they are brother and sister. Today was a tough day for Tammy. She cried from the time her mom left her until she came to pick her up. The whole time nothing pleased her. I knew she was angry about something because she whined when anyone tried to play with her.

We all have days when nothing pleases our child—when everything and anything kicks them into a temper tantrum. We usually blame it on a poor night's sleep or no nap. Or we conclude that they are just cranky.

Did you know that you can talk with a child and work out those feelings? Tammy's mom and I decided to try. We talked with Tammy and played out her feelings with her stuffed animals. As it turned out, Tammy was angry with me because I had been giving my two children more attention than I had been giving to her. She missed my attention and felt hurt.

Children have lots of feelings inside. We can help them work through their feelings by encouraging them to get their feelings out in the open.

▼ *God, help me to know how to deal with my children's feelings through good communication.*

LB

ACTIVE LISTENING

For if anyone is a hearer of the word and not a doer, he is like a man observing his natural face in a mirror; for he observes himself, goes away, and immediately forgets what kind of man he was. —JAMES 1:23–24

*H*ave you heard the one about the daughter who cried to her father, "You never listen to me." "Of course I do," he responded. "I always discipline you."

From time to time most kids complain that their parents don't listen to them. What they most often mean is that their parents don't give them what they want or let them do what they want to do. This is a very manipulative complaint. What they really want and *need* is to feel understood. This will happen only when we respond with action.

What should our response be? Start with the basics. Keep good eye contact. Repeat what you hear them say. Follow their conversation. The goal is to show your children that they have significance by how you act toward them. When they converse in an acceptable manner, respond to them by paying attention. Listen attentively. Put the newspaper down to give them your undivided attention. Look into the mirror today. Do you see a good listener? And remember, being a good listener means you need to respond when your child talks to you. You need to be a doer, not just a hearer.

▼ *With your help, O Lord, I will be an active doer, not just a passive listener, to You and my children.*

GC

FORGIVENESS IS A FAMILY MATTER

And be kind to one another, tenderhearted,
forgiving one another, just as God in Christ
also forgave you.   —EPH. 4:32

*F*orgiveness is a cornerstone of the Christian faith. We need to ask each other for forgiveness as well as be willing to forgive those who misuse us. Forgiveness also needs to be a family matter. Most children are taught early to say they are sorry when they have mistreated someone or disobeyed. Parents are many times a different matter.

Patti's mother was very angry when she arrived home from work to find the kitchen was not clean and the clothes were not folded as she had requested. She blasted her daughter, expressing not only her displeasure but also her disappointment. Her fatigue from work added to the intensity of her lecture. Later her husband came home and explained that he had asked Patti to do an important errand for him. This left no time for Patti to do the chores. Even though Patti's mother realized her mistake, she was reluctant to say she was sorry. She felt it would diminish her authority.

Parents need to ask their children to forgive them when they fail. What a role model for your child! It's the perfect way to clear the air. It makes them feel better about themselves as well as you.

▼ *Dear Lord, remind me of how graciously You forgive*
   when I have just blown it with my child.

JS

STRONGER THAN SUPERMAN

The LORD is my light and my salvation;
Whom shall I fear?
The LORD is the strength of my life;
Of whom shall I be afraid?

—PS. 27:1

*U*nfortunately the television and sometimes even books make children *afraid of* monsters, sharks, and tigers. I know a child like that, my own Jesse. He's afraid of all three. One day as Jesse was going to bed, he said, "Mommy, the tigers and monsters are gone." I was pleased but confused. "You know how Superman protects people?" he said. "Well Jesus protects me from all the bad guys. He is stronger than Superman. I love Jesus!"

I about fell out of my chair. Jesse is correct and knows Jesus the way a lot of us don't. Jesus will protect us, especially when we ask. I'm glad my two-year-old has picked up this important lesson. It's important that we also learn that God is always there to help calm our fears and protect us.

▼ *Thank You, God, for Your promises and the lessons You teach me through my son.*

LB

TWO STANDARDS

*All things are lawful for me, but all things
are not helpful; all things are lawful for me,
but all things do not edify.*
—1 COR. 10:23

*A*fter dinner it was always the same. You could smell the aroma of a fine cigar as the father contemplated the day's events or perhaps pondered the solutions for the world's problems. Whatever the case, you could count on him having an after dinner cigar. It was an extension of his hand after a hearty meal.

So was it a big surprise that his teenage son smoked an occasional cigarette? Maybe not a surprise, but certainly not acceptable. It was unsightly, odious, and harmful to his health. His grandmother had died of lung cancer. His father was not about to allow his son to suffer a similar fate. He loved his son too much.

Unfortunately, logic and love seemed to have little impact. And why should they? It was ridiculous to expect this young boy not to smoke with the example his father set for him. But argue they did about this issue. Over time much damage was done to their relationship.

The example we set will have more impact than our logic or the "I love you" statements we make. Let us be mindful of the costs and rewards of the example we set for our children.

▼ *Dear God, help me to follow the example set by my Lord Jesus.*

GC

DAY-CARE

Surely I have calmed and quieted my soul,
Like a weaned child with his mother.
—PS. 131:2

$\mathcal{D}$ay-care is the new way of raising children. Scary isn't it! Both parents work in lots of families so day-care is a necessity. But make no mistake about it, day-care does not take the place of parenting. It only offers care for your child until you return home. Parenting is a two person job just like earning the family income. If there is only one parent, caring for your children is going to be as hard as earning enough income.

Brandon went to an excellent day-care. Fortunately the staff was stable and he had his friends there, but he could hardly wait until Mom picked him up. Many days he was frustrated because there were errands to run and supper to prepare. Soon things deteriorated into a scene. One day Mom decided a change was in order. She began going home immediately and sitting down with Brandon to talk, play, hug, and listen. When he was finished, she got up to take care of dinner with Brandon's help. When his father came home, it was his turn with Brandon. Mom and Dad had their time after Brandon went to bed.

In working families something has to give. Make sure it is not family relationships. Scrambled eggs for supper are better than scrambled feelings.

▼ *Please help us, Lord, to work together as parents to make our family solid.*

JS

ROLE MODELING

I write to you, little children,
Because you have known the Father.
—1 JOHN 2:13

I have heard that our perception of God is often affected by our relationship with our earthly fathers. If we do not trust our fathers or are angry with them, our distrust and anger at times may spill over onto God.

If our father is not loving, it may be very difficult for us to perceive God as a loving heavenly Father.

As parents we are also models for our children's perception of God. If we are not honest and faithful, our relationship with them suffers—and so does their relationship with God. If we do not set limits when disciplining them, they do not learn how to obey God's commands. If we are too overbearing and discipline too much, then they may think God is out to get them. They may feel as if God is waiting around every corner for them to make a mistake.

Raising our children to have good, healthy relationships with their fathers is like walking a tightrope. We need our heavenly Father's help to keep in balance. And we need to keep our eyes focused on Him as we keep putting one step in front of the other. With His help both we and our children will one day meet Him face to face.

▼ *Father, thank You for walking that tightrope with me. I need Your balancing hand for every step.*

LB

ADDICTIONS

*And do not be drunk with wine, in which is
dissipation; but be filled with the Spirit.*
—EPH. 5:18

There is an epidemic raging through our country. It is
called alcoholism. The statistics are staggering. Three
out of every four teenagers are drinking by the time they
reach eighteen years of age. Children as early as nine
years old are beginning to drink and show the early
signs of alcoholism. Three million teenage alcoholics
exist in this great land of ours, and that number is increasing every year. How very sad.

Addictions come in many different packages—drug
addiction, sex addiction, work addiction. All contain the
same destiny—avoidance of true emotions, real intimacy, and life as God wants us to live it. Of all the addictions, alcoholism is perhaps the most available and
most deadly for our children and teens.

Make sure your children do not physically, spiritually, or emotionally die. Make available opportunity for
emotional, relational, and spiritual growth by investing
in their lives. Allow them to be intoxicated with God's
love rather than wine.

 *Help me, O God, to walk with my children and pro-
vide them the intimacy and strength they need to
face their emotions.*

GC

A FAMILY DISEASE

*"For I, the LORD your God, am a jealous
God, visiting the iniquity of the fathers on the
children to the third and fourth generations
of those who hate Me."* —EX. 20:5

$\mathcal{A}$lcoholism is a serious family disease. It affects
everyone and is passed down from one generation to the
next. Children know something is wrong and assume it
is them. They think the drinking will stop if only they
are good enough. Then the alcoholic will love them.
Adult children of alcoholics face a lifetime battle with
these feelings.

Donna's father was an evening drinker. He never
missed a day of work because of alcohol, but his whole
life revolved around drinking so he was not involved in
family matters. He never went to PTA meetings or drove
his children to the movies. Mother was angry at him
most of the time, but covered for him whenever necessary. Donna's role in the family was to be perfect. When
she failed, there was a major crisis. She decided she
was responsible for the problems. It never occurred to
her that her parents were the ones with problems.

Children crave a nurturing family. Alcoholics and
their spouses are not able to provide this nurturing.
This leaves their children wounded. It is imperative to
break through the denial and secure treatment.

▼ *Father God, help me to face my problems boldly and
to address them so I do not hurt my children.*

JS

PRAYING FOR OUR UNBORN CHILD

*"May God Almighty bless you,
And make you fruitful and multiply you,
That you may be an assembly of peoples."*
—GEN. 28:3

*J*ennifer and Joe were trying to have a child. Each day they prayed: as a couple, in their church prayer group, they even asked their friends to pray. Not only did they pray for conception, but also that the child would be protected and guided by God each day. Soon, Jennifer was fortunate enough to be pregnant. Every day of her pregnancy Jennifer and Joe asked God for their child's health and spiritual growth. Not only did this help their child, but both Jennifer and Joe became closer and closer to God and to each other.

Prayer for our children really helps before they are conceived. It is important to pray to God to help mold that child while it is inside you and after it is born. For it is up to us to help each child grow in a likeness of Jesus. This is a tough test, believe me. Therefore, we have to have God in charge, guiding us, teaching us, disciplining us every step of the way.

 Dear Father, we need You. Show us how to pray for our children both before and after they are born.

LB

TEACH THEM DILIGENTLY

"You shall teach them diligently to your children, and shall talk of them when you sit in your house, when you walk by the way, when you lie down, and when you rise up."
—DEUT. 6:7

*L*ittle Janie was so excited she couldn't sleep. She would be spending the next day with her daddy. They would walk through the park and run in the sun chasing butterflies and each other. Then they'd picnic near the pond and feed the ducks. After a short nap back home, they would dine at her favorite restaurant. She'd have a hamburger, fries, and a small Coke.™ They'd walk through the mall to window shop and finally come back home. Of course, Daddy would read the perfect bedtime story to end a perfect day.

As the years passed, Janie remembered little of her special day with her dad. But she did remember the love and warmth she felt as her father made her a priority and shared in her life.

Today's Scripture makes clear that we are to teach our children about God through every aspect of our daily lives—in the mornings, at night, in our homes, and along the roads we walk. We do this as we walk with our children down their various roads, sharing in their lives.

▼ *Dear God, I will love and worship You with all my heart, soul, and might.*

GC

PUPPIES AND BABY SISTERS

But when his brothers saw that their father loved him more than all his brothers, they hated him and could not speak peaceably to him.
— GEN. 37:4

Sibling rivalry is a natural part of family life. Sometimes it is loud and raucous. Other times it is never spoken. But be sure it is there. There isn't a child in this world who wouldn't prefer a puppy to a baby sister. We are kidding ourselves if we think otherwise. However, just like broccoli, it's good for you.

Jerry was an excellent student who loved to read and play the piano. Matt was athletic and gregarious. Each felt his parents appreciated the other more. Their parents enjoyed each one's special assets and attempted to give each equal attention. But it never seemed that way to Jerry and Matt. Each was convinced the other was favored. They frequently argued and fought.

There is no way to have everything equal between siblings. Sometimes one has a legitimate need for more attention, or the other needs a show of extra affection. Parents need to love and appreciate their children for their uniqueness and respond according to their needs. And, of course, they need to expect conflict between them. Part of the rivalry is to define their place in the family. That's not easy because it keeps changing.

▼ *Dear Lord, help me respond to each child's individual needs and help them accept the differences.*

JS

TEACH THEM TO PRAY

*Bring them up in the training and
admonition of the Lord.* —EPH. 6:4

$\mathscr{M}$rs. Jones has a set routine with her three-year-old each night to help him get to sleep. First he has his bath. Then she holds him in the rocking chair and reads two to three books. Finally she prays with him— not a memorized prayer, but one they work on together. "Father," she prays, "thank you for . . ." She stops and waits for her son.

"For Mommy and Daddy and going to the park today."

She continues, "Forgive us for . . ."

He fills in, "For hitting Tommy and throwing my books, but I was angry, God."

"Please protect us all, tonight and tomorrow," she prays.

They close their prayer time by praying together, "We love you. Amen."

It is so important not only to pray every night with our children, but also to begin teaching them how to pray. Long before they are even three years old, they can get into the habit of praying and learn to depend upon the Lord. What a great habit it can be!

▼ *Father, thank You for prayer and for the privilege of teaching our children to pray.*

LB

RELATIONSHIPS

"If you bring your gift to the altar, and there remember that your brother has something against you, leave your gift there before the altar, and go your way. First be reconciled to your brother, and then come and offer your gift."

—MATT. 5:23–24

*G*eorge grew up in a fairly normal family. Although his parents were not believers, they were good people and good parents. George was fairly successful in high school. He left his family to go on to college. He fell in love and got married. He and his wife had two children. George was moderately successful in the corporate world. It was some years after his second child was born when a business colleague introduced George to Christ.

George's life became dramatically different after he accepted Jesus as his personal Savior. He became enthusiastic in his study and worship of his Lord. He could not get enough. He attended Bible studies, seminars, and worship services as often as he could. The most important thing he could do, George believed, was to worship God. It became his priority. His spiritual duty. Unfortunately, in his zeal to please God, he often neglected his wife and kids. Today's Scripture shows the importance God places on relationships. Don't substitute religion for relationships with your family. Be in good standing with them before you worship.

▼ *Dear God, help me to evaluate my relationships today.*

GC

ADOPTION

*And the child grew, and she brought him to
Pharaoh's daughter, and he became her son.
So she called his name Moses, saying,
"Because I drew him out of the water."*
—EX. 2:10

*D*eanna was adopted when she was two days old. Her adoptive parents were there when she was born and held her immediately. By the time Deanna was three, she could tell the story of her adoption better than her parents. Throughout elementary school, she had plenty of questions. When she reached adolescence, she had to rethink the whole issue and understand that her red hair came from someone other than her parents. This required some examination because it involved her sense of identity. Deanna was able to work through these stages because of the openness and lack of defensiveness from her parents.

No matter how wanted and accepted the child is, it must be understood that before he was adopted he suffered a major separation trauma. At some point the child must deal with this loss. Adoption, therefore, needs to be an open family topic throughout a child's life. Otherwise it gets cloaked with mystery and secretiveness. That stifles a child's natural curiosity. It also hinders him from working through his feelings.

▼ *Dear Lord, You knew of our special need and blessed us with many ways to have children.*

JS

*Confess your trespasses to one another, and
pray for one another.*   **—JAMES 5:16**

*S*ally was crying in the other room. Her husband
came in to comfort her. "What's wrong, dear?" he
asked.

"I yelled at little Tommy today and I feel so guilty,"
she blurted out. "But I was so angry after he spilled his
juice on purpose."

Tom, her husband, was a wise man. "Dear, you're
not perfect," he said. "We all blow up once in a while.
It's impossible sometimes not to get angry and yell. As
long as we don't make a habit of it, I don't see how it
can hurt our children."

"But I just feel so guilty," Sally said. "I need to be in
control and never blow up or get angry."

Her husband replied in a loving manner, "It's okay
that you're not perfect. It shows our children that they
don't have to be perfect."

None of us are perfect—parents or children. We all
make mistakes. The important thing is what we do *after*
we've made a mistake. If we follow the counsel of today's Scripture, God can use our mistakes to bring us
closer to our children and to teach them how to handle
their own mistakes.

▼ *Lord, please make me aware of those times when I
need to apologize to my children. Help me to say
"I'm sorry."*

LB

MANOAH'S EXAMPLE

*Then Manoah prayed to the LORD, and said,
"O my Lord, please let the Man of God
whom You sent come to us again and teach
us what we shall do for the child who will be
born."*
—JUDG. 13:8

*M*anoah's wife had not borne any children when the angel of the Lord appeared to her and told her she would conceive and give birth to a son.

When Manoah heard of this encounter, he entreated God to have the Angel of the Lord reveal to them what to do for their expected newborn. The Angel of the Lord instructed Manoah's wife to abstain from wine, not to eat anything unclean, and not to let a razor touch her son's head. What a revealing passage for parents!

First, Manoah's son was a miracle from God—a gracious gift to a barren woman. Second, Manoah prayed for wisdom to teach his child. Third, Manoah and his wife had a teachable spirit—they were willing to learn and grow as parents. Finally, the Angel of the Lord told Manoah's wife what to do, placing the initial responsibility for his life upon her.

Our children are also a gift from God. We need to pray for wisdom and keep a teachable spirit. We need to be willing to grow and to assume the responsibility of parenthood, and expect God to teach us along the way.

▼ *Lord God, instruct me in the ways to raise my children. Reveal to me Your truths.*

GC

WE MAKE THE SAME MISTAKES

> *[God's Son] being the brightness of His glory and the express image of His person, and upholding all things by the word of His power, when He had by Himself purged our sins, sat down at the right hand of the Majesty on high.*
>
> **—HEB. 1:3**

I will never make the same mistakes my parents did! I sincerely mean it, but I find myself doing the same thing my parents did. It is understandable since they are the ones who taught me all I know about being a parent.

A man I once counseled regarding his abusive treatment of his child bragged, "My father used to whip me the same way. That made me the man I am today." To myself I agreed. *Yes, it turned you into a child abuser.*

This man was only doing what he learned, but it was no more effective on his child than it had been on him.

Behavior modeled by our parents carries a lot of authority. Without a positive role model, changing the behavior they modeled is difficult. But it is not impossible! The first step is to notice areas of your behavior that you have vowed not to repeat. The second step is verbally to acknowledge this to yourself and family. With your family's help you can slowly begin to change to a healthier model. Believe me, if you have confessed it, they will help you.

 Dear God, let me use Jesus as my role model.

JS

EXPRESSING ANGER

Be angry, and do not sin.
—PS. 4:4

$\mathscr{B}$ecause I'm a therapist, I sometimes am amazed at what I learn from my children. The other day my two-year-old son was angry at me because I wouldn't give him what he wanted. Jesse began to throw a temper tantrum. At first I ignored him. Then I began to talk with him about it. He became even angrier and ran upstairs. I followed him, so he came back downstairs. I left him alone and watched. Jesse went into his playroom and began to pound his play hammer as hard as he could on his workbench. Around fifteen minutes later he came to me with a smile on his face. "All better," he said.

It's important to help children learn not only how to talk about their feelings, but also how to express them in a healthy way. For my son it was a physical expression. Then he let it go. Other healthy ways we might express our feelings could be through exercise, a punching bag, or hitting a pillow.

The Lord has given us muscles and strength. May we learn how to express our feelings in safe ways so we don't hurt ourselves or others.

▼ *Dear God, when I get angry, please remind me that my children are watching. Help me to show them appropriate ways to express angry feelings.*

LB

ACTING OUT

But now I have written to you not to keep company with anyone named a brother, who is a fornicator, or covetous, or an idolater, or a reviler, or a drunkard, or an extortioner— not even to eat with such a person.

—1 COR. 5:11

*P*eggy and John were angry about their son's behavior. He was drinking and wearing weird clothes. He had even been caught sneaking out after curfew with his friends. The family had a neatly packaged answer. "It's his friends. They're a bad influence."

Of course, his friends were not a positive influence. Yet the more his parents pointed this out, the more he defended them. After listening for some time to both sides, we attempted to look at the real issue.

We looked at the family's values. For a long time they had been more achievement oriented than relationship oriented. They had placed a lot of pressure on their son and provided little nurturing or support. He was angry and stressed and was displaying his anger and distress in his acting out behavior, the clothes he wore, and the friends he chose. His friends were a source of comfort. After all, they understood and felt the same way. Unfortunately, his parents only saw the "bad influence" they had on him—not the pain their son was enduring or the choices he was making to try and cope.

▼ *Help me, Lord, to understand the choices my children make, and help them to choose You as their friend.*

GC

PEOPLE IN OUR CORNER

Edify one another.
—1 THESS. 5:11

Scott came running into the house and told his father he had been nominated for class president. His father assured him he would have a good chance to win since he was such a good speaker. Then Scott realized that his father was home early. When he inquired, his dad told him he got laid off his job. Immediately the roles shifted and Scott began to encourage his dad. He let him know he had great confidence in his ability to deal with the situation.

There are always people to point out our shortcomings—friends, enemies, teachers, bosses, parents, and other children. What we need are people who will stand in our corner—people who will be quick to cheer our successes and able to put our failures into the right perspective. Without people standing in our corner, few of us would have the courage to face and deal with our problems. Our focus tends to be on the enormity of our problem and all the things that may go wrong. But someone in our corner lets us know we can overcome any obstacle.

The ultimate encourager is Jesus. He promises us we can do anything with His help.

▼ *Dear Lord, help me to be an encourager to my family and friends.*

JS

THE AWAKENING AGE

"And I will bless her and also give you a son by her."
—GEN. 17:16

$\mathcal{I}$ was amazed the day I noticed that my eight-month-old son, Justin, had crawled from one room to the next. I thought he was playing on the floor in front of me as I worked, but when I looked up, I saw him standing in the next room, smiling proudly and hanging on to the edge of a table.

Our children grow and change before our eyes. Each day they learn a new movement, skill, or sound. At eight months, babies develop personalities. I call this age the awakening age because they are no longer infants. They are more responsive and aware of what is going on. Some can sit up. Others begin to get up on all fours. They are on a mission to explore, and they are serious about their work. For the next year or so, we are in a race to keep up with them—preventing them from exploring physically painful territory.

One of God's great blessings in our lives is the gift of raising His children. What a joy and thrill it can be.

▼ *Father, I praise You for the children You have given me. Help me to love them and not to miss the ways they are changing and growing.*

LB

CHOOSING GOOD FRIENDS

> *Do not be deceived: "Evil company corrupts*
> *good habits."*
> —1 COR. 15:33

We don't like the friends our son is hanging around with. What can we do?" Here are some suggestions to help your children and teens choose good friends.

Start early. Share with your children the qualities you appreciate in your own friends. Tell them about trust and loyalty, integrity and high standards. Allow your children to get to know your friends. Let them see you interact with them so they can know how friends treat each other.

Get to know your child's friends. Open your home. Invite them over. Entertain with food or games, but give them space to do their own thing.

Be honest about your feelings about their friends. Don't be judgmental or critical, but do share your concerns. Point out the negative and the positive traits you see. Ask them how they feel and what they like about their friends.

Finally, don't be afraid to allow your children and teens freedom to make their own decisions and their own mistakes. Show them you have confidence in their ability to make good decisions and their ability to handle things when they don't.

▼ *Dear God, help me to impart the qualities of a*
friend in my relationship with my children.

GC

CHEER THEM ON

I have confidence in you in everything.
        —2 COR. 7:16

*B*obby never started any project without his father telling him, "That is not the way to do it. It will not work that way. Let me show you how to do it." Bobby's confidence in himself was as low as his father's confidence in him. No matter how many times Bobby made an "A" in school or reached a goal he had set for himself, he always thought he couldn't do anything well.

Children need to know that we expect them to be successful in whatever they do. Of course they will make mistakes and errors in judgment. But they need to know we have confidence in their ability to attain their goal whether it is to build a boat or get a passing grade in math. When we don't have confidence in them, they may not have enough confidence in themselves to succeed.

Success breeds success. When children are successful in a small endeavor, they need their parents to cheer them on. This will prepare them to tackle the big things in life as they get older and become adults.

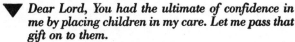

▼ *Dear Lord, You had the ultimate of confidence in me by placing children in my care. Let me pass that gift on to them.*

                                    JS

TEASING

See that no one renders evil for evil to anyone, but always pursue what is good both for yourselves and for all.
—1 THESS. 5:15

*W*ere you ever teased by your older brother or sister? You could probably spend all day telling stories if you were the one doing the teasing. If you were on the receiving end, you may prefer not to remember the teasing you endured. One of my favorite stories is when the oldest of three sisters dyed her two younger sisters' hair purple. She later teased them about this many times.

Some teasing is just for fun, but it may be more fun for the person dishing it out than the one on the receiving end. Some teasing ends up hurting people and is really passive-aggressive behavior. Usually, passive-aggressive behavior comes out when you're angry with someone. When our children are complaining about something or are cranky, we may be tempted to tease them to try to make them feel better. Resist the temptation! Instead acknowledge their feelings and help them work through them.

How does God feel about teasing? I believe He is concerned that we love each other and ourselves. He wants us to build each other up, not tear each other down.

▼ *Help me, Lord, to know when the teasing in my home is getting out of hand, and show me how to intervene.*

LB

A UNITED FRONT

But did He not make them one,
Having a remnant of the Spirit?
And why one?
He seeks godly offspring.
                    —MAL. 2:15

*F*ourteen-year-old Eric was prone to lie quite a bit.

He was a real smooth character who always had an answer for everything and a way out of trouble. Some said he was destined to be a successful salesman or maybe a politician! But most everyone who knew Eric also knew he was not to be trusted.

When I met with Eric's parents, they asked why he lied so much. One possible reason quickly became evident in their first few statements to me. "My husband's too strict." "My wife's too lenient."

When God brings a man and woman together for marriage, the two become one. One reason for this is so the two can better reflect God's character. Remember God is steadfast and so should we be as parents. It is important for parents to present a unified front—to agree on important issues about the children.

Don't sabotage your spouse's efforts or the respect your children have for him or her by a contradictory philosophy of parenting. Provide consistent accountability and also you'll develop consistency in your children's character.

▼ *Father, please help me talk openly with my spouse about my views of parenting.*

GC

JUST LISTEN

Hear me when I call,
O God of my righteousness!
You have relieved me when I was
in distress. —PS. 4:1

$\mathscr{R}$ecently I was working with a mother of a sixteen-year-old faced with some decisions about the family relationships. The mother reported that their relationship improved considerably when she quit talking and started listening. At first her daughter's ideas were not very realistic, but they did embody her thoughts about what she wanted to do. Each time she talked with her mother, her ideas changed. Finally she was able to express a very good plan for handling the situation. The mother also commented that when she quit talking and started listening, her daughter processed the problem and was able to use good judgment.

Children learn how to think by expressing their thoughts, feelings, and ideas. They need to bounce their thoughts off of someone. Sometimes they are illogical and not always grounded in reality. But as they talk about them, they adjust their ideas a little and take a different approach. The one thing they do *not* need is someone always pointing out the flaws in their thinking. One of the best gifts we can give our children is just to listen to them.

▼ *Thank You, Lord, for being here to listen to me as I*
work through the issues dealing with my children.

JS

PARENT'S PET

*"He makes His sun rise on the evil and on
the good, and sends rains on the just and on
the unjust."*
—MATT. 5:45

*B*rian was his mother's favorite child. He was the oldest of the two boys and, in his mother's eyes, did everything right. His brother, Randy, was another story. His mother never bragged about Randy. She always complained that though she knew what Brian thought, she could never figure out Randy.

Brian was the pet and knew it. He loved it but hated it. He knew his brother resented him, and he was always afraid of losing his mother's love if he failed. Brian grew up feeling fearful of everything, especially failure. By the time he was twelve, he was very depressed. He was failing in school and many other things.

Randy felt like a nobody because his mother didn't acknowledge him at all. He was constantly trying to win her approval. He grew up with poor self-esteem.

Favoritism hurts everyone. If you have a favorite child, I encourage you to find the cause for your feelings and to work them through to avoid hurting any of your children.

 *God, help me to love my children as You do and not
to pick favorites.*

LB

PUPPY LOVE

Love suffers long. . . .
—1 COR. 13:4

*K*aren came home after school with that puppy love glimmer in her eyes. Her mother couldn't wait to ask her, "What's his name?"

"Oh mother, I'm in love!" fifteen-year-old Karen exclaimed.

They went to the yogurt shop to share a vanilla with fruit topping and they talked for more than an hour. Karen told her mother how handsome he was and how nice he treated her. "He really respects me," she lauded.

Finally, the inevitable question came. "How do you know when you're in love?" Karen asked.

Her mother told her how she met her father. The courting. The exciting feelings. Their first argument. She told her how infatuation came and went with other boys, but how over time real love grew between her and Karen's father.

Share in the excitement when your children fall in love. Let them know infatuation is okay—that it's part of the falling in love process. But remind them that, just like a beautiful flower, love takes time to grow.

▼ *Dear God, protect my children as they fall in love. Help them know that love is patient.*

GC

A LITTLE RESPECT PLEASE

*"Listen, O coastlands, to Me,
And take heed,
    you peoples from afar!"*
—ISA. 49:1

*A*dults do not always treat teens politely! At times, sales people in stores ignore them in favor of an adult customer. They don't always take a teen's complaints seriously. Sometimes, without cause, they are even very rude to teens.

My teenage daughter ordered a burger at the window of a drive-in restaurant. She paid with a five dollar bill and did not receive the correct change in return. The manager gave her the disputed dollar, but he made it clear that he did not believe her. He was very rude. She was extremely angry when she came home. She told her dad. He became her instant hero when he went to the drive-in and told the manager he did not appreciate the way she had been treated. This validated her feelings.

Parents need to be aware that their teens are not always treated fairly outside of the family. Sometimes our teens may want and need us to come to their defense. Other times all they may really want and need is a listening ear. Knowing that we're on their side, that we respect them, can help to make up for the rudeness they may encounter.

▼ *Dear Lord, give me wisdom to know what my teen needs when he has been treated rudely.*

JS

Children, obey your parents in all things, for this is well pleasing to the Lord.
—COL. 3:20

Susie and Jimmy were at it again. Their mother was in the kitchen and could hear the fight growing. She quickly went to break it up.

"Susie hit me," Jimmy said.

"Jimmy hit me first," Susie accused. "He took my train."

"No, you took *my* train," Jimmy insisted. And the fighting started again.

The frustrated mother said, "Jimmy, it's not okay to hit your sister. Susie, it's not okay to hit your brother. This train is Jimmy's, but you may play with it."

"No, it's mine," Jimmy shouted.

"We share, Jimmy," mother said in her most patient voice. Jimmy became angry and ran off.

Should we referee every fight or should we let our children work it out? Some experts say fighting increases if you do interfere. Others say if you don't referee, they will never learn healthy ways of resolving conflicts. Whatever you choose to do, know that fighting among siblings is normal. All children and adults fight, but not all ways of fighting are healthy. It's important to learn the productive ways.

▼ *Lord, You know how I feel when my children begin to fight. Please give me the wisdom I need.*

LB

FORGIVENESS

The discretion of a man makes
him slow to anger,
And it is to his glory to overlook
a transgression.
—PROV. 19:11

*M*elissa was a single mom. Life had been difficult for her and her eight-year-old son since the divorce.

That day had been a particular trying day. Late hours at work left little time for Melissa to spend with her son. Her little boy playfully bounced on the bed as she hurriedly prepared for the next day. Then it happened. Crash! The beautifully framed inscription over the bed fell to the floor. It was a gift from a dear friend. Now it lay broken in pieces.

Jeff looked at his mom, his eyes filled with fear and guilt. She looked at him with eyes filled with rage. But before words were spoken, her attention was drawn to the inscription. In part it read:

> *Forgiveness is a treasure*
> *That is passed between friends.*
> *When hearts are broken*
> *Tis kindness that mends.*

This time there was no scolding, no discipline. Her words were understanding and gentle and healing.

▼ *Dear God, may forgiveness and mercy fill my heart.*
                                                    GC

DEALING WITH THE SYSTEM

Remove falsehood and lies far from me.
—PROV. 30:8

$\mathscr{A}$ high school student applied for a job with the city. It required filling out a job application and taking a test in a downtown office that was open Monday through Friday from eight to three. The student had good grades and excellent attendance. Her father had no problem getting off work to take her, but the school refused to let her leave. The alternatives were to miss the job opportunity, leave without permission (jeopardizing her school record and grades), or lie and say she was sick.

Many times adults expect behavior from children and teens that they do not require of themselves. They demand total allegiance with little flexibility for extraneous circumstances. Schools expect perfect attendance. Sports activities demand unfailing participation. Church choirs and youth activities have high performance expectations. Adults need to realize that youth have special circumstances that do not always fit the norm. Teens also need flexibility. It certainly does not enhance relationships with adults if lying or rebellion are the only way to deal with the system.

▼ *Dear Lord, help other adults to be flexible and understanding when dealing with my teens.*

JS

SHARING FRIENDS

For the LORD gives wisdom.
—PROV. 2:6

*M*ichael repeatedly complained that his younger brother was taking over his friends. Because of his brother, he said some of his friends wouldn't come to his house anymore. When he complained to his mother, he got nowhere. She just told him, "He's younger and needs you. You use him as an excuse too much."

But Michael had a point. He was angry and hurt that he was losing friends because of his brother, John. I encouraged his parents to listen to Michael's feelings and to work on possible solutions. I recommended that John invite his own friends over. I also recommended that when one of the boys had a friend over, the other one go and visit at a friend's house and vice versa. It worked! John developed his own friends and stopped chasing and stealing friends from Michael.

If your children are having a problem with sharing friends, take the time to listen to their complaints. Find out how they feel. Respect their feelings, and work together to find a solution. And remember, no problem is unsolvable with the Lord's help.

▼ *Dear God, show me how to work with my children to find solutions to their problems. Make me sensitive to their needs.*

LB

AIM IN THE RIGHT DIRECTION

"For everyone to whom much is given, from him much will be required; and to whom much has been committed, of him they will ask the more."
                                    —LUKE 12:48

*C*onsider the beautiful and wondrous creation of a child. One must humbly proclaim, "There is a God!"

I once attended a field trip with some third graders. Keeping charge over 100 eight and nine-year-olds was no easy task. I remember their excited innocence as they walked through the museum and the awe in their faces. Each child brought with him or her uniqueness of personality and experience, and a reservoir of unlimited potential. All were magnificently and uniquely fashioned by God.

Children are a precious gift from God. "Like arrows in the hand of a warrior" (Psalm 127:4), they are a prized possession. Much is required from us. What will we teach our children? What experiences will we expose them to? Will we nurture their potential toward positive goals?

Like a warrior's arrow, children may be directed toward a target for harmful destruction or be used to defend what is honorable and right. Much has been entrusted to us as parents. Take great pains to aim your children in the right direction.

▼ *Thank You, Lord, for giving me the great gift of a child. Help me to be faithful in accomplishing that which You ask of me as a parent.*

GC

WHEN SIBLINGS LEAVE HOME

*Then he [Joseph] fell on his brother
Benjamin's neck and wept, and Benjamin
wept on his neck.* —GEN. 45:14

*W*hen Elizabeth was married, everyone was excited,
including her ten-year-old sister—especially since she
was getting her room. No one was prepared for the
younger sister's intense feelings of loss after Elizabeth's
marriage. She was depressed and irritable. It took several months for her to feel better, but the sense of loss
continued to come back at times. Fortunately her parents were sensitive to her feelings and were able to talk
with her about it.

When siblings leave home, it presents a special problem for the ones left behind. There is a sense of loss that
needs to be grieved. Many times these departures are
considered happy events like college, marriage, or a
new job. That makes it more difficult for the younger
child to grieve.

Parents may rush past their child's feeling of loss because they may be having grief of their own. Sharing
feelings about the loss within the family will probably
help everyone get through it. Grief is something we can
and should share, and it does not always have to be
about death.

▼ *Dear Father, heighten my sensitivity when my child
needs special understanding.*

JS

KEEPING THE PEACE

The fruit of the Spirit is love, joy, peace.
—GAL. 5:22

*M*r. and Mrs. Conover had two girls who were only one year apart. When one got something, the other had to have exactly the same thing. And so the Conovers bought two of everything—two swings, two bikes, two Barbie® dolls. . . . However, they found what research has proved, This didn't really help. The girls continued to compare and fight.

The Conovers' plan failed because their daughters' rivalry wasn't so much over things but over their parents. What the girls needed was reassurance that their parents loved them equally.

If you have two or more children vying for your attention and love, tell them, "I have enough love for both of you." If one happens to get a smaller gift, point out that you don't love them less. Your love is equal. It's important to acknowledge and work with how children feel, not with what they demand.

▼ *Father God, please let love, joy, and peace reign in my home and in my heart.*

LB

GOALS AND PRINCIPLES

Through wisdom a house is built,
And by understanding it is established;
By knowledge the rooms are filled
With all precious and pleasant riches.
—PROV. 24:3–4

*T*he young father decided to become a student of parenting. He attended seminars, read books, and sought godly wisdom concerning his role as a father. He took stock in the positive model his own father provided. He knew he did not want to establish his household haphazardly. After all, "If you aim for nothing, you will surely hit your mark," he thought. Foundational to his goals as a father were three principles he shared with me:

First, there was no room for pride. He determined to pray for humility and to consider others (his family) as more important than himself.

Second, he had a vision for the future. He understood the things he did with his family would have consequences later on.

Third, recognizing he might need to make many sacrifices, he made a commitment always to ask God for a giving heart. Like this young father, we also need to seek wisdom and knowledge. We need to set goals and prayerfully consider how we will attain them. And we need to be vigilant so the rooms of our household will be filled with the riches of healthy family.

▼ *Lord, please help me to apply Your principles to my life and to act on them.*

GC

FRIENDS

A man who has friends must himself be friendly. —PROV. 18:24

$\mathcal{I}$n the eighth grade, April spent all of her time at home talking on the phone. She wanted to sleep over with her friends every Friday and Saturday. When they were together, they had endless hours of nonstop conversation punctuated by giggles. April's mother understood how important friends were to her daughter. She made their home available whenever possible. She also knew when to be accessible and when to be scarce. This enabled April to interact with her friends. Meanwhile her mother knew who April was with and what they were doing.

Parents who underestimate the importance of friends have problems relating to their teens. Friends are vitally important to teens and many times take priority over the family. In order for the family to have the necessary place, they need to open their home to their teen's friends and enjoy a casual, unobtrusive relationship with them. It can be fun because teens are full of energy and enthusiasm. It may be just what is needed to keep you young.

▼ *Dear Lord, I know how important friendships are. Help me include my teen's friends.*

JS

DEALING WITH JEALOUSY

A soft answer turns away wrath,
But a harsh word stirs up anger.
—PROV. 15:1

*K*evin was four years old—two years older than his brother, Dustin. Kevin was very jealous of his younger brother and had been ever since Dustin was born. He would do anything to upset his brother. One afternoon Dustin was having great fun stacking his blocks as high as he could reach. Of course Kevin could not resist knocking them down. Dustin started screaming and crying. Mother came running. Huge tears rolled down Dustin's cheeks as mother held him on her lap while Kevin was in "time-out." Kevin's anger and jealousy grew.

Kevin's mother realized something needed to be done. She talked with Kevin about his feelings and started to spend more time with him.

If one of your children is showing signs of anger and jealousy toward a brother or sister, don't ignore his feelings. The answer is not to be found in passively or aggressively striking out at your child, but in listening and loving.

 Please show me, Lord, how to help my children deal with jealousy, and help me not to take sides.

LB

PRIORITIES

*Let nothing be done through selfish ambition
or conceit, but in lowliness of mind let each
esteem others better than himself.*
—PHIL. 2:3

$\mathcal{A}$s we sat and talked, I felt a little intimidated. The Italian suit, silk tie, and all those gold rings clearly stated that he was extremely successful in his business. I even noticed the fluid motion of his watch's second hand. Must have been a Rolex.

He told me of his business ventures and travels. In fact, our session was cut short because of his travel to another state for more business. He left without really accomplishing much regarding his family. With so little time to talk, he talked mostly about himself.

Unfortunately, like many other parents in his situation, this gentleman thought more of his corporation than he did of his family. Of course, when the question was put to him, he emphatically voiced his love for his wife and children. But his actions spoke louder than his words. He fed his ego by his business accomplishments.

Each of us has a choice in determining our priorities. With God's help let us always choose to put our family first.

▼ *Dear God, create in me a humble heart.*

GC

SPOILING OUR CHILDREN

But his sons did not walk in his ways.
—1 SAM. 8:3

"I want to be careful so I won't spoil my child." Most of the time this is not a parenting problem. Sometimes parents overindulge their children, but usually they don't spoil them.

Ricky was a child who was always throwing temper tantrums and demanding his way. He was hard to get along with. Frequently he was verbally abusive to his parents, teachers, and friends. These are symptoms of an extremely angry or depressed child. Many times lack of time and attention create this type of behavior. In talking with Ricky's parents, it was obvious they both had careers and active social lives. They had little time for Ricky. To make it up to him, they were willing to buy him almost anything he wanted. Even though he acted like a spoiled child, he was a neglected and deprived child.

Your children can never get an overabundance of love and care. As long as you are not intrusive and you take your cues from your children, you won't spoil them with too much affection. Enjoy your children and love them as much as possible. They grow up too quickly to miss out on any of it.

▼ *Dear Lord, help me not to be too busy to give my children the love and affection they need.*

JS

WHAT THEY SEE IS WHAT THEY DO

My son, do not forget my law,
But let your heart keep my commands.
—PROV. 3:1

Frank and Marsha admitted to me that they fight a lot. They never hit each other, but they are constantly yelling. This never resolves anything except allowing them to ventilate their anger. They complained that their two children also fight constantly, and that their fighting had increased in the last month. They didn't know why. After talking, they soon saw the pattern. When they fight, their kids fight.

What children see is what they do! One of the hardest parts of being a parent is knowing they are going to pick up our behavior—good and bad. It's like looking in a mirror, and it can hurt.

If you find yourself in a situation similar to Frank and Marsha's where you are frequently fighting with your spouse and not resolving anything, seek help. In the end it will not only help you and your marriage, it will also help your child.

▼ *Lord, I know my children are watching everything I say and do, and I know oftentimes I fail to set a good example. I want my home to be happy, to be filled with peace and love.*

LB

WHEN WE LACK WISDOM

If any of you lacks wisdom, let him ask of God, who gives to all liberally and without reproach, and it will be given to him.
— JAMES 1:5

$\mathscr{A}$ couple came to me and asked an important question. "Should our child attend a private or public school?"

We talked about the pros and cons. There were many. One school had more extracurricular activities. The other had stronger academic requirements. They had made a list of what they liked and did not like about each school. Still they were frozen in indecisiveness. Their child also had no particular preference.

We talked about their child's development. I asked if he had any special needs. "No," they replied. Again no swaying aspect to make the decision easier.

I remember saying that God is most concerned with *who* we are rather than *where* we are. That sometimes the process of faith building is more important than the outcome when final consequences are unclear. We prayed together and asked for God's wisdom. There was no voice from on high, but they felt assured God would lead them.

Some months later they called to say their decision turned out well. Did they make the best choice? Only God knows. That's why we need to seek His wisdom.

▼ *Heavenly Father, please help me not to hesitate in seeking Your wisdom in all areas of my life.*

GC

DUAL CAREER FAMILIES

"Let the children be filled first."
—MARK 7:27

$\mathscr{A}$fter school can be a lonely two hours until parents start arriving home from work. It is probably better when there are siblings to keep each other company. Children pretty much stay in a holding pattern awaiting their parents' arrival. TV is frequently the baby-sitter along with milk and cookies. For entertainment between commercials, they pick on each other or make the fifth call to mother to ask what's for supper.

Parents rush home and start supper or start washing clothes. They feel so frazzled, they don't realize their children are waiting for their return and need some positive attention. This is part of the world of a dual career family. "Hectic" and "not enough time" are the most descriptive words.

Parents do not mean to rush past their children to get on with the chores. Probably everyone needs to slow down to rescue the children from their boredom and Mom and Dad from nervous exhaustion.

A playful interlude would probably be the best medicine for everyone and might increase the family bonding. It may be time for other things to wait. Giggles probably would help everyone's digestion.

▼ *Father God, help me to remember that my children are my first priority and that I need to stop and enjoy them.*

JS

THE NEW BABY ARRIVED

One who rules his own house well, having his
children in submission with all reverence.
>   —1 TIM. 3:4

*M*egan was almost three years old when Kyle, her new baby brother, arrived. She clung to her mother, cried, and acted out whenever her mother fed him. Megan became increasingly jealous of Kyle. She began to poke, hit, and push him. Her mother got angry and yelled at her. She told Megan she could not go near the baby. Every time Kyle cried, her mother accused her of touching him. "Megan, leave your brother alone," she'd say in an angry, accusing voice. Megan became more and more resentful and bitter.

It's important to let children love their new brother or sister. Let them hold the baby with your help. They will be imitating you. If the baby is crying, don't assume the older sibling is hurting the baby. Instead of excluding the older child from being involved in the baby's care, give him the supervision he needs so that he does not hurt the baby.

To lessen jealousy, give equal love and attention to both children. Ask a relative or friend to care for the baby while you take time for your older child. Remember, just as young children need to learn to share their toys, they also need to learn to share you.

▼ *Father, help me to know how to protect my newborn,*
and how to teach his brothers and sisters to do the
same.

                                                              LB

CLEAR MESSAGES

"Whom will he teach knowledge?
And whom will he make to
understand the message?
Those just weaned from milk?
Those just drawn from the breasts?
For precept must be upon precept, . . .
Line upon line." —ISA. 28:9–10

*B*ut why? You treat me just like a baby! You never give me a reason good enough."

How often have you answered, "Just because"?

Back in the days of the prophet Isaiah the people of Judah had a similar complaint. They didn't like the way God was revealing His truth to them. They did not feel God was respecting their intellect and understanding. "Who does God think we are—little children?" they might have asked.

God gave them the Truth through the prophets in simple fashion, as a teacher would write a word and have a child trace it—line upon line. His message is clear and without elaborate illustration.

Our expectations and messages to our children also should be clear and not necessarily accompanied by a lot of explanations. It's likely they won't understand our reasons anyway. What they do need to understand is what we expect of them. Understanding is the key so accountability cannot be questioned.

▼ *Please help me, Lord, to give clear messages to my children.*

GC

ALWAYS READY FOR A STORY

Then He spoke many things to them in parables.
                                  —MATT. 13:3

O. B. was a rugged rancher with a handlebar mustache and a cowboy hat. He knew I was always ready for a story. As soon as he saw me, he would say, using his nickname for me, "Come on Old Scout." He'd take me to a porch that surveyed a large pasture and tell me tales about Frank and Jesse James, the Sundance Kid, and the Seminole Indians. I could see them riding through the pasture and stopping at the brook for water. Hours later I would emerge from this adventure. I still remember the magic of those days and how real it all seemed. O.B. is my all time favorite folk hero.

Storytelling is a dying art, but children love it. Painting a picture with words is also lots of fun for the storyteller. It sparks parts of your imagination you have forgotten. Stories add color and adventure to life. They create a special bond between the storyteller and listener. Parents can tell stories about their children and their lives. Children are spellbound especially if the stories are about them.

The Bible is rich with stories and storytellers. Jesus knew stories were a wonderful way to make a point.

▼ *Dear Lord, You know the importance of storytelling. Help me to incorporate that into my life.*

                                                JS

THE CRITICAL PARENT

*Bless those who persecute you; bless and do
not curse.*   —ROM. 12:14

*C*raig and Sue were getting ready for bed when Craig
said, "What's wrong, Sue? You've been so critical with
the children lately." Sue said nothing as she slipped into
bed. That night she tossed and turned. *Why am I like
this?* she asked herself. All night she criticized herself
for being a terrible mother. The next morning she felt
very down. A few weeks went by and her husband said
something again. When Craig mentioned it a third time,
Sue yelled at him to leave her alone.

Sue is a critical parent. First she's critical of herself.
Then she's critical of her children. If you are critical of
your children and they seem to frustrate you beyond
your limits, listen to what you are saying to yourself. If
it's negative, then you're going to be negative of whoever is around. Your children will be the first ones you
criticize. This creates children with critical parents inside themselves as well as poor self-esteem and sometimes depression.

What's the solution? Work on nurturing yourself and
that critical parent inside you. If you can't change that
critical parent into a nurturing parent, seek help. You'll
feel better and so will your family.

▼ *Dear God, please help me not to be so critical of
myself and others.*

LB

VANITY

Charm is deceitful and beauty is vain,
But a woman who fears the LORD, she
shall be praised. —PROV. 31:30

*F*ourteen-year-old girls seem to spend hours in front of their mirrors. It's really no surprise. With the millions of dollars spent advertising beauty products, it's a wonder they are not permanently affixed to the mirrors on top of their vanities. Vanity. It's an interesting name, isn't it!

As our children navigate through the teenage years, they are especially susceptible to society's idea of who they should be and how they should look. This is especially true for our young girls.

Teenage girls' bodies are changing fast. Their hips fill out and they develop breast tissue. Hair begins to grow under their arms and in their pubic area. The first time they menstruate can be a traumatic experience. They struggle with feelings of acceptance and identity while everything about them is in flux.

Provide emotional support and acceptance during this time. Talk openly about self-perceptions and what all those magazine ads tell us about real identity. Is it really better to look good than to feel good? Focus on the character not the clothes, the attitude not the appearance. Help your daughters find their identity in Christ.

▼ *Lord, I want to reflect the true beauty that comes from within. Please help me.*

GC

RAINBOWS AND YELLOW SUNS

"I set My rainbow in the cloud, and it shall be for the sign of the covenant between Me and the earth."
—GEN. 9:13

*R*ainbows and yellow suns with smiley faces are incorporated into almost every picture children bring home from school. What a wonderful outlook on life! From a child's perspective everything is wonderful. Even if things are bad, they will get better. There has to be some truth in that because parents probably smile when they see the picture. For that moment the day has brightened.

One day my husband and I took a getaway weekend for relief from all the normal stress. I was still uptight as we drove to our destination. Suddenly the sky turned black and threatening. *This is just what I need,* I thought. *A thunderstorm to add to my stress.* Just at that moment the most beautiful rainbow spanned the sky from horizon to horizon. It was the most glorious sight I had seen in a long time. My heart felt like singing, and my stress was immediately removed. My husband shared my enthusiasm.

God has planted little gems in this world to help us make it through the dark times. What a way to do it with a bucket full of color—red, yellow, blue, green, orange, and purple! It is amazing how that can lighten the load.

▼ *Dear Lord, give me a child's eye to see rainbows and yellow suns with smiley faces everywhere.*

JS

THE NURTURING PARENT

Be transformed by the renewing of your mind.
—ROM. 12:2

*P*arental figures are formed within ourselves when we are young. Guess who helps form them? Our parents! Many adults have childhood memories of parental criticism that make them pretty unhappy with themselves. But others, who have had words from nurturing parents, take good care of themselves and have a happy, positive outlook.

One of the ways these two counterpart parents operate inside us is through our own self talk. Listen to what you say about yourself. Do you beat yourself up, or do you nurture yourself with encouragement? Having a nurturing parent within yourself is very important to you and your children. It builds a strong nurturing parent in them, and you'll be a lot healthier yourself.

Those with critical parents don't have to stay stuck in their pain. Start with your own dialogue, analyze it, and begin to change it as needed. Try some positive statements like, "It's okay if you fail. You'll do better next time." Or tell yourself, "I love you, you're a neat person. I'm here for you. Take it one day at a time." It really works!

▼ *God, help me to nurture my inner child so I in turn can nurture my children.*

LB

PROTECTED

> *"We ourselves will be armed, ready to go before the children of Israel until we have brought them to their place; and our little ones will dwell in the fortified cities because of the inhabitants of the land."*
>
> —NUM. 32:17

*H*ave you ever overheard children when they begin to brag about their families? "My daddy can beat up your daddy!"

One of the basic needs children have is to feel they belong in the family unit. Part of that need is met when they have a sense of protection in the family. An important role we have as a parent is to provide that protection.

Imagine in your mind your home is a fortified castle that is impenetrable. It provides refuge and shelter from the outside elements. Among its many rooms is a battle chamber and a jousting run for training. It also has a round table where you and your knights (family) meet regularly.

Sometimes you must lead a force to do battle against an enemy. You do so to maintain your family's respect and to defend its honor. When you return, there is celebration and much merriment. Your family feels secure and protected.

▼ *Lord God, help me to realize the times when I am to do battle for my children—not only from outside elements, but also from the Enemy. May my home always be a place of refuge.*

GC

BLENDING VOICES AND LIVES

*I will sing to the LORD as long as
I live;
I will sing praise to my God while
I have my being.*

—PS. 104:33

Singing is good for the soul! Maybe because it is the best way to praise the Lord. Singing is the way parents bond to their infants and play with their toddlers. It's how our children bond to their Scout troop and romance their true love. If singing is that important, it should be nurtured every chance that presents itself.

When I go to church, the songs that I love to sing are the ones sung by my parents and grandparents. Besides enjoying the familiar music and the comforting words, it seems to bring a little of them into the worship time. Maybe that's why Christmas carols are so precious. They bring more to the season than just beautiful music. Maybe a touch of nostalgia or a connection with the past.

Families need to sing together to deepen their family bonds. The lovely sound is not nearly as important as blending voices and lives together. I am sure that is acceptable in God's sight.

▼ *Dear Lord, quiet my self-consciousness and encourage my family to bond together through singing.*

JS

YOU ARE AWESOME

Put on the new man which was created according to God, in righteousness and true holiness.
—EPH. 4:24

*B*eth is fourteen years old and blames everything on herself. When someone is arguing, she thinks it's about her. When someone looks at her the wrong way, she thinks they hate her. When her mother and father scold her, she feels she has failed them. This makes her hate herself even more.

Beth's parents cannot understand why she hates herself so much. She is good looking, smart, and has always succeeded in everything she does. They expect her to succeed and praise her for all her accomplishments. Now, because she can't get straight A's or seem to do anything else exceptionally well, Beth feels worthless.

Beth's parents did not realize it, but they had created an unhealthy pattern. They did everything for their daughter and praised her only when she was doing well. As a result Beth learned to feel good only because of what she does, not for who she is.

Beth and others like her need to learn about God's love. They need to learn that He loves them no matter what they do. Whether they get A's, B's, or D's, God sees them as special. Speaking their language, He says, "You are awesome."

▼ *God, help me to love my children not for what they do but for who they are inside.*

LB

GREEN PASTURES

"You shall therefore keep His statutes and His commandments which I command you today, that it may go well with you and with your children after you, and that you may prolong your days in the land which the LORD your God is giving you for all time."

—DEUT. 4:40

*O*ne of the ways to simplify successful parenting is to make sure we, as parents, are keeping God's commandments in our own lives.

I think of the old horse trainer who often quipped, "A horse has got to be trained from the head on back." The massive power of a horse can be directed or held in check by controlling his head. The direction a horse runs depends on where its nose is pointed. The same is true for our families. As the head goes so will the body.

Is the head in our household pointed in the right direction? If we are loving God with all we have and loving others as well, the lives of our children are more likely to go well. Hopefully, they will follow the example we set before them so their days will be prolonged. Allow your children the privilege to experience life in green pastures. Provide the direction and example for your children to follow. Keep His statutes and commandments.

▼ *Your Word, O Lord, will be my trainer. Your Spirit will be the reins to guide me.*

GC

FOLLOWING THE RULES—CHEERFULLY

. . . And they said, "All that the LORD has said we will do, and be obedient."
—EX 24:7

"Follows rules cheerfully," Bobby's teacher checked in the box on his report card. How many parents follow these guidelines? Children in elementary school accept it as a given. Rules are a natural part of life. They expect consequences when they disobey. In junior high they begin to question this premise. By the time they become an adult, they are ready to be the ones to make the rules. Never mind following other people's rules cheerfully. That's obvious listening to conversations about the IRS or traffic tickets. Cheerfulness doesn't have anything to do with it.

Bobby reminded his mother that she was at the wrong checkout counter. The sign read "eight items or less," but she had a full cart. She assured him it was okay. Bobby felt extremely embarrassed at remarks from the other customers. His mother didn't mind a bit. She may have been cheerful, but she was not following the rules.

Parents many times expect behavior from their children that they do not expect from themselves. Maybe it's time for us to set a better example by following the rules cheerfully.

▼ *Dear Lord, You know I would like to make all the rules but that would never work. Help me to follow the rules cheerfully.*

JS

A TEAM EFFORT

*Therefore do not be unwise, but understand
what the will of the Lord is.*

—EPH. 5:17

*T*he other day, the pediatrician's nurse said to Mrs.
Epstein, "Why doesn't your husband bring the kids in
for their appointment with the doctor? He's not working
and you are. You know, you need to let him do some of
the work. That's the only way he'll learn."

Mrs. Epstein thought for a moment. "No," she said,
"he'd never know what to ask, and I need to be here to
comfort the kids."

So many times we overlook the ways our husbands
can help. If we just ask, most are more than willing. The
important thing is not to be critical and not to expect
that they will do everything the same way we would.

The nurse was right. Fathers can and need to help,
but it's hard for some mothers to let go. Some prefer to
be in charge and do things their own way. But God's
plan is for a child to be parented by a mother and father.
That means one can't sit on the sidelines while the other
assumes all the responsibility. Our children need both
of us. And we need to work together as a team acknowledging that God is the One in charge. After all, our
children really belong to Him.

▼ *God, thank You for my husband and for the children
You have given us. Help us to share the responsibilities and joys of parenting.*

LB

TRUE HAPPINESS

"These things I have spoken to you, that My joy may remain in you, and that your joy may be full."
—JOHN 15:11

*F*rom where does true happiness come? Fame and fortune? For our children, too often it seems happiness or pleasure comes only when they get their way or get something they want. As Christian parents, we know better. We know true happiness comes from the knowledge of our Lord and Savior Jesus. We also know the decision to invite Christ into our lives is one we make on our own. No one can make that decision for us.

It is important for our children to learn to deal with their feelings and circumstances on their own rather than to be dependent on others or on "pacifiers." How do they deal with their feelings and circumstances? What choices are they making? The decisions are, of course, their own.

Do you feel responsible for your children's happiness? What is your reaction when they are unhappy or uncomfortable? Do you always attempt to help them feel happy? Frequently, when children are left to their own, they eventually will learn to deal with their feelings and make good decisions. In most cases, happiness is a choice our children can and should make for themselves.

▼ *Dear Lord, I pray my children will seek true joy in knowing You as their Lord and Savior.*

GC

THROUGH A CHILD'S EYES

*How much better it is to get wisdom
than gold!
And to get understanding is to be
chosen rather than silver.*
—PROV. 16:16

*I*n our church we sing a song with the line, "God reigns." When asked to draw a picture about the song, a child drew God in the heavens dropping raindrops.

Knowing that children take things literally, we need to be careful to say what we mean to avoid misconceptions.

A friend told the story of sitting in the beauty shop with her mother. The hairdresser was sharing some gossip. The mother warned her saying, "Little girls have big ears." My friend took that literally. She grew up thinking her ears were unusually large. She always was careful to choose hairstyles that covered her ears. Years later she was surprised when the hairdresser said her ears were normal and did not need to be hidden.

Of course misunderstandings will occur, but many times they can be avoided if we're careful to view our words through a child's eyes.

▼ *Heavenly Father, I don't ever want to confuse or mislead my children. Help me to think before I speak.*
JS

WE ARE BLESSED

And God is able to make all grace abound toward you. —2 COR. 9:8

You know that feeling you get when you watch your children sleeping? It's that peaceful, warm, fuzzy feeling of really being blessed. It also comes to you when your little one says something that hits your heart like, "Mommy, I love you."

The other day, my son, who is now three years old, was getting on top of a double swing. I shouted to him, "Be careful, don't fall!"

He yelled back, "Don't worry, Mommy. I'll be careful."

I will carry his words with me for a long time.

Children are one of God's richest blessings. Every day we see them grow, learn, and explore. I praise God each day for both of my kids. Praise God for yours, for the little things they say that are so special you will remember them forever. Even with all the illnesses and troubles of life, praise God that He blessed you with the joyful gift of children.

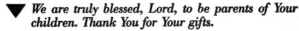 *We are truly blessed, Lord, to be parents of Your children. Thank You for Your gifts.*

LB

CONTENT

I have learned in whatever state I am, to be content.
—PHIL. 4:11

$\mathcal{O}$nce upon a time there was a far-off land where only teenagers lived. There was no school, so of course there were no teachers to give pop quizzes and there was no homework to worry about. There were no parents to nag about dirty rooms and make sure curfews were met. And everyone was popular. Looks were not at all important. But everyone had clear skin and nice clothes anyway. Everyone had a car to drive too.

The teens in this land never had any of those embarrassing moments when you don't know exactly what to say. Best friends were always honest and loyal. Everyone knew what the future held—what kind of job he would get and who he would marry. And in the meantime, everyone had dates Friday and Saturday nights.

Contentment would be easy in a world like this. Unfortunately, life is not a fairy tale. When your teens complain about their less than fairy-tale lives, you can encourage them to be content by listening to their feelings and opinions. And you can help them consider ways to change things that can be changed.

▼ *Lord, may my children learn to be content in every circumstance as they grow in You.*

GC

MULTI-GENERATIONAL FRIENDSHIPS

Gather the people,
Sanctify the congregation,
Assemble the elders,
Gather the children and nursing babies . . .
—JOEL 2:16

*Y*ears ago I moved to a new city to start a job. I only knew my great aunt and her daughter with whom she lived. My aunt was almost eighty. She was very lonely when her daughter worked. She lived for the days the Avon saleslady came because she would have someone to talk to. I started dropping by with my lunch once a week. It became a precious time for both of us. She always was so happy to see me, and being with her filled a lonely spot for me. She told me stories about the family with vivid details. She shared her thoughts and opinions and rounded out some of my impressions.

Unlike generations past, our society is segregated into age groups. Schools, churches, work places, and recreation do not encourage a lot of multi-generational friendships. Children and young people have little need to mingle with elderly people. In a way it is even discouraged. But life loses much of its savor without the wisdom of the previous generations. Children, youth, adults, and elderly adults all need each other to offer the full perspective God intended.

▼ *Dear Lord, help me not to be too busy to learn from those who are older and wiser.*

JS

LITTLE HELPERS

Train up a child in the way
he should go,
And when he is old he will
not depart from it.
—PROV. 22:6

*E*mily's new baby sister arrived just a few weeks ago. Emily insists on helping her mother with everything from diapering to bathing the baby. "I want to take care of the baby," she says. "I want to feed her, wash her, change her." When anyone comes over, Emily is the first to tell everyone exactly what her baby sister has been doing.

Some experts say we should encourage our older children to help with younger siblings, especially a baby. They say this will help resolve any anger or competitiveness they may feel. This is also a healthy way for them to get attention.

An older child may try to help because he is jealous of the time we give to a new baby. If that is the case, we need to make time to spend just with him to reassure him of our love.

If a big brother or sister wants to help, that's great. But remember that they need to feel free to be children, not assistant parents.

▼ *Lord, give mothers of new babies time, energy, and wisdom to meet the needs of their newborn and their other children. Thank You for the gift of little helpers.*

LB

TRUE LOVE

"If you then, being evil, know how to give good gifts to your children, how much more will your Father who is in heaven give good things to those who ask Him!"

—MATT. 7:11

*Q*uick, think about this. How do you feel when your child says, "You really don't love me!" What do you do?

Your child may not actually ever say these exact words, but may so in other ways. "You never let me . . ." "Everybody else gets to . . ." For many parents these statements suggest that if we really loved our kids, we would give them everything they want.

In today's Scripture, we see that God's love for His children is perfect and not to be questioned. He gives good things to all His children—what is best for each of us as we keep asking, seeking, and knocking. Neither should the love we have for our children necessarily be questioned. Would you give your son or daughter a stone if they asked for a piece of bread? Of course not.

Children may do many things to manipulate parents. One powerful means of manipulation is to redefine or distort true love and healthy relationships.

You know you love your children. God knows your heart too. Show your love by doing what you know is best for your children.

▼ *Show me, Lord, if I'm trying to prove my love to my children based on their standards.*

GC

GOD, MAKE MY DAY

*This is the day which the LORD
   has made;
We will rejoice and be glad in it.*
                                —PS. 118:24

*M*any times teens are so sensitive they get their feelings hurt over the slightest remarks by their friends, teachers, or family. They can go to school in a wonderful mood, feeling good about themselves. When they get to school, they can speak to someone and be ignored by them, or hear someone giggle and assume it is about them. Instantly they are in the depths of depression. The sad part is that the other person does not think another thing about it. In reality the teen has given the other person the ability to make or break his day.

When my teens came home from a bad day in school, I listened carefully. Then I'd say to them, "How dare you let anyone ruin your day?" I'd point out that the other person was only as powerful as they let them be. Their attitude did not change immediately, but in time I think they realized they had more control in their life.

Adults often have the same problem. We allow others the power to make or ruin our day. But we don't have to. With God's help we can enjoy each day to the fullest and rejoice in it.

▼ *Dear Lord, You made every day to glorify You. Help me to remember to rejoice in it.*

                                                        JS

FATHERS CAN HELP

Husbands, love your wives, just as Christ also loved the church and gave Himself for it.
—EPH. 5:25

The other day, my two-year-old son starting calling my husband Mommy and me Daddy. Our roles have switched! I'm working and my husband has become a house husband. My two-year-old was right in calling him Mommy, because right now that is his role.

Fathers can do an excellent job of mothering—with a little training, of course. Even if they are not forced into this role, they can really help at home after work or on weekends. They can feed, bathe, and help potty train their children. In other words, they can and need to be more than just a baby sitter.

It is important for fathers to help raise their children, not only for the mother's sanity, but also because it forms a bond with his children. I've seen how both of our boys have grown much closer to their father since he has taken over caring for them. As hard as it is for me to go out to work instead of stay home with my children, I know God is doing something special during this time. He is using it to build a solid base that all families need.

 God, thank You for my husband and for the joy of watching him care for the children You have given us.

LB

RESCUING

"The fathers shall not be put to death for their children, nor shall the children be put to death for their fathers; a person shall be put to death for his own sin."

—DEUT 24:16

*E*very morning it was a battle and constant reminding. "It's time to get up." "Make your bed." "Don't forget your books." "You're going to be late for school."

Obviously, it was more hectic for the mother than for her son. Sometimes she would not have time to get herself ready for work with all the time she spent reminding her son. Of course, he couldn't be late for school another day. He would have to visit the principal. That would be horrible! Or would it?

Sometimes it is important for children and teenagers to suffer the natural consequences of their behavior. Often it's only when they experience the consequences that they choose to become more responsible. Sometimes this is the only means for true self-motivation.

Be careful not to rescue your children from the learning experiences in life. Help them to be responsible by allowing them to endure the natural consequences of their actions.

▼ *Dear God, thank You for loving me so much that instead of rescuing me, You let me learn from my experiences.*

GC

TEEN SUICIDE

For You are my hope, O Lord GOD;
You are my trust from my youth.
—PS. 71:5

A young teen was upset over breaking up with her boyfriend and over failing grades. She wrote a suicide note. As a last thought, she called to tell her boyfriend goodbye. Then she went to the medicine cabinet and took all the pills she could find. Fortunately the ambulance got there in time. After pumping her stomach, she was physically okay. Emotionally she was seriously depressed. For the first time her parents were forced to recognize that she needed professional help.

Parents need to be aware of the danger signs of depression that can lead to suicide attempts. Broken relationships, withdrawing from family and friends, academic failures, changes in eating and sleep habits— all may signal the teen is in trouble. We need to be in touch with our teens. We need to know what's going on in their lives and to be sensitive to their feelings. And we always need to take suicide threats seriously and get help immediately. Without help for the emotional as well as the physical problems, the threat of suicide persits.

 Lord God, please protect my children from ever considering suicide as an option, and please help me not to overlook their needs.

JS

REGRESSION

*"Whoever humbles himself as this little child
is the greatest in the kingdom of heaven."*
—MATT. 18:4

*T*hose who have more than one child will understand
this and those who don't will learn. There is a backward
behavior called regression that happens to some children when younger siblings come along. It is normal,
expected, and makes perfect sense.

Here is a child's mommy, who used to put all her
energy and attention into him. Now she is giving that
attention to another child. Anger and jealousy are part
of the deal. It's like your spouse marrying someone else
and bringing her home. I think we'd regress too!

Two- and three-year-old children who are already
potty trained may regress to wetting their beds and
pants. My two-year-old son wants a bottle like his
brother. There are times he also wants to be carried
instead of walking. Having two kids can be tough!

If our children regress, they don't need our criticism.
They need our love and our comfort, so they can adjust.

▼ *God, help me to give my older children the attention
they need when they are struggling to cope with a
new baby brother or sister.*

LB

LOST AND FOUND

"What woman, having ten silver coins, if she loses one coin, does not light a lamp, sweep the house, and seek diligently until she finds it?"
                                          —LUKE 15:8

*I*t's a familiar story. The young boy wanted to buy a new baseball glove. He had no money of his own, but a wise father allowed him to work at odd jobs to earn the necessary dollars.

Fifty cents here, and a dollar there, and finally the glove was his. And what a prized possession it was. It even was autographed by a national league all-star!

Then one Saturday night, the boy realized his glove was missing. He had left it at the ballpark after playing all day. He frantically pleaded his case to his father. They drove across town to the park to look, but it was gone.

The drive back was quiet, the boy obviously downtrodden. The father thought of how precious God's children are to Him, how He grieves when we are lost and rejoices when we are found. He would eventually help his son buy another glove. Now, he thanked God for his son and prayed he would learn the lesson of caring for things he valued. How do we prize our children? Would we stop everything to look for them or help them if they were lost?

▼ *Thank You, Lord, for calling me Your own and allowing me to know Your voice.*

                                                    GC

GO FLY A KITE!

And He rode upon a cherub, and flew;
He flew upon the wings of the wind.
—PS. 18:10

*G*o fly a kite!" Sounds like a great idea to me. As a child, kite flying was hard for me to do. But the new kites are easier and are in the air with little expertise needed.

Kite flying is a perfect stress reliever. Watching the kite float through the sky with the greatest of ease is soothing and relaxing. It has no redeeming value which is essential for relaxation. It's an opportunity to enjoy the wonders of God's creation—blue skies with gentle breezes and the quietness of nature. It's also a wonderful way to bond with your children. It can be a way to interact with your children and to ease into conversation or play.

The point is not necessarily kite flying. It's stopping to enjoy life. It's slowing down our busy lives and taking time to do nothing but enjoy God's creation including our children. God blesses us in many ways but we frequently are too busy to notice. Kite flying, because it cannot be rushed, is a way to take time to notice.

▼ *Dear Lord, help me enjoy the simple pleasures of Your creation.*

JS

SPACE

*Be kind to one another, tenderhearted,
forgiving one another, just as God in Christ
also forgave you.* —EPH. 4:32

$\mathcal{K}$aren and her older brother, Pete, were playing together. Pete was building a tower with blocks. Karen, who was angry at Pete for hitting her earlier, got revenge by knocking his tower down.

Some say we need to keep the peace at home and to have strict law and order. That means Karen would need to be punished. Others say to let children resolve their own conflicts. Choosing the latter, however, doesn't mean that we allow one child to retaliate by beating up on the other as Pete is likely to do if he thinks mother isn't watching.

One way we can help maintain a balance of peace and law and order is through establishing space and boundaries. These are vital concepts for children. They need certain areas, like their own room, where their brothers and sisters are not allowed. Then if they have special projects, they can't be destroyed. It's important that children don't violate each other's boundaries and that they have space apart from each other. They also need to have time apart so one sibling is not always crowding the other. Sometimes they just need time alone the same as we do!

▼ *Lord, show me when to intervene in my children's conflicts and when to let them solve their own conflicts.*

LB

WRESTLING IN PRAYER

*Epaphras, who is one of you, a servant of
Christ, greets you, always laboring fervently
for you in prayers, that you may stand perfect
and complete in all the will of God.*
—COL. 4:12

*H*e had been a high school wrestling champion in
upper state New York. He was solid as a rock—someone
you would not want to cross. Yet when you heard him
speak, he had a gentle confidence about him that was
disarming.

He told me of his many wrestling matches—of all the
bloody noses and bruises and the long, hard hours of
training. He even showed me a few wrestling holds that
made me, frankly, regret having volunteered. He also
told of the rush of excitement and satisfaction he felt
after winning a match well fought.

We sometimes are called to wrestle in prayer for our
children. The struggle may be long and hard, with
many points of disappointment and many bruises. But
we must continue to pray fervently for them and God's
will. The victory of having our children stand complete
in the will of the heavenly Father is worth the fight.

▼ *Train me, Lord, for the spiritual battles that are
part of parenting. Help me to wrestle in prayer for
my children.*

GC

WHEN ILLNESS COMES

*Now Jesus went about all Galilee, teaching in
their synagogues, preaching the gospel of the
kingdom, and healing all kinds of sickness
and all kinds of disease among the people.*
—MATT. 4:23

*N*o one likes surprises unless they are pleasant ones.
Parents often think they are protecting their children by
not telling them about unpleasant events. Not so! Children are always aware when things are not as they
should be. They feel more secure in knowing what is
happening so they can deal with their feelings about it.

A teen's father was about to have surgery. It was presented as a minor procedure even though there was a
potential that it could be more serious. The son picked
up his father's anxiety, but it did not compute with the
information he had been given. It is understandable
why the teen was extremely angry when his father's surgery was almost fatal and involved a more prolonged
period of hospitalization.

Hospitalization is a heavy-duty experience, but children as well as adults handle anxiety better if the fear is
spoken. Then the family can be involved in the situation
and help each other through it together.

▼ *Dear Lord, be our source of strength when illness
comes. Bind us together so we can face it in Your
strength.*

JS

UNRESOLVED ISSUES

*The beginning of strife is like
  releasing water;
Therefore stop contention before
  a quarrel starts.*
            —PROV. 17:14

*I*n the movie *For Keeps,* the mother lives her whole life through her daughter and hates her ex-husband. She is afraid of losing her child and of men hurting her child. This causes her daughter to push her away.

When a couple separates or is divorced, it is crucial that they work through any unresolved issues so they don't hinder their child's growth and their own. Issues left unresolved will affect every facet of their lives, from their workplace to their home. They will affect everyone they come in contact with and especially those with whom they live.

If we want to make sure our child is healthy emotionally, we need to work on ourselves first. It's not easy to change and to look at ourselves. But we need to ask God to open our eyes to see where we are unhealthy and then seek professional help or work on those areas ourselves.

▼ *Open my eyes, God. I want to be more like Jesus every day.*

LB

FEARING THE FUTURE

*"But seek first the kingdom of God and His
righteousness, and all these things shall be
added to you."* —MATT. 6:33

*M*any of us are motivated, and sometimes paralyzed, by a fear of the future. We find it hard to trust
God, especially in the area of finances. We may make
several sacrifices based on this fear that will almost
always result in diverting God's perfect will for us. Unfortunately, the real sacrifice may be our children.

Of course, it's wise to plan for the future, but when
most people think about planning ahead they think only
of finances. We are not accustomed to thinking about
the future in terms of relationships.

What kind of people do you want your children to
be? What kind of relationship do you want to have with
them? Do you want your grandchildren to visit you?

When we are motivated by fear in the area of our
finances, we may rob God by not tithing. We also may
rob our children. How? Our preoccupation with financial concerns may be taking from them the thing necessary to build godly character—knowing our character.

Seek God's kingdom first. Know the importance of
fellowship not only with Him but with your children.

▼ *Dear God, thank You for all Your provisions in my
life. Thank You for being a God I can trust in.*

GC

STEP ASIDE

My brethren, count it all joy when you fall
into various trials, knowing that the testing of
your faith produces patience.
                                —JAMES 1:2–3

$\mathcal{C}$ontrary to the opinion of many that perfect parents provide a problem-free existence for their teens, a parent's role in life is *not* to make everything wonderful for his or her children. Actually that would create a very dysfunctional relationship. Parental tasks involve teaching their teen to learn problem solving techniques. One way teens do that is to encounter some problems and not handle them well. The next time they will know what does not work. An axiom of life is that the words that are misspelled and have a big "X" by them are the ones that are learned and never forgotten.

The hardest thing to do is to watch your teen mishandle a situation without stepping in. However, balance is necessary. Your children need to start handling some of their own problems while the problems are small enough to handle. That gives them the experience of finding their own solutions and thus building their self-confidence. It prepares an adolescent for the larger problems he will face. But sometimes our teens will face problems that are beyond their maturity to handle. We need God's wisdom to know when to step aside and when to step in.

▼ *Dear God, give me wisdom and restraint in helping*
   my child problem solve.

JS

BIRTHDAY WAR

*The wisdom that is from above is first pure,
then peaceable, gentle, willing to yield, full
of mercy and good fruits, without partiality
and without hypocrisy.* —JAMES 3:17

*J*eremy and Joey are brothers. Today is Jeremy's birthday. He is so excited. He knows he is going to have a party and receive lots of presents. Everyone, like his grandmother and grandfather, is calling to wish him a happy birthday.

On the other hand, Joey is pretty down. His birthday isn't for six months. He feels left out. Their mother notices how Joey is acting and says to him, "Come here, I've got extra hugs for you. You are very special."

Throughout the day mother continues to show Joey that he is equally loved. She reminds him of all the presents he received on his birthday. Right before his brother's birthday party starts, she gives Joey a token gift. It is smaller than his brother's gifts but something he has been wanting.

Because of this mother's wisdom and sensitivity, there wasn't a birthday war in her home. Both boys enjoyed the party and the cake, ice cream, and games. Most of all, both Jeremy and Joey felt loved.

▼ *Dear God, please help me to show my children that they are equally loved.*

LB

FAMILY FIRST

*Appoint elders in every city as I commanded
you—if a man is blameless, the husband of
one wife, having faithful children not
accused of dissipation or insubordination.*
—TITUS 1:5–6

J know of a man who has held a position of authority
in his church for some time. He is a very wise man who
knows much about not only the worth of his children,
but the development of *worthiness* that children must
have.

Some time ago, when his teenage son went through a
particularly difficult time, this man resigned from his
position of church leadership. He resigned not because
he feared setting a bad example in a highly visible position, but because he knew his son needed more attention. After a time, he was able to be reinstated as a
church leader.

When children are neglected, they may develop a
sense of worthlessness or shame. In order to deal with
these feelings, they may turn to drugs, alcohol, or even
contemplate suicide.

We need to make sure our children are given opportunity to develop positive feelings of self-worth. And we
need to remember God never calls anyone into a position of leadership or ministry and asks them to neglect
their children.

▼ *Dear God, I will prayerfully consider Your call.*

GC

UNMADE BEDS

The LORD is merciful and gracious,
Slow to anger, and abounding in
mercy. —PS. 103:8

*T*he "unmade bed" look is the home fashion statement of the nineties in homes where there are teenagers. "Why should you make a bed when you are going to crawl back into it at the end of the day?" Does that sound familiar? I've heard it frequently as a therapist. You have to admit it contains a certain amount of logic. But from a parent's point of view, an unmade bed represents other issues like rebellion, defying authority, laziness, slovenliness, control, and proof that he has done a poor job raising the child.

When children are eight through twelve years of age, they can make a bed as well as any adult. The day they turn thirteen, they completely forget how. The amazing thing is that they suddenly know how to do it again when they turn twenty-three, especially if it really matters to them personally.

That's the real issue. Does it really matter? You can be a good parent, and he can be an energetic and successful teen even if his bed remains unmade for a decade. Parents need to evaluate how much of their relationship is dependent on whether or not a bed is made.

▼ *Dear heavenly Father, focus my attention on important things rather than trivial annoyances.*

JS

[Love] bears all things, believes all things,
hopes all things, endures all things.
—1 COR. 13:7

*W*hen we were kids, my brother and I would fight as if there were no tomorrow. We hit, we yelled, we made lines across the car seat so the other could not cross and then hit each other when we did. But if anyone else hit us, we defended each other to the end.

Sibling loyalty is astounding. It protects the other from the harsh words of a parent and from the wounds of a friend.

Kelly's mother yelled at her little brother. Kelly immediately went over and comforted him by saying, "Mommy is just tired. She still loves you." Timmy's younger brother was rejected by a friend. Timmy comforted him by saying, "I'm your friend, Pete. He's probably just mad. You'll see."

On those days when we think our children will never be friends, let's choose to remember their fighting is a normal part of growing up. And let's trust that when they have a real need they will be there for one another.

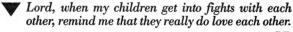 *Lord, when my children get into fights with each other, remind me that they really do love each other.*
LB

HOLDING ON

"And I give them eternal life, and they shall never perish; neither shall anyone snatch them out of My hand. My father, who has given them to Me, is greater than all; and no one is able to snatch them out of My Father's hand."
—JOHN 10:28–29

A small town preacher told the story of a father and his young son as they walked down a country road in the springtime. "Grab hold of my finger, son," the father said. But because the road was well-traveled and full of potholes, the son often stumbled and lost his grip. After several tumbles where gravel met tender bare knees, the boy looked up at his dad. In brilliant innocence he said, "Why don't you hold *my* hand so I won't get hurt anymore."

Sometimes we need to be reminded that as children of God it is He who is holding our hand rather than us holding on to Him. His mighty hand, the same hand that fashioned the heavens and the earth, holds us tightly so no one is able to snatch us from Him. We are safe and protected in His loving care.

Our children also need to be reminded that we are holding on to them—that our commitment to them is unchangeable. They need to know that our love for them is not dependent on their strength or desire to hold on to us.

▼ *Thank You, Lord, for Your strong and gentle hand.*
GC

CREATING SPECIAL MEMORIES

Delight yourself also in the LORD,
And He shall give you the desires
of your heart. —PS. 37:4

*Y*ou can't have your cake and eat it too—unless your mom makes cupcakes!" This is a proverb my daughter coined. It reminds me of how parents can create special moments with their children that can leave a mark on their lives if only as nothing more than a fond memory and brief smile.

One year my daughter had a Barbie® doll cake for her birthday. It was a masterpiece. Her delight turned to distress, however, when she realized it would be cut into pieces to serve her guests. The solution was obvious. I made cupcakes to serve at the party so she could enjoy the cake.

Of course she would have survived and maybe even learned a valuable lesson, but why was that necessary when I was able to provide an easy solution. It made her know that I heard her distress and acknowledged the importance of it. We felt close to each other then, and even now, when we remember it.

Was it worth the extra effort? Sure it was. It turned into a priceless moment for both of us.

▼ *Dear Lord, show me things I can do that will create*
special memories for my children and for me.

JS

LOVE

"For God so loved the world that He gave His only begotten Son." —JOHN 3:16

*H*ave you ever seen a mother look at her new infant? I've never seen so much love. It's a love beyond words. Now reverse that. Have you seen a child's eyes light up when he sees his mother? The bond between a mother and her child is like no other. It is a peak of life.

My brother told me that the love I would have for my children would be very strong. He was right. It is wonderful. At times I don't feel it as strongly, and yet I know love is more than a feeling. It is a commitment I have made to them.

There is another love beyond our understanding—a love ten million times greater than the love we have for our children. This love is the love God has for His children—for you and for me.

▼ *God, thank You for Your love. Help me experience it daily.*

LB

REAL WINNERS

He does not delight in the strength of
the horse;
He takes no pleasure in the legs of a man.
—PS. 147:10

There was a certain young man who dreamed of being a football star. Perhaps he wanted to achieve the fame and fortune of today's sports heroes. Or perhaps this young man sensed the frustrated desires of his father to be a star athlete in high school. Whatever the case, his dreams never came true. This not-so-athletic boy experienced much disappointment sitting on the bench on second string teams.

Gratefully God does not value us based on our performance. Having the strength of a horse and the agility of a foot solider are not important to Him. Rather, He takes pleasure in having a relationship with us.

So, too, we need to guard against sports, or anything else for that matter, becoming more important than our relationship with our children. We need to communicate love regardless of performance; to emphasize that exercise and good health are what's important, not winning. And we need to let our teen decide whether or not he wants to be an athlete.

Do you take pleasure in performance and winning? Remember, you are the real winner when you have communion with God and a relationship with your teens.

▼ *Dear God, help me to be strong in Your ways.*

GC

HANDICAPS

*"My grace is sufficient for you, for My
strength is made perfect in weakness."*
—2 COR. 12:9

*H*aving a handicapped child is a complicated issue.
After accepting and handling your own feelings, it is
essential to help your child learn to live with his handicap. Each new developmental phase requires a new
level of acceptance. Ultimately the teen years are prob-
lematic because they are attempting independence.

A friend had a daughter who was born deaf. The
family did a good job of raising her to be as independent as possible. When the teen years came, the family
was very protective and upset because she didn't fit into
the church youth group. They expected the other teens
to reach out to her. Finally their daughter realized that if
she was going to fit in, she would have to take the initia-
tive just like all the other teens. When she did, she was
able to find her niche.

Everyone has areas in their lives where they feel
handicapped. Being too short or having a nose that's too
big are as much a handicap to a teen as deafness. Helping them to accept their "deficiencies" and to embrace
their attributes can do more than orchestrating peer relationships. They are the ones who have to reach out
and let others get to know them.

▼ *Dear Lord, You have given me a big responsibility in
raising a child with special needs. Now, please, give
me the wisdom to do it well.*

JS

CREATING A MONSTER?

If any of you lacks wisdom, let him ask of God, who gives to all liberally and without reproach, and it will be given to him.

—JAMES 1:5

*J*ane was a first-time mom. Her new baby girl, Laura, was three months old. Whenever Laura cried, Jane immediately picked her up. She never let her baby cry long. Everyone told her that she was spoiling her child. Laura was soon eight months old. Now she cried not only for food and a dry diaper, but for her mother's attention. Jane was perplexed. *Should I pick her up every time or not?* she asked herself. *Could I be spoiling this child and creating a monster?*

Some specialists say you can never spoil a baby. Others say that by the age of eight months, babies begin to manipulate by their cries. Still others say that an eight-month-old can't talk. All he or she can do to communicate is to cry.

Our world is loaded with plenty of advice. A lot of it contradicts itself. That's why we need to go to God and ask Him to help us. Beginning at our child's birth, we need to ask Him for the wisdom to know how to treat our child. God knows more than anyone else if we are spoiling our baby.

▼ *Dear Father, I praise You for Your wisdom and guidance that is greater than any book or the advice of any expert.*

LB

ALLOWANCES

"If you have not been faithful in the unrighteous mammon, . . . who will give you what is your own?" —LUKE 16:11–12

$\mathscr{D}$o you remember getting an allowance when you were a kid? How did you learn the value of a dollar?

I believe in giving allowances. They can be an important part of helping children learn how to handle money early in life. Weekly responsibilities can be established with specific guidelines about expectations. A word of warning, though. Money given for each chore accomplished can be tedious and puts the wrong focus on helping around the house.

Money can be given for lunch at school. This can be done on a daily or weekly basis. This gives children an opportunity to plan their spending. If done weekly, when a child runs out of money, they run out—no borrowing from the bank!

Many parents also wonder about money for grades. Motivation for good grades should come from within. Furthermore, rewards for grades devalues the important things—learning and effort.

Finally, a weekly allowance gives our children opportunity to learn about tithing and giving. Let's not forget to teach our children how to handle money in a spiritual manner.

▼ *Help me, Lord, to be a good steward and to store up riches in heaven rather than on earth.*

GC

A CHILD'S PERSPECTIVE

"Assuredly, I say to you, inasmuch as you did not do it to one of the least of these, you did not do it to Me." —MATT. 25:45

$\mathcal{R}$ecently I was at an adult meeting where a parent came accompanied by a child. The topic of discussion was inappropriate for the child's ears. Besides being adult and boring, it contained material that could be frightening and/or suggestive. I became more distressed when the parent took no responsibility for protecting the child and appeared unconcerned.

Parents have the responsibility to protect their children from inappropriate experiences even if it means exiting an adult forum. A child's perception is much different from an adult's. Useful, meaningful information about the adult world is inappropriate for children because they do not have the experience or knowledge of the world to make sense of it. Add a little imagination, and that is how nightmares are created.

Sensitivity can turn potentially unhealthy experiences into ones that are nurturing. Seeing things through a child's perspective helps to accomplish that.

▼ *Dear Father, help me to be sensitive to my child's need and to know when and how to protect him from harmful experiences.*

JS

EGOCENTRIC

Most men will proclaim each his
own goodness,
But who can find a faithful man?
—PROV. 20:6

*Y*oung children view life as revolving around them! They are in the center of everyone and everything.

Four-year-old Christy said to her mother, "I want that and that and that." When her mother got her the toys she wanted, she screeched, "Those aren't the ones." Another time, Christy demanded a waffle. Her mother baked it and cut it up. Christy's response was to cry loudly, "No, no, I wanted it frozen and not cut," and she threw the waffle on the floor.

I wonder if we adults behave toward God any differently. I hear some adults say, "No, God, that's not the job I wanted. I don't want to move. I want that job over there." If we're honest, we have to admit that we, too, are egocentric. How does God handle us? He is patient, loving, and kind, but He also disciplines us when we need it. He's given us a good example to follow in dealing with our own children.

▼ *Thank You, God, for putting up with my selfishness.*
Help me to be as patient, loving, and kind toward
my children.

LB

ATTACHED

Make me to hear joy and gladness,
That the bones which You have broken
may rejoice.
                        —PS. 51:8

The shepherd was concerned about one of his lambs. It constantly kept straying from the flock as if it were on its own trail. The shepherd knew the only way the lamb would survive would be for it to become attached to him. It needed to know his smell and his voice as signals of the place where it belonged. And so the shepherd took the little lamb and broke its leg. Until it mended, he carried it on his shoulder. By the time the leg had healed, the lamb knew its master well. The lamb would never stray beyond the safety of the shepherd's care again.

Our children attach to us through the nurturing, protection, and respect we give to them. It is vital for us to be available to them from the time of birth so they can know our genuine love for them. From time to time our attachment may be hindered by a child taking its own trail, or we may be on our own path. That's when we must sacrifice and break a few "bones" in order to rebuild our parent-child bond. The importance of children being attached to their parents cannot be overemphasized. It's the foundation for healthy development. It also sets the stage for a healthy separation. You cannot properly leave someone you've never belonged to!

▼ *Dear God, I am committed to do whatever is necessary to "attach" to my children in healthy ways.*

GC

FAMILY SECRETS

*"But he who does the truth comes to the
light, that his deeds may be clearly seen, that
they have been done in God."*

—JOHN 3:21

*M*any families have family secrets. Sometimes they
are as simple as, "We don't have a perfect family."
Other times they are things everyone knows but are
afraid to talk about. If they remain secret, they can perpetuate emotionally unhealthy behavior patterns for the
whole family.

A teenage girl frequently ran away from home, much
to the dismay of her parents. Finally, when directly
asked what the problem was, she revealed that her
father had been molesting her for several years. The
mother and siblings were shocked; however, they were
all aware that the father frequently visited the girl's
room at night. The family secret was to avoid talking
about the obvious. Once it was out in the open, the family could do something about it.

Honesty in communication clears up the misconceptions and unfounded fears that secrets may create. It
also makes relationships much less complicated. Ask
yourself, "Who made the rule that we can't talk about
this?" "What will happen if we do?" Developing honest
communication within the family will disarm the power
of the family secret.

▼ *Dear God, give me the courage to develop honest
communications and to eliminate family secrets.*

JS

ENOUGH TIME?

Meditate within your heart on your bed, and be still.
—PS. 4:4

*C*harlotte," Jeanne called, entering the room where her children were playing, "you still have to put on your shoes for school. And Griffin, you still need to brush your teeth." Jeanne fumbled with the zipper to her own dress as she reached out to scoot the children toward their tasks.

"Mom," Charlotte complained. Griffin wrestled his arm away from his mother as he silently continued playing.

"Kids. We're late. We've got to go!"

As parents, we often wonder what we did with all the extra time we had when we didn't have kids. A lot of mothers say it takes two to three hours to get their young children up, fed, and dressed. Other moms have tighter schedules and have to push their children until they're exhausted.

We spend so much time with our children. But how much time do we spend with God? How much time does God have to spend with us to get us ready for His Kingdom? Do we fight Him all the way?

▼ *God, I need energy and encouragement to keep going. Help me take some time to be with You today.*

LB

KNOWING THE DIFFERENCE

The LORD will guide you continually,
And satisfy your soul in drought,
And strengthen your bones;
You shall be like a watered garden,
And like a spring of water, whose
waters do not fail.

—ISA. 58:11

*H*is school grades were not good enough. He could only make the second string football team. At home he constantly broke things. Even at church, so-called friends excluded him because of the "bad luck" that followed him. What a failure!

This would be a harsh and undeserving description of anyone, but unfortunately it is often how a child or teenager perceives himself. Failures are a normal part of any child's development. But when failures are not dealt with properly, they can result in intense frustration or depression. When failures become intense or frequent, they may impact a child's identity. He may become convinced that he is a failure.

Parents need to help their children make the distinction between failing and being a failure. Let them know who they are in Christ, how God sees them, and what He promises. Reassure them that when they do fail, God will continue to guide, satisfy, and strengthen them.

▼ *Dear God, I thank You that I am never a failure in Your eyes.*

GC

PRIVATE! KEEP OUT!

And He said to them, "Come aside by yourselves to a deserted place and rest a while."
—MARK 6:31

*P*rivacy is necessary for everyone. Teens are no exception. They need parents to respect their privacy and to protect it from invasion by anyone else, including a sibling.

Privacy is especially important to teens because they are trying out new ideas and ways of doing things. They have no idea if they are going to work, but they don't want to be embarrassed by exposure if they don't. As they mature, they will discard the failures and begin to share the successes.

Frequently parents ask, "Is it valid to invade their privacy to insure they are not involved in something we disapprove of or something that is harmful?" There will probably be other telltale signs long before you would find drugs and alcohol in their room. Invading their privacy usually just increases the rift between parent and teen and decreases the trust.

▼ *Dear Father, I need to remember to treat others, including my teen, with the respect I need for myself.*
JS

NEVER ALONE MOMS

*Now may the God of hope fill you with all joy
and peace in believing, that you may abound
in hope by the power of the Holy Spirit.*
—ROM. 15:13

*W*hen you have children, you will have an audience
most of your waking hours, and even through the night.
You will have a hard time escaping, even to the bathroom. Your children will follow you and question you
through the door: "Mommy, where are you? Let me in.
What are you doing? What's that? I want to be held!"

Our kids like to be with us because they feel secure
and safe with us. I wonder if God doesn't want us to
depend on Him as our children depend on us—
constantly seeking Him, talking to Him, wanting to be
near Him every minute of our day. We need the same
comfort and safety our children seek. God is available
to us every minute of our day and night, and He never
gets tired.

 *Thank You, God, for being a trusting parent we can
cling to day and night.*

LB

CONFIDENCE

Also I heard the voice of the Lord, saying:
"Whom shall I send,
And who will go for Us?"   —ISA. 6:8

Someone once said that you fail only when you fail to try.

Perhaps the most common reason children fail is a fear of failure. They fear failing in the growing up process. Believe it or not, many kids really are afraid of growing up!

Even when children argue or complain about too many restrictions and not enough freedom, underneath they are likely to feel anxious or fear the unknown—of the uncertainty of handling the stress and responsibility of young adulthood.

Every child has these fears to some degree, but sometimes they can become immobilizing. Some children may choose not to try. Others may become reclusive. If an unhealthy dependency on someone or something exists (i.e. drugs, alcohol, or even overprotective parents), it must be honestly addressed and resolved.

We all want our children to have the confidence to step forward and announce, "Here am I! Send me." Let us teach and show our children how to be dependent on Him who will never fail us.

▼ *Dear God, I will attempt to go forth today in the confidence that You will never fail me.*

GC

TAKE CARE OF YOURSELF

"You shall love your neighbor as yourself."
—MATT. 22:39

*L*ove your neighbor as yourself." Many times people forget that that Bible verse includes the part about yourself. We feel it is selfish to take care of ourselves, yet it is an essential ingredient to being a healthy parent and raising healthy children. It really has more to do with self-care than selfishness.

Raising children is an especially draining job. Small children interfere with all your normal functions, like getting enough sleep, eating relaxing meals, and spending time with other adults. They are demanding and emotionally and physically exhausting. As they grow older, they drain you in different ways. Without caring for yourself with the same vigor as you care for your family, you can be all used up.

It doesn't have to be that way. Many times we deliberately have to choose to love ourselves and to let others know our needs. A spouse is the natural person to meet those needs, especially since they are in on this adventure of parenthood. Taking good care of yourself means you will be physically, emotionally, and spiritually able to take care of others.

▼ *Dear heavenly Father, remind me to take good care of myself so I can be a better caretaker of my family.*

JS

IT'S NOT A DIRTY WORD

*"Have you not read that He who made them
at the beginning 'made them male and
female'?"*
　　　　　　　　　　　　　—MATT. 19:4

The other day a mother asked me what she should tell
her ten-year-old boy about sex. At first she wanted to
ignore the details. Then she admitted, "But he needs to
know."

Ignoring our children's questions about sex will not
dampen their curiosity. It will only make them ask more
questions. If we don't answer their questions, they may
feel insecure, confused, and frightened. They also may
get their answers from someone else.

Children need to know that sex is not a dirty word.
They need to hear us call the body parts by their real
names so they won't feel guilty or embarrassed about
their bodies or their desires. We need to tell them, for
example, that the male organ is a penis, not a tee-tee or
a wee-wee or whatever. Or, a wet dream is masturbation
in your sleep.

Our children need to hear from us God's perspective
on sex. We can use their questions as an opportunity to
teach them about this beautiful gift God has given to
husbands and wives.

▼ *Dear God, help me to talk with my children about
sex. Give me the right words to answer their questions.*

　　　　　　　　　　　　　　　　　　　　LB

RISKING FAILURE

The God of my strength,
in Him I will trust,
My shield and the horn of my salvation,
My stronghold and my refuge;
My Savior, You save me from violence.
—2 SAM. 22:3

$\mathcal{I}$ think of Thomas Edison and the innumerable failures he experienced. He failed over 6,000 times before he perfected the first electric light bulb! What if he had been too emotionally upset to continue his endeavors? What if he had considered himself a failure? I wonder about his parents. I suspect they didn't try to protect him from emotional hurts by not allowing him to risk failure. Instead, I suspect they encouraged him to take risks and taught him how to handle failure.

The consequences for failure as a child are often less intense and less far reaching than as an adult. They sometimes can even be reversible. For adults the stakes are much higher and people are less forgiving. Children can learn valuable lessons without having to pay the highest price.

We need to allow our children to deal with failures while it is still safe. Our home should be a sanctuary for our children. It should be a refuge where restoration and revitalization can occur. Through troubled times, our children can be strengthened to withstand future failures.

▼ *Lord, please help me to make my home a refuge for my children.*

GC

UNIQUELY MADE

"But the very hairs of your head are all numbered."
                                    —MATT. 10:30

We have this picture of how our children should be. We try to thrust them into a special mold. Society tells us they should make A's and B's, sit quietly in their desks, be superstars in sports, or prima ballerinas. These demands start very young and continue through high school and into adulthood. As parents, we quickly try to conform because we don't want our children left behind. We want them to be the best that they can be.

The truth is that God made each of our children, and they already are the best they can be. He made them with unique personalities, temperaments, gifts, and talents. No one else has the exact combination they have. The more they are in touch with their uniqueness, the better they will function and the more the world will be blessed. The problem comes in trying to be someone else.

Our children learn early to try to be like their parents, friends, and teachers. They learn to be what others expect of them. Peer pressure to conform is strong, but love and acceptance are stronger.

▼ *Dear God, help me to appreciate the uniqueness of each of my children and to love them unconditionally.*

JS

RELATIONSHIPS AFFECT A LIFETIME

> *"And he will turn*
> *The hearts of the fathers to*
> *the children,*
> *And the hearts of the children*
> *to their fathers."*
>
> —MAL. 4:6

*C*indy is only six years old and is living with her mother. Her parents divorced when she was very young. It was a bitter divorce with a lot of anger between her mother and father. It got to the point where they no longer spoke to each other except through their lawyers. Cindy was caught in the middle, going back and forth, mainly living with her mother. She missed her father, especially when her visits with him were over. She felt guilty and depressed telling her mother she wanted to live with her dad.

Cindy is not alone. Thousands of children like her feel confused, guilty, and most of all, hurt deep inside. Cindy has been able to work through her pain through counseling. She has finally been able to express her feelings and to be understood. The key was working on the relationship between herself and her parents.

It is crucial that every child, whether the parents are divorced or not, have healthy, open relationships with each parent. A relationship that's not healthy will affect their whole life. May we all learn how to be heard.

▼ *God, help us to work through our hang-ups with our parents so we can be healthy parents and hear our own children.*

LB

TRUE SUCCESS

*What then shall we say to these things? If
God is for us, who can be against us?*
—ROM. 8:31

*W*e all want to be successful. Perhaps even more, we
want our children to be successful. But what does being
a success really mean? Let's look at three myths of success.

The first myth is, "Success will make me happy."
People who are successful by the world's standards are
never really satisfied. They are always striving for more
and better. Yet, we know there is no true happiness in
what we accomplish or possess.

A second myth is, "Success is being popular." When
a teen values popularity, life can be hard. They can become envious and hateful toward those in the "in"
group if they are "out."

A third myth is, "Success equals self-sufficiency."
Our society has taught us to be independent and strong.
When we teach our children these values, they may
choose to isolate themselves and thus feel a devastating
loneliness or emptiness.

True success is knowing God's love and having the
assurance of salvation. It is knowing God is "for" us,
thus nothing and no one can come against us. True failure is an eternal life of separation from God.

▼ *Dear God, help me teach my children You are "for"
them and that true success is in knowing You.*

GC

APPEARANCES CAN BE DECEPTIVE

Do you look at things according to the
outward appearance? —2 COR. 10:7

*A*ppearance can be a deceptive thing. Teenagers use it to get attention from their parents. Hair is especially useful. It's too long, too short, or wild and crazy. Rebellion is a necessary element for teenagers to grow up, become adults, and start a life of their own. If they are to leave adolescence successfully behind them, they will rebel. But it's hard for parents who want to point with pride to their offspring to discover that they have spiked hair.

It is appropriate to be shocked and react negatively, otherwise your child's rebelliousness has not succeeded. But don't overreact. It's probably just a phase. It's unlikely when your child becomes an adult that he will wear a spiked haircut with his three piece suit. This is just part of the growing up process.

When I was a teenager, boys violated the dress code by having long hair. When my son was in high school, boys violated the dress code by having their hair cut too short.

Teens have always used hair and appearance to get reactions from parents and teachers. Try to relax and enjoy it.

▼ *Dear Lord, let me keep things in proper perspective*
and not overreact.

JS

DEATH—DON'T DENY REALITY

"I, even I, am He who comforts you."
—ISA. 51:12

*J*ulia was about to turn sixteen, but she said she didn't really care. She said she felt numb. Her mother had died just two days earlier. Everyone knew Julia's mother was going to die—everyone but Julia. Because they protected her, Julia never knew the reality of pain until her mother was dead. The night her mother slipped into a coma, Julia sensed her mother was going to die. She wanted to stay with her. Instead she was again protected and rushed away.

The funeral came. Julia didn't cry. She just felt anger. Time passed. No one talked about the death of her mother. No one asked, "How do you feel?" It took Julia ten years and professional help finally to grieve through her mother's death.

Children need to know the truth about pain and death. When a parent, relative, or friend is ill, talk about it. If a loved one dies, share your feelings—talk and cry together as a family, no matter what the age of each member.

▼ *Dear God, help us to mourn death in healthy ways, and help us to guide our children through each step of the grieving process.*

LB

THE RIGHT FOCUS

*"O our God, will You not judge them? For we
have no power against this great multitude
that is coming against us; nor do we know
what to do, but our eyes are upon You."*
—2 CHRON. 20:12

The story is told about a famous race between three young boys. This race was peculiar. The object was not who could finish first, but who could run the straightest line. Everyone was there as the gun sounded the start.

The first boy soon began to sway off course as did the second. It was the third boy who ran a true straight line from start to finish. Afterward they each explained how they ran the race.

The first thought to run straight he would place one foot in front of the other. He kept his eyes upon himself. The second boy figured he would keep an equal distance between himself and the other boys. Because the first swayed, so did he. His eyes were on those around him. The third boy had help from his father. His father stood at the finish line in clear sight. He told his son to look his way and run towards him. "Keep your eyes on me, son. Never look away and you'll win the race."

Sometimes our children are not so sure what to do. Sometimes as parents we are not sure what to do either. But we can remember to keep our eyes upon the Lord. He will guide us.

▼ *Lord, please help me be a worthy example to my children.*

GC

LICENSED TO DRIVE

*For He shall give His angels
  charge over you,
To keep you in all your ways.*
—PS. 91:11

*D*riving a car is perhaps the toughest milestone in a teen's life. Turning an immature person loose on the street in a 3,000 pound automobile is really a scary thing to do. That's what makes nightmares. But sixteen is the magic age when society says they are old enough to hit the streets. Parents are a little more cautious and approach this rite of passage with trepidation.

When my teen passed his driver's test, it was a time of great celebration. To him that meant driving home from the test. I wasn't ready for that and decided the real miracle was that all the cars managed to stay out of his way.

Parents know their teen better than the state trooper who gives them a license to drive. You also hold in your hands the one thing your teen needs to gain freedom—the car keys. You need to assess his ability to assume responsibility by short experiences with his newfound independence. If he handles it successfully, you can give him more responsibility. If your teen is not responsible, do not increase the privilege.

▼ *Dear Lord, driving a car may be the scariest thing I have to let my teen do. We need Your guidance as well as Your protection.*

JS

LISTENING

*A brother offended is harder to win
than a strong city,
And contentions are like the bars
of a castle.*   —PROV. 18:19

*T*racy and Cathy are sisters. They are very close, but they argue nonstop. Usually, they both end up yelling and crying, and then running out of the room. Where did they learn their behavior?

Tracy and Cathy's parents frequently argue. Their mother screams at their father until he storms out of the house. Then she screams at the girls.

The members of this family rarely listen to each other. Their communication consists solely of accusations and attacks. But the cycle of anger is being broken through counseling. The family is learning how to listen and how to hear what is really being said. It is like talking with God.

So many times God tries to tell us something, but instead of listening, we argue with Him, just like this family did with each other. We question, "But God, why did You let this happen?" It is difficult to be quiet and stand in God's presence, giving Him our attention. But with practice, we do learn to listen, even when we disagree.

 Dear God, help me to listen to You and to my spouse and children.

LB

SILENCE ISN'T GOLDEN

"But when they arrest you and deliver you up, do not worry beforehand, or premeditate what you will speak. But whatever is given you in that hour, speak that; for it is not you who speak, but the Holy Spirit."

—MARK 13:11

*F*or some parents, it is extremely taxing to express their thoughts and feelings when conflicts arise. Many report they are afraid they may say the wrong thing. Still others report no matter what they say, it most often falls on deaf ears and does nothing to resolve conflict between them and their teen.

Unfortunately, this fear or reluctance to intervene can cause much harm to relationships. Children may interpret silence as neglect, dislike, or even hatred. This may do much damage to self-esteem and identity. Furthermore, children may see silence as fear or incompetence. They may bitterly resent the failure or weakness of the parent. Perhaps they may try to take charge of the household themselves. Many parents who intervene timidly must ask themselves, "Who is in charge?"

Never be afraid to speak the truth in love. Ask the Holy Spirit to lead you. And remember, in most cases, something said is better than nothing said.

▼ *Dear God, in my own weakness and fears, You will be glorified. Teach me to trust Your Spirit in times of conflict.*

GC

WHO BROKE THE WINDOW?

*I have not written to you because you do not
know the truth, but because you know it, and
that no lie is of the truth.*

—1 JOHN 2:21

*T*ruth and honesty are important principles to teach
children. It also is a difficult principle to get across because there are many nuances. When you are molding
your children's behavior, it is important to be clear
about the point you want to impart.

"Who broke the window?" you ask as you watch
your son drop the bat. I may be wrong, but I think any
self-respecting boy is probably going to answer, "Not
me." Therein lies the dilemma. At first you had a problem of carelessness. Now it is a moral and ethical issue.

Many times parents set their children up to lie by
asking an obvious question that is going to marshal the
child's self-protective instincts. Then the child is la-
beled a liar which is destructive to his self-esteem. It
also undermines the relationship with the parent.

To avoid this entrapment, parents can always state the
information they know that does not require a child to
tell on himself. That clears out the ethical consideration
and allows you to deal with the problem at hand. In
other words, don't ask a question when you already
know the answer. Clearly state what you know and then
discipline accordingly.

▼ *Dear Lord, help me to have an honest relationship
with my child.*

JS

NIGHTMARES AND NIGHT TERRORS

*The day is Yours, the night
also is Yours;
You have prepared the light
and the sun.*
—PS. 74:16

$\mathcal{B}$obby was three years old and full of energy. His family had just moved from Washington to Wisconsin. He seemed to adapt easily and to be excited about starting preschool. When his older brother and sister started school, Bobby began having night terrors. One evening his mother heard him screaming. When she awakened him, he was confused and didn't know her. She couldn't understand what was happening.

Moving is stressful for children even if they don't show it. Bobby was releasing some of his stress in his sleep. Through counseling Bobby's mother learned how to help him. They began talking about his feelings and playing out his fears with therapeutic games.

Night terrors and nightmares are a sign that stress is high. The child is frightened of something but usually doesn't know what. Bad dreams may also frequently occur between ages one and six. This is part of a developmental stage and a good sign that whatever is going on, they are working out their fears in their sleep. God has given us dreams so things don't build up.

▼ *Dear God, help us understand our children's fears. May we all work through our anxieties and learn to depend on You to feel safe.*

LB

PARENT CARE

Now for the third time I am ready to come to you. And I will not be burdensome to you; for I do not seek yours, but you. For the children ought not to lay up for the parents, but the parents for the children.

—2 COR. 12:14

Should you take care of your parents when they are elderly? Many people have strong feelings about this issue. Most feel we need to provide for the elderly. That's why our government attempts to do so.

Scripture does indeed teach us to care for and respect our parents when they grow in years. But I don't believe this means children that are not yet grown are meant to care for their parents.

Many problems arise when parents expect their children to meet their needs. This is especially true when parents expect to get their emotional needs met.

Children are simply unable to do so, and it's unfair to ask this of them. If we do, we will be disappointed. Remember, we are the adult, not our child. We need to get our needs met by God, our spouse, or friends.

Children will become angry, manipulative, or sometimes be forced to grow up too fast when parents expect too much of them. Instead we need to teach them how to get their own needs met in good ways, rather than constantly giving of themselves.

▼ *Dear God, thank You for being the giver of all good things. Today, I will look to You to meet my needs.*

GC

BIRTHDAYS

"For there is born to you this day in the city of David a Savior, who is Christ the Lord."
—LUKE 2:11

$\mathscr{B}$irthdays are magic and should be treated that way. It is the one day of the year set aside to recognize the importance of a person. It is worth celebrating to acknowledge the joy that person brings to the family.

Each family has unique rituals designed to make the birthday person feel special. In our family, birthday cakes were always unusual because it was my job to design them. Realize that I am a therapist, not a baker. But I have made a race car, R2D2, Barbie, gingerbread house, elephant, and bear cakes. Of course the cake isn't important. It's the person's birthday we're celebrating that's important, but the cake makes it memorable.

There are so many experiences in life that make us feel ordinary or less than perfect. That's why it's so important to take time to embrace our children and make them feel special.

A forgotten birthday can be painful. So can one that is barely noticed. Birthdays can be celebrated in special ways without spending money. A fancy sign, a big fuss at mealtime, singing happy birthday are all designed to make anyone king for the day.

▼ *Dear Father, thank You for the special gift You gave to me on my child's birthday.*

JS

CONFLICTS

*Fathers, do not provoke your children to
wrath.*   —EPH. 6:4

*J*ohn and Susie could hear their parents fighting
again. Susie ran to her big brother's room and crawled
under his bed. "Please hold me, John," she cried.
"I'm scared. Are Mommy and Daddy going to leave?"

John tried to calm his own fears and to reassure his
little sister. "It's okay. They'll stay. They'll stop soon.
Try and sleep, I'm right here."

Sometimes we forget our children are listening when
we are fighting. We don't stop to think how we may be
worrying them. Children are sharp. They know when
something is wrong between their parents even when we
try to cover it. If you are fighting frequently with your
spouse and cannot resolve the issues, go to a counselor
for help. And don't ignore your children's feelings. Talk
to them. They need you.

▼ *God, help us to work through our anger with our
spouses, and help our children to work out their feelings.*

LB

FAILURES AS SUCCESS

*We also glory in tribulations, knowing that
tribulation produces perseverance; and
perseverance, character; and character, hope.*
—ROM. 5:3–4

*M*atthew was a gifted child—very bright, very athletic, very likeable. During his elementary school years he easily succeeded. He made straight A's and was a star on the football and soccer teams. Everyone thought Matthew was on his way to a success-filled life. But when he entered high school, something drastically changed.

Matthew became withdrawn and irritable. Sports and other activities where he had once excelled now held no interest for him. Why? For the first time, Matthew faced the possibility of failure. The competition was a lot tougher now. Things were not as easy. Perhaps he would no longer be the star. The possibility of not succeeding paralyzed him.

Matthew did experience failure. But with the help of his parents and his counselor, he made it through high school. His parents understood the importance of being involved in his life. They communicated unconditional love. They were realistic with their expectations. And most important, they helped Matthew view his trials as learning and growing experiences. They helped him see his failures were an integral part of becoming a success.

▼ *Lord, show me how to help my children fail successfully.*

GC

SUGAR COOKIES AND POEMS

*I call to remembrance the genuine faith that
is in you, which dwelt first in your
grandmother Lois and your mother Eunice,
and I am persuaded is in you also.*
—2 TIM. 1:5

Sugar cookies and poems—what a legacy my grandma left for me! I remember never finding the cookie jar empty. Her cookies were the best I have ever eaten. Next best was sitting on her lap as she recited poems to me like "Little Orphan Annie" and "The Raggedy, Raggedy Man." Those poems were alive for me as only my grandma could make them. I have her cookie jar, her cookie recipe, and her poetry books. But I can never recreate the wonder of those moments with her.

I guess that's why God made grandmothers. They can add that extra touch when parents don't have the time or patience to give unconditional love that has nothing to prove. They completed their job with the parents, so the grandchild is theirs for joy and companionship. What better way than poetry and cookies?

It's important that parents respect this special relationship and not be threatened by it. There is no way a parent can offer this relationship to their children. Only grandparents have the qualifications.

▼ *Dear God, help me to encourage the relationship my children have with their grandparents.*

JS

PLAY

*Better is a poor and wise youth
Than an old and foolish king who will
be admonished no more.*
—ECCL. 4:13

*A*nnie and Kathie are sisters. They have a cute new kitten who plays from morning to night. The kitten intently watches the ball of yarn. Suddenly he pounces.

Annie and Kathie also enjoy playing. They play school. Annie likes to play the teacher. They also play house. They take turns pretending one is the mommy and the other is the daddy. Like the kitten, children have a purpose in their play. The kitten is learning how to hunt. Annie and Kathie are learning how to cope with life. They are learning the role of mother and father and how to care for themselves.

Children take what they observe and act it out in their play. Playtime also works out their fears and frustrations. For example, if you've ever had a car accident, your kids probably play out the wreck over and over with their toy cars. What an ingenious way God has provided for our children to work through their feelings.

▼ *Dear God, thank You for giving my children the gift of play.*

LB

GUILT AND SHAME

*I do not write these things to shame you, but
as my beloved children I warn you.*
—1 COR. 4:14

*W*e all experience guilt at one time or another. It's a
normal part of life. Scripture tells us that sadness or
guilt that leads to repentance is a good thing. But many
people, children too, experience false guilt. They feel
responsible when they are not. They feel overly embarrassed or unduly blamed.

Sometimes children experience a deeper, more intense form of false guilt—shame. Shame is when a child
feels worthless or discounted. It affects their identity
and abilities. Sometimes shame results from physical or
sexual abuse. Other times it results from unhealthy relationships with the adults around them. Messages are
given that they are not important—that they cannot do
anything right. There is always something they can do
better. They are stupid and usually wrong in their
actions, thoughts, or feelings. These children never feel
accepted, and they never feel able to accept themselves.

Scripture tells us "there is therefore now no condem-
nation" (Rom. 8:1). If God can accept our children in
His knowledge of all their sinfulness, why can't we? He
accepts us as imperfect parents doesn't He?

▼ *Dear God, help me to know the difference between
true guilt and false guilt. Help me never to shame
my children.*

GC

LET GO AND TRUST

"Which of you by worrying can add one cubit to his stature?"　　—MATT. 6:27

*F*ear can be a paralyzing emotion for a parent of a teen, especially when they are exercising their new found freedom. The world seems like such a dangerous place with drugs, alcohol, crime, and accidents. Parents would like to move to a desert island until their children are responsible adults.

Whenever my teens were out at night, the sound of a siren would bring tragic scenes into my thoughts. My imagination was more vivid than most TV programs. It became such a problem that I never wanted them to leave the house without me. That is when I realized I had to let go a little and trust God to take care of them. My worry and fear was not protecting them from danger. It was only giving me an ulcer.

I have to depend on God to help me with my fear and not place that responsibility on my children. However, I also have to accept my fear as normal. What parent who has loved, cared for, and protected a child for sixteen years isn't going to feel fearful when facing the prospect of turning a teen loose in a hostile world? The only armor you can provide is your prayers.

▼ *Dear Lord, protect my child because we both love him.*

JS

THE PET RABBIT

"Blessed are those who mourn,
For they shall be comforted."
—MATT. 5:4

Debbie and Joanie had a pet rabbit, Fluff. For almost four years, they loved and cared for Fluff. Then one day their father discovered that Fluff had died. Thinking the girls wouldn't notice, he immediately ran out and bought another rabbit almost exactly like Fluff. Debbie and Joanie came home that afternoon and, as usual, went to let Fluff out of his cage. Debbie was the first to come running in. "Where's Fluff, Mom? You didn't give him away? Where is he, and who is this?" she asked holding up the new rabbit.

"That's your new rabbit," Dad said. "Fluff isn't here anymore."

"Well, where is he?" Joanie demanded, running in behind Debbie. "Did he run away?"

Finally, the girls' father decided he had to tell the truth. Saddened, the girls handed the new rabbit to their father and went off to be alone. They didn't want the new rabbit. They only wanted Fluff.

Children need to experience the pain of loss so they can grow and mature. Covering losses will only make them lose touch with reality and can eventually make them angry.

▼ *Please help me, God, to guide my children through pain and not to avoid it.*

LB

YOUR ROD AND STAFF

*Yea, though I walk through the valley
of the shadow of death,
I will fear no evil;
For You are with me;
Your rod and Your staff, they comfort
me.* —PS. 23:4

This Scripture is a beautiful depiction of a healthy relationship between parent and child.

Hopefully we are always in a state of development. For children, developmental changes are much more drastic and significant than perhaps at any other time in their lives. Problems arise when transitions and changes do not come easily. When impediments occur, the change may be particularly stormy. A child may walk through a valley with a shadow lurking over them.

Notice the psalmist's understanding of his Father's response to difficult times. "Your rod and Your staff, they comfort me." The rod is for protection and the staff for guidance.

Scripture does not teach us that the Father will keep us from shadows in our lives. Neither does it lead us to believe that He will completely rescue us from difficulty, or that He will fight for us in our place. What we do know is He will protect and direct us.

Do we guide and protect our children when they are in the shadows?

▼ *As I walk through the valleys in my life, help me to model trust in You.*

GC

STEPPARENTING

Now the birth of Jesus Christ was as follows:
After His mother Mary was betrothed to
Joseph, before they came together, she was
found with child of the Holy Spirit.
—MATT. 1:18

𝒦asey was seventeen when her father married her stepmother. She complained her stepmother was fussing over her too much and trying too hard to be the perfect parent. I interjected with my opinion that it was difficult to be a mother, especially to teenage children, and being a stepmother must be infinitely more complex and difficult. Kasey smiled and acknowledged that her stepmother was at least trying. They went on to become best friends.

Probably the most frequent pitfall for stepparents is in trying to take the place of the natural parent. That is impossible and unnecessary. Only the natural parent can fill that spot, even if he or she doesn't do a good job. The relationship with the stepparent can be fulfilling, but it must evolve over time. It usually takes several years before everyone is comfortable.

▼ *Dear Lord, please guide my decisions regarding my*
new family.

JS

UNLOADING

The rod and reproof give wisdom,
But a child left to himself brings
shame to his mother.
—PROV. 29:15

*R*achel and her mother were in therapy together. "You blow up at me every time you've had a bad day," Rachel's mother said. "It's like I'm your punching bag."

"You're the only one who's safe," Rachel said. "It helps me to unload on you."

"Well, you may not have any problems at school," mother responded, "but you do at home. You don't have these yelling tantrums except with me and that hurts."

Often a child feels safe to unload anger on a parent. Is this wrong? No, it's important for children to get their feelings out. If we stuff things, we may take it out on others as well as ourselves. Parents need to draw some boundaries and set some limits. If parents allow a child to abuse them verbally, it's not helping the child or them. The more they allow this behavior to continue, the more a child will lose respect for himself and his parents. Encourage your child to go to his room and pound on his pillow when he is beginning to take his anger out on you. He will feel better and so will you.

▼ *Father God, please help me to guide my children to process their anger in healthy ways.*

LB

THE BOOGIE MAN

*"In disquieting thoughts from the
    visions of the night,
When deep sleep falls on men,
Fear came upon me, and trembling."*
—JOB 4:13–14

How many of you have gone through the ritual of checking under the bed or in the closet for the boogie man? How many of you have been awakened by the knock on the bedroom door and the feeble cry, "I've had a bad dream. Can I sleep with you?"

About grade school age, a unique mixture occurs for our children. Blend one part of an increasingly imaginative mind and two parts of an increasing exposure to a very scary world, and you have concocted the perfect scenario for nightmares and late night visits to their parents' bedroom.

Scary movies should be monitored, if not kept entirely from the child, at this age. Bedtime stories also should be chosen with care. Be careful not to expose children to situations that may be fear producing. Remember, they may not know enough about their world or about themselves to filter out concerns of which they need not be fearful. Sometimes the evening news falls into this category! Also remember to take every opportunity to reassure a young child of his or her safety in an otherwise threatening and cruel world.

▼ *Dear God, I will trust that Your angels are watching
over me and my family.*

GC

PART OF GOD'S PLAN

"And the two shall become one flesh."
—MARK 10:8

Sex is a powerful word. It has almost as many meanings as there are people who talk about it. Everyone has something to say about it, even if they don't understand what to do about it. Therefore, as a parent, it is essential that you discuss sex with your child to impart your value system and Christian principles. If you don't, you can be sure your principles are not what they will learn on the playground or at the movies.

At ten, a boy gingerly asked his mother the meaning of graffiti written on the bathroom walls at school. As she explained, he responded, "I will never do that." She had her opportunity to explain that sex is part of God's creation. It is beautiful and wonderful when used according to God's principles. The conversation started on a gross note, but ended with an important set of values in place.

If parents don't explain sex and how to use it according to God's principles, they take their chances that it will be described as a tool for pleasure and self-satisfaction. This can deprive their children of the wonders God has in store for them.

▼ *Dear Lord, use me as an instrument to impart Your wisdom about life and the proper place for sexual pleasure.*

JS

Then God said, "Let Us make man in Our image, according to Our likeness."
—GEN. 1:26

$\mathcal{O}$ne of my favorite things to do is just to sit back and watch my two-year-old and six-month-old play and explore. I especially like to watch for familiar characteristics in each of them—a twinkle in my son's eyes or a laugh from my son that reminds me of my husband, the tenacity in each that remind me of both my husband and myself.

God watches us with the same joy we have as we watch our children. He delights in our every move and loves us more than we can comprehend. He enjoys watching us grow spiritually, as well as physically, seeing in us characteristics that make us like Him.

▼ *Thank You, Lord, for Your great love. I want to enjoy my children the way You enjoy me.*

LB

BONDING

"Lo, I am with you always, even to the end of the age."
—MATT. 28:20

The most important thing we can give our children is ourselves! In doing so we give our children a sense of safety. The message should be clear. Someone is with me. I am not alone. Indeed, surveys tell us one of the greatest fears children have is a fear of abandonment.

Have you ever felt alone, misunderstood, and vulnerable? Now think about a child experiencing these feelings. They can fear so much that their development may become misdirected or stifled.

So many studies tell us of the importance of "bonding" with our children. Most conclude bonding is necessary for relationships and the development of like values—moral or behavioral. But bonding meets a need far more important. It allows a child to feel protected, safe, and not alone.

Bond with your children early in life. Be with them. Understand that in many ways as God relates to us, so should we relate to our children.

▼ *Dear God, help me to look at my own fears of abandonment.*

GC

VACATIONS

His parents went to Jerusalem every year at the Feast of the Passover. —LUKE 2:41

$\mathcal{V}$acations are necessary to keep families on track. Many times in counseling sessions, vacations are the only pleasant childhood memories. Perhaps that's because they are a time set aside to be together without the usual daily expectations. People tend to treat each other better because there are no places to retreat.

My teenagers were delightful on a trip to the Grand Canyon. After one day in the car away from shopping malls, telephones, and friends, they actually began to talk about their thoughts, ideas, and plans. At first it was probably sheer boredom, but the surprising thing was that I had plenty of time to listen between Albuquerque and Flagstaff.

Time away is essential to real communication. We stay on the run, so vacation time is important for the family to regroup, recharge, and realign relationships. Put it on your must-do list and realize it is one thing you can't afford to pass up.

▼ *Dear God, remind me that time apart with my family is the maintenance care it needs.*

JS

SEVEN MONTHS PREGNANT

"For with God nothing will be impossible."
—LUKE 1:37

*C*hrissy was seven months pregnant and beginning to feel the weight of pregnancy. In the past she had kept herself in shape and felt okay about the way she looked. Now she was feeling very out of shape, very heavy, and just plain ugly. All of her friends kept saying, "You look so cute with that tummy of yours." But Chrissy wasn't feeling cute. Her maternity clothes weren't fitting anymore. She couldn't reach her shoes to tie them. And she could barely get out of the bathtub.

The last few months of pregnancy can be difficult, especially with your first baby. You may not sleep well at night, which doesn't help—everyone feels miserable when they are overtired.

When you're feeling ugly, it helps to remember that God loves us not because of how we look, but just because we are ourselves. We need to love ourselves the same way.

 Thank You, God, for loving and accepting me, especially when I am having a hard time loving and accepting myself.

LB

KNOW YOUR LIMITS

Do not reprove a scoffer,
lest he hate you.
—PROV. 9:8

*M*any times teenagers come to my office unwillingly, only under duress of their parents. They feel no problem exists. They'd rather be doing anything than sit in a counselor's office talking to a total stranger. When asked why they came, they simply reply, "I don't know." They usually do know why, but they just don't want to admit anything or talk about bothersome topics.

The air is so full of resistance in these situations that you can cut it with a knife. Developing trust becomes a priority. Once accomplished, it is my job to make observations to help teens gain insight that may lead to a change of behavior. Sometimes what I say is fully accepted. Sometimes it isn't. Sometimes, when my words fall on deaf ears, it is very frustrating.

Parents relate the same experience. "They just won't listen!" Know that in some situations you as a parent can only do so much. It becomes your teen's responsibility to either accept or reject what you have to say to them. Sometimes parents have to shake the dust off their sandals and move on.

▼ *Dear God, help me to know my limits as a parent.*
GC

RESPONSIBILITIES AND SOLUTIONS

My son, pay attention to my wisdom;
Lend your ear to my understanding.
—PROV. 5:1

*W*ashing clothes is a never ending task. It also can be a source of many conflicts. "Why isn't my baseball uniform clean?" "Where is my favorite shirt?" Parents somehow are automatically supposed to solve these problems without any help from their teen.

When my son was sixteen, he constantly complained that his favorite shirt wasn't clean. But he took no responsibility to pick it up from his floor and put it in the laundry. I would get extremely angry during these arguments and lose all perspective. My husband intervened and decided our son could do his own laundry in preparation for leaving home. It took some work on all our parts, but instantly our relationship improved. It surprised me how my anger decreased when I gave him the responsibility to take care of his clothes. If he didn't have his favorite shirt clean, he could only blame himself.

Truthfully, that is teaching responsibility in a practical way. Many times the best way to solve an argument is just to step away and put the responsibility and the solution where it belongs.

▼ *Dear heavenly Father, help me to remember I am not the solution to all my child's problems.*

JS

DRIFTING APART

Beloved, let us love one another, for love is of God. —1 JOHN 4:7

*E*ileen and George had a baby boy four weeks ago. Together, they have decided Eileen will stay at home and be a full-time mother. George is now feeling a little angry and jealous because Eileen seems to have a new man in her life. He feels like he's been put on the shelf. Instead of talking with his wife about how he is feeling, George pulls away and begins to work longer hours. Soon Eileen is angry with George because he is gone all the time and she is always with the baby. She also begins to pull away.

It's a familiar pattern that can become a real problem if nothing is done to stop the process. But it can be reversed. We do not need to allow ourselves to continue to drift apart.

Arrange for a special time alone—just you and your spouse *without* the baby. Talk about your feelings. Ask him to forgive you if you have hurt him in any way. Encourage him to tell you what he has been feeling, remembering it's usually not as easy for men to talk about their feelings. Make a renewed commitment to each other. And set a time for another date with your mate!

▼ *God, help us to nurture each other and our love for one another.*

LB

LOVE YOUR SPOUSE

*Nevertheless let each one of you in particular
so love his own wife as himself, and let the
wife see that she respects her husband.*
—EPH. 5:33

*G*ary and Mary were having difficulty with their daughter. When they finally decided to seek help, she had been verbally abusive. She also was drinking some and sneaking out at night.

They came to my office, feeling frustrated and desperate. They felt they had tried everything to restrict their daughter and prevent her from continuing her destructive behavior. They told me of endless trials, behavior contracts, and every consequence that could possibly be given.

"Let's try looking at your daughter's problems a little differently," I suggested. Gently I asked if any marital problems existed. Hesitantly they said "yes," but they assured me that had little to do with their daughter's behavior. We had much work to do.

The acknowledgement of their marital problems was the first step toward helping their daughter change her self-destructive lifestyle. Children always suffer when mother and father are in conflict. They may be unable to cope with unresolved tensions, experience extreme guilt, or feel the need to express angry emotions when a spouse silently endures abuse.

▼ *Lord, I want to love my spouse from this day forward as You love me. Please help me.*

GC

LOSING PRIVILEGE

"So why do you worry about clothing?
Consider the lilies of the field, how they
grow; they neither toil nor spin."
—MATT. 6:28

*P*at pulled her favorite blouse out of the dryer only to find a large brown stain on the front. When she confronted her daughter about the stain, she was angry that her daughter didn't accept responsibility even though she had spilled chocolate ice cream on the shirt. Pat was enraged and felt misused. This is the time to employ natural consequences in a perfect cause and effect relationship. If you don't use borrowed clothes responsibly, then you lose the privilege to borrow them.

Parents many times feel inclined to give a twenty minute dissertation about what should have been done or how to be more careful in the future. However, that only avoids the issue and usually results in everyone being angry and nothing being resolved. It is healthier to keep the issue simple without lengthy explanations or belaboring the point. If you are not responsible, you lose the privilege.

▼ *Dear God, responsibility is a difficult lesson to learn. Help me keep it as simple as cause and effect whenever possible.*

JS

PUTTING ACTION BEHIND OUR WORDS

*Do not provoke your children to wrath, but
bring them up in the training and
admonition of the Lord.* —EPH. 6:4

*N*o, William," Amanda said firmly when she saw her
two-year-old climbing onto the counter to reach the
cookies in the cupboards. Amanda was afraid William
would fall and get hurt. When she saw him climbing
back onto the counter after she had turned away and
back, she yelled at him. "William, get down!"

William frequently tested the boundaries Amanda
set. And Amanda frequently found herself yelling at
him to reinforce those boundaries. Eventually, he began ignoring her yelling. To toddlers, *no* means nothing.
But if you yell a lot, they tune you out.

We need to put actions with our words to make our
discipline effective. Our children's choices need to
bring consequences they feel. "Time out" often works.
Sometimes spanking is needed, especially if our youngster does something dangerous like running across the
street after he's been told not to. But the most effective
discipline is consistent limit setting with concrete consequences. It takes a lot more effort than yelling or spanking, but you won't end up with laryngitis or a sore hand.

▼ *Dear Father, thank You for the way You patiently
discipline me as Your child.*

LB

PERFECT LOVE

"Greater love has no one than this, than to lay down one's life for his friends."
—JOHN 15:13

*O*utside of our heavenly Father's love for us, there is no greater love than the love of parents for their children. It seems almost instinctive. And it has no limits. A mother bear or mountain lion has this kind of love for her young. She will fight to her death to protect her cubs. But this instinct to protect ends when the cubs are old enough to be on their own.

I knew a young man who was old enough to be on his own. Unfortunately, he had been involved in drugs for some time and had rejected many attempts by his parents to get help. One day I got a phone call from his parents. Their son had died of an overdose at the young age of twenty-one!

As I listened to the weeping over the phone, I felt angry and empty inside. Later, his parents and I met and talked. I will never forget his father telling me that if he could, he would give his own life and allow his son to live. I think that every parent has that type of love.

▼ *Dear God, thank You for loving us perfectly. Help me love my children as You love me, and help them receive this love.*

GC

SAY WHAT YOU MEAN

Wrath is cruel and anger a torrent.
—PROV. 27:4

*M*any times we do not mean what we say. We agree to things we really do not want to do and then we are angry. That is an unfair response. We need to take responsibility for our own feelings.

One day, George asked his father if he could use the automobile. Without pause, this father threw him the keys to the car realizing he would have to rely on a friend to take him to a meeting. He fumed as his son drove away. The father subjected his needs in favor of his son, but the clincher is that he was very angry. That is too high of a price for his son to pay for the use of the car. His father, however, made the choice for him so he didn't have any control over the situation. A healthier way to handle it would have been to make a decision based on what the father could do without being angry.

Not expressing your true feelings may make others the victims of your anger without their knowledge.

▼ *Dear heavenly Father, let me take responsibility for my anger and not place it on other members of my family.*

JS

NOT WITHIN EARSHOT

*Whatever things are of good report, if there
is any virtue and if there is anything
praiseworthy—meditate on these things.*
—PHIL. 4:8

*F*or about the fourth time that day Sarah overheard
her mother talking about her behavior. She felt embarrassed. Why did her mother have to tell everyone what
she did? But Sarah also saw how much attention she
was getting for this behavior. *In a way,* she thought,
Mom really gets a kick out of me doing these things. So
naturally Sarah continued to do them over and over
again.

There are times we do get frustrated with our children, and times we need to share that frustration with
someone who will listen and understand. But we need
to be careful not to talk about our children when they
are within earshot. If they overhear what we say, it gives
them more reason to repeat the behavior frustrating us.
Instead, if we suspect our child is listening, we need to
make a positive comment like, "It will be so neat when
Timothy is gentle with his brother."

We all tend to live up to the expectations—good or
bad—that others have of us. Let's make sure we give our
children positive expectations to live up to.

▼ *Lord, You know how frustrated I get with my children. Please give me patience and show me positive
ways to express my feelings without hurting them.*

LB

UGLY DUCKLINGS

"The LORD does not see as man sees; for man looks at the outward appearance, but the LORD looks at the heart."

—1 SAM. 16:7

*W*e all have seen or know of children who are not quite like the rest. They were perhaps malformed at birth or maligned by disease or accident. Yet even more tragic are the ways these children are often rejected by those around them. Kids can be so cruel. But to be honest, even we as adults are often guilty of making a child feel like an outcast through our subtle and hurtful messages.

I know a young man who, as a child, underwent surgery for a brain tumor. He was subjected to radiation and chemotherapy. As a result of his tumor and treatment, his growth was significantly stunted. He became physically uncoordinated and developed learning disabilities. Yet inside, this young man is a spiritual giant who has already accomplished much in his young life. I know this young man's heart is in pursuit of God. He is a prayer warrior and a student of God's Word. In my eyes he is not small in stature but a giant among men.

We are all familiar with the Ugly Duckling story. What an invaluable lesson to be learned by our children and ourselves.

▼ *Help me, Lord, to see my children as You see them.*

GC

CHILDREN ARE WATCHING

Therefore God also gave them up to uncleanness, in the lusts of their hearts, to dishonor their bodies among themselves.
—ROM. 1:24

*T*hirteen-year-old Connie was very excited when her father and his girlfriend of three weeks took off for Las Vegas one week after his divorce from her mother was final. Connie thought the whole thing was romantic and glamorous. It was certainly out of character from the relationship he had with her mother. At that moment, all the heartbreak and sorrow of the divorce was forgotten. This was like TV and the movies. What thirteen-year-old girl wouldn't be excited?

What a mixed message for a child! The humdrum daily life of paying bills, getting kids off to school, and working on a marriage that has some problems looks drab compared to the exciting jet set life of parties and vacations. What kind of statement does that make to a young and impressionable mind? A parent would be distressed to witness that same behavior in their children in seven years, yet that is exactly where children learn their value system. In this generation of "anything goes" it is essential to preserve the life-style you feel is important because your children are watching.

▼ *Dear Lord, no matter what my desires are, help me to live by Your principles and to be a living example to my children.*

JS

QUIET MOMENTS

Be still, and know that I am God.
—PS. 46:10

$\mathcal{I}$t's about 10:00 P.M. The windows are open for the cool breeze. I can hear the crickets chirping busily. It's just me and Justin, my eight month old, lying on my bed. He's finally getting sleepy. Justin is tummy down on my belly with his head snuggled up on my chest. Off and on he reaches his small, chubby hand up to my face. He gives it a good squeeze, then a soft touch, and then leaves it there. What a wonderfully quiet moment—no crying, no screaming, just peace. I cherish these moments with my children when we can enjoy snuggling and loving each other.

I believe God is filled with joy when we look to Him as children, snuggling up on His chest, laying our heads down, and letting Him rock us back and forth as we absorb His comfort. During those quiet times, He talks to us. He gives us strength and guidance as we pray silently. Sometimes we need to talk to Him. Sometimes we need just to be still and know that He is God.

▼ *Father, I praise You so much for being here with me always. Thank You for the quiet times when I can rest and renew my strength in Your presence. Thank You, Lord, for Your peace.*

LB

EXAMINE YOURSELVES

Examine yourselves as to whether you are in the faith. Prove yourselves. Do you not know yourselves, that Jesus Christ is in you?—unless indeed you are disqualified.

—2 COR. 13:5

 $\mathcal{D}$ riving down the highway, a sleek black Corvette jumped lanes and zoomed past me. I got a glimpse of a Christian symbol on its bumper. *What a jerk,* I thought to myself, *to drive like that while advertising his Christianity!* Of course, I didn't immediately realize I was over the speed limit myself! It's funny how God gives us opportunity to examine ourselves.

I think it's especially imperative we examine our parenting skills and habits. Give yourself a test:

Do you feel you have a positive influence on your children?

Do they come to you when they need help?

Do you feel they respect and admire your behavior?

Are you consistent in your character?

Do your children know Christ is the most important person in your life followed by your spouse and them?

Spend time to evaluate the results of your test and your recent behavior. Does your life reflect your love for Christ? And does your parenting reflect your love for your children?

▼ *Dear God, search my heart and allow me to examine honestly my relationship with You and my children.*

GC

LET KIDS BE KIDS

I have taught you in the way of wisdom;
I have led you in right paths.
When you walk, your steps will not be
*   hindered,*
And when you run, you will not stumble.
                                        —PROV. 4:11–12

$\mathscr{P}$atrick was eight when his father left with another woman. His mother was concerned about how to be both mother and father. She shared everything with Patrick. When she got a raise, when she argued with her mother, and when she had a headache, Patrick was the one she told. She expected him to do the same by sharing his life. By the time he was thirteen, they had more of a husband and wife relationship than mother and son. That made it very difficult for Patrick to separate from his mother and grow up in a healthy way.

Close relationships strengthen a child's security and self-confidence. In a world where single parent homes and workaholism are becoming the norm, it is important to develop a healthy, balanced relationship. It is inappropriate to use children as best friend or confidant. They are not mature enough to shoulder their parents' concerns and responsibilities. They need to experience being a child.

▼ *Dear Lord, let my child enjoy every last minute of his childhood.*

                                                            JS

SET LIMITS

*Correct your son, and he will give
   you rest;
Yes, he will give delight to your soul.*
                    —PROV. 29:17

essica is seven years old and a real holy terror. She has manipulated her parents into giving her whatever she wants. If her mother denies her something, she runs crying to her father. Usually he gives in to her demands, even if it means arguing with his wife. Sometimes Jessica's mother still refuses to give in. Then Jessica throws one or two major temper tantrums to remind her parents she's the boss. Her mother tries ignoring her, but this only teaches Jessica that she needs to scream longer and louder to break her mother. Jessica definitely is running this home. Both her mother and father are miserable, angry at each other, and fed up with their daughter. Is there any hope for Jessica and her family? Definitely, but it needs to start with Jessica's parents' regaining control of her. They need to set firm limits on her behavior with specific consequences. And they must not rescue her by caving in when she disobeys.

I believe that is why God is so tough on us. He sets firm limits and doesn't budge in order to teach us what is healthy for us and what is not.

▼ *Dear Father, You are so patient with us. Discipline us so we will become responsible and mature.*

LB

ANSWERING QUESTIONS

"For there is nothing covered that will not be revealed, nor hidden that will not be known."
—LUKE 12:2

*M*any parents struggle with whether or not to tell their children certain things. For example, issues such as divorce or adoption. They often ask, "How much does my child need to know? How much can my child handle?" These are always difficult questions to answer. There are many variables involved. How old is the child? How much does the information involve the child? How should you relate the information?

At some point children need answers to the questions they are likely already to be asking. Kids are usually not given enough credit. They deserve to know why their parents are no longer living with each other. If adopted, they probably suspect they might be. Do you want them to find out from somebody else? I saw an eighteen-year-old find out about her adoption from a friend of the family who was a total stranger to her. She was more than devastated.

The general rule is twofold: 1. Honesty is the best policy although you may not need to relate every detail. 2. Know your child. Understand your child's ability to handle information. You may need to talk about the same issue later on as they grow older. The important thing is to keep the door of communication open.

▼ *Dear God, give me wisdom and strength to speak truth in love.*

GC

PERSEVERING

Indeed we count them blessed who endure.
—JAMES 5:11

*P*arenting often feels like a water torture experience. You wipe up spilled milk at every meal, referee the same argument every day about who sits by the car window, get three glasses of water for your child every night before he will go to sleep. You tell her to cover her mouth every time she coughs. You help him with an endless parade of math problems while he is telling you that is not the way his teacher does it. Like a constant dripping of water on your forehead, the monotony makes you wonder if you are going to lose your mind or if you should quit. But there is a pay off down the road.

One day you will hear your child say thank you without your having prompted, "What do you say?" She will get along with others without your guidance. He will do the math problems by following the example in the book. And at first you will wonder what happened. Then you will think your child doesn't need you anymore. *But* you will finally realize that your job as a parent is over—and you've done a good job. That's the way God planned it.

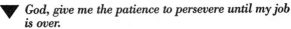 *God, give me the patience to persevere until my job is over.*

JS

I WANT IT!

Men will be lovers of themselves, . . . without self-control, . . . headstrong.

—2 TIM. 3:2–4

*M*y infant son loves to chew on pizza crust. If I take one away because it's become too soft, he dissolves into a screaming fit. If he can hang on to the crust and not allow me to take it away, he will.

Babies grab at everything they see that they want. They reach up and seize your fork while you are eating, sending food flying in every direction. They rip book pages and snatch pens if you are reading or writing around them. My eight month old especially loves to grab my hair. If you try to take anything away from them, they hang on with fierce strength.

How many times have we had fits when God didn't give us what we wanted? Perhaps we were denied something we truly believed we needed—a new job, a new friend, some special vacation time, or just some peace and quiet. Sometimes it's hard to trust God if we feel that He denies us something we want or even takes away something we think we must have.

Our Father really does know what is best. He is looking out for us and helps us, as we do our kids, even if we throw a fit!

▼ *Father, increase our trust in You. You really do know what is best for us. Help us keep our infants safe.*

LB

LYING

*Lying lips are an abomination to the LORD,
But those who deal truthfully are His delight.*
—PROV. 12:22

$\mathcal{I}$ don't think there is anything more hurtful to parents than to have their children lie to them. Let's look at a few reasons why children lie.

Anger—Kids often lie to get even or to hurt their parents. It's a way to show disrespect and all kids know it hurts to be told a lie.

Fear—While kids fear negative consequences, they may fear rejection even more. To tell the truth may mean admitting something is not right or that they failed. If they fail, they risk not being accepted.

Selfishness—At the root of selfishness is pride. This type of lying may start early in life, especially when there are no consistent limits. They may think, *I want it, and I'll do whatever is necessary to get it.*

Habit—Lying for the sake of lying. This may occur when lying goes unchecked, or when parents are careless about lying themselves. Do you cheat on your income taxes? Do you make excuses to avoid parties? Make sure to examine your own life. Take time to consider why your child may be lying.

▼ *Lord God, hold me accountable to speak the truth, today and every day.*

GC

GET INVOLVED

And suddenly a voice came from heaven, saying, "This is My beloved Son, in whom I am well pleased." —MATT. 3:17

$\mathcal{A}$ frequent complaint among emotionally disturbed adults is that their parents were never involved in their school or extracurricular activities. Their parents never saw a championship soccer game; they never attended a church play. These children never felt important to their parents, hence they never felt important to anyone else—a contributing factor in their illness.

If you want your children to be loved and respected by their teachers and friends, get to know them and let them know you. When you attend parent-teacher conferences, for example, your children will see you value them and their achievements. And as the teachers see you are on their team—you are supporting their efforts to help your children learn—they will respect your children.

Good self-esteem starts with your positive perception of your children and your ability to convey that to others. Your children will know they are important as they see you attend their school, church, and sports events and realize you care for them. And others will believe your children are important too and treat them that way.

▼ *Father, help me to show my child and the world that this is my child in whom I am well pleased.*

JS

IF YOU'RE BEING ABUSED

*Do not let them depart from your eyes;
Keep them in the midst of your heart.*
—PROV. 4:21

*C*hristopher is eight. He and his two younger siblings, five-year-old Jennifer and three-year-old Sarah, live with their mother who has to work full-time. Their father no longer lives with them because their parents are divorced. While Christopher's father has never physically hurt him or his sisters, he often comes over and beats his mother. His mother is afraid to call the police because she fears losing his financial support. When his father comes to the house, Christopher grabs his younger sisters and takes them to hide in the woods behind the house until his father is gone.

Christopher is in therapy. He is failing third grade because he is overly worried about his mother's and sisters', as well as his own safety. Christopher does not act like an eight year old. He behaves like a small adult, trying to take care of his mother.

If anyone is abusing you, *please seek professional help.* You need to protect yourself and your children. If you're afraid to seek help, pray for God's help. He will provide for every need, from finances to the person who will protect you. He will protect you as you ask Him. Yes, it may be a risk. But when we ask, He always provides ways to keep us safe.

▼ *Father, answer our prayers for protection. Guard us and our children in this world.*

LB

REJECTED OR ACCEPTED?

He is despised and rejected by men,
A Man of sorrows and acquainted
* with grief.*
And we hid, as it were, our faces
* from Him;*
He was despised, and we did not
* esteem Him.*
                              —ISA. 53:3

$\mathcal{B}$eing a child or teenager can sometimes be very hard. Some children and teens are just plain cruel. Can you remember your most embarrassing moment growing up? Would you like to relive your teen years and all those awkward blunders you made?

Young Jimmy was a clumsy child and not so bright. He wore thick glasses and sometimes stuttered when he was nervous. He was always the last one picked in gym class, and the first one the school bully picked on.

Compared to most kids his age, Jimmy had little success in life. Yet through it all Jimmy was happy and self-confident. How so? It was due to the careful nurturing of his parents. They communicated to Jimmy a very important message in how they treated him.

The message was simply this: You are the best at who you are—our beloved Jimmy, loved by us and by God. Strengthen your children against the rejection of this world.

▼ *Dear God, I cherish Your acceptance of me as a parent.*

                                                    GC

A NAME

> *"You shall call His name JESUS, for He will save His people from their sins."*
> —MATT. 1:21

*F*our-year-old D. J. was given a droopy-eyed, floppy-eared, spot-ridden baby beagle for Christmas. D. J.'s parents decided to let D. J. give the new puppy a name. For two days D. J. called the puppy all sorts of names. "Here Spot," he would say, "Roll over Rufus." "Beg Blotches." "Come'ere Cuddles."

As D. J. tried out each new name, he looked at his puppy and wondered if the name fit his new friend. He wanted to make sure the name was just right because he loved his puppy so much. D. J. finally chose *Pete*, saying, "<u>Pete</u> is the best name in the whole world!"

The following Sunday D. J. listened intently in church as the minister discussed why God named His Son Jesus. After the service D. J. said to his parents, "God named His Son Jesus because He loved Him so much. I named my puppy Pete and I love him. You must have named me D. J. because you loved me too!"

▼ *Dear Lord, help me to teach my child that his name is special, just as Your name is special.*

JS

BUSINESS TRIPS

Cast your burden on the LORD,
And He shall sustain you.
— PS. 55:22

*F*or three long weeks Mrs. Davis was a single parent. Her husband was away on a business trip, and she was left to take care of four-year-old Harrison and ten-month-old Rob. She tried to be strong like all her friends whose husbands also traveled on business. But she was having a difficult time.

Mrs. Davis was exhausted because she had trouble sleeping when her husband was gone. She had no breaks away from her children or time to get her work done. Each evening she prayed, "Lord, help me to get through tonight and tomorrow. I'm so tired, Father, and I feel so angry at Joe for being gone all the time. I barely see him anymore!"

When a parent has to travel on business, it's not easy for anyone—the parent and children at home or the parent on the road. But there are some things you can do to get through those times. If you are left at home, you need to find a way to take a break. Try to get someone to help with the children—maybe a teenager after school, another mother of young children who will trade days baby sitting, a Mother's Day Out program. When your spouse gets home, make sure you set a date just for the two of you.

▼ *Father, please be with those families who have one*
traveling parent.

LB

WE NEED EACH OTHER

Two are better than one,
Because they have a good reward
for their labor.
For if they fall, one will lift up
his companion.
—ECCL. 4:9–10

$\mathcal{A}$s counseling progressed over several weeks, the focus of their concerns changed. At first they complained about their son's behavior and disrespectful attitude. Now their focus was on each other.

They were divided on some issues and often were in conflict with each other. Their son, they realized, was taking full advantage of these times either to avoid consequences or to get his way. As we talked, it became obvious he enjoyed the power he attained whenever his parents were in conflict.

Ultimately they were forced to address their division and its harm to their household. First, they needed each other for their wisdom. It was hard to make good decisions on their own. Second, it was impossible to have any consistency in their household. An inconsistent household is unfair to children and will lead to insecurities, anger, and chaos. Finally, they needed each other for support and encouragement, They needed each other to help the other one up when they fell.

▼ *Dear God, thank You that I am needed by my spouse. I will be an encourager and supporter.*

GC

TOUCHING

And He took them up in His arms, put His hands on them, and blessed them.
—MARK 10:16

*M*y son's attitude changed abruptly when he started junior high school. He was disgruntled by everything and was quick to let you know. I didn't understand and felt disconnected from him until I realized that I wasn't hugging and kissing him as I used to. I thought a junior high student wouldn't want to be hugged and kissed by his mother, so I had withdrawn showing my affection like this. And he made no attempt to pursue this activity. But I missed this part of our relationship and wondered if he missed it too.

I decided to begin touching Brian in some way, every time he walked by. I playfully patted him, ruffled his hair, or just nudged him. Within two weeks, his previous disposition returned. He was happier, more sure of himself, and certainly happier with me. We still weren't hugging and kissing, but touching was part of the daily routine.

Touch is essential to our well-being—some say we need five hugs a day. Children of all ages need touching to feel secure and cared for.

▼ *Lord, remind me, daily, that touching feels good and makes others feel good too.*

JS

SHARING

*Do not forget to do good and to share, for
with such sacrifices God is well pleased.*
—HEB. 13:16

*T*hat's *my* plane," Alex cried. "You can't have it!"
"No, it's mine," Mark screeched back. "I want it!" The
fight escalated between the two children. If ignored,
their fight would probably have ended in hitting and
screaming. At least one child would be crying.

When Alex's mom heard the loud voices, she decided to intervene. "We need to share the toys, Alex,"
she said. "You need to put away the ones you don't
want to share. You can play with those later." Alex pro-
tested again, to which his mother responded, "Sounds
like it's hard to share. Okay, you can each play with the
toy for five minutes." She went and got the timer.

Sharing is a tough concept at any age, not just for a
two year old. God wants us to share our possessions,
and has even taught us to share by declaring, "What
you have given to the least of these, you have given unto
me, saith the Lord."

▼ *Help us, Lord, to set a good example for our children by sharing what we have with others.*

LB

TEACHING RESPONSIBILITY

For even when we were with you, we commanded you this: If anyone will not work, neither shall he eat.

—2 THESS. 3:10

*O*nce upon a time life was simple. An honest day's work brought an honest day's pay. If you worked, you got to eat. If not, then you went hungry. Today, it's not quite that simple.

Parents struggle constantly with how to teach their children responsibility. The object is to devise a plan that provides good or bad consequences for behavior. Followed consistently, the plan will teach children responsibility.

Of course, it's always best to allow children to suffer natural consequences. If there are none, however, then a few parent-made consequences might be in order. We can make them sit during "time out." We can take away the phone, the keys to the car, or, the most dreaded of all consequences, we can take away the Nintendo®!

For some children there are no consequences severe enough to cause them to change their behavior. But don't let discouragement cause you to give up. Your child will still be learning about making choices and discovering that some type of consequence will always follow.

▼ *Help me, Lord, not to ignore my children. Help me to show them that their behavior has an effect on them and the world in which they live.*

GC

DOING THINGS MY WAY

"And all things, whatever you ask in prayer, believing, you will receive."
—MATT. 21:22

I had reached my limit! I was in a daily battle with one of my children over a chore and I had lost my temper and my perspective. I called out to God for immediate help.

As soon as the words were out of my mouth, my husband walked in the door. Seeing that I was out of control, he offered to intervene. But I refused. Instead I continued, out of control, and mismanaged the situation. My child and I ended up in tears, and my husband and I had an argument.

Two hours later when we were all calmed, I asked God where He had been. I then realized He had sent my husband to help. But I was too busy doing things my way to see God had a better way in mind.

Being a parent is too important a job to do alone. You need all the help you can get. God is your most available resource. And many times, He has built help right into your situation. That's what He did for me. Now all I have to do is be open to His answer and use it.

▼ *I need Your wisdom, Father, to access the solutions You have provided.*

JS

TIME JUST FOR US

Commit your way to the LORD,
Trust also in Him,
And He shall bring it to pass.
—PS. 37:5

Two mothers were talking over a cup of coffee while their babies fussed and their toddlers crawled under their feet. "You know, Janet," Susan complained, "I never seem to have time with their father anymore. The kids monopolize us. When Stephen came home last night, I really wanted to talk to him without any interruptions. But my four-year-old had to have him first. Then there was dinner and baths. By the time we got them to bed, we were both too exhausted to talk."

"I know," Janet said. "Alan and I also have a tough time spending any time together. Even though we try to go on a date once a month, it's not enough. I worry that we'll end up like other couples. You know—not really together anymore. They live under the same roof but in two separate worlds."

Many couples find it difficult to spend time with each other. But if we don't, we usually find ourselves drifting farther and farther apart. It is critical that a mother and father have a strong bond. Otherwise it's almost impossible to be a united front with the children. Sometimes it takes as much work getting together as it does taking care of the kids. But in the long run it's worth the effort.

▼ *Lord, help us to find time just for the two of us.*

LB

PICK FIGHTS CAREFULLY

*"And you shall know the truth, and the truth
shall make you free."* —JOHN 8:32

*H*ow many times have you argued with your children
and then realized you forgot what you were angry
about? Sometimes it's almost funny to listen to families
gripe about something or another. Then sometimes it
isn't.

Many times behind the closed door of a counseling
office, parents and teens argue about who is right and
who is wrong. I remember a particular family that argued violently about who forgot to feed the family dog.
Sides were clearly drawn with one parent pulled to the
middle to act as the mediator. The parent and teen built
their case and even presented witnesses—all in the pursuit of the truth. It was a courtroom drama of which
even Perry Mason would be proud!

But what did it matter? Was it really worth all the
effort or cost? Blood pressures were up and relationships were strained.

As one wise fellow once said, "This kind of truth will
not set you free."

Pick your fights carefully. Ask yourself, "Is it worth
it? What's the real issue here?"

▼ *Lord God, give me Your perspective on the issues
facing my family.*

GC

WORKAHOLICS

*You know how we exhorted, and comforted,
and charged every one of you, as a father
does his own children, that you would have a
walk worthy of God who calls you into His
own kingdom and glory.*
                    —1 THESS. 2:11–12

The value system of our country is to work until you get the job done. No one ever mentions that the job never gets done or, if it does, that next time it is bigger.

This philosophy has bred a generation of workaholics who thrive on the Protestant work ethic.

A workaholic's top priority is his work, his money, and the power and recognition that goes with it. He has little regard to the sacrifices it demands.

Family relationships are frequently one of those sacrifices. A relationship isn't something you sandwich between appointments. Relationships need nurturing in the form of time and attention. They have to be a priority because otherwise there is never time for them. When did you last take time to evaluate your priorities and set boundaries? You only get one chance to raise your children. They are the most important job you will ever have.

▼ *Dear Lord, help me keep my priorities straight and
to remember the special job You have given me to do
as a parent.*

JS

WHEN WE CAN'T BE WITH THEM

He will gather the lambs with His arm,
And carry them in His bosom.
—ISA. 40:11

*L*ately I've had to be away from home more and more. It's not been easy on my children. My baby wants to be held more. He fusses when I put him down. He's waking up more at night. My toddler is frustrated more quickly and loses his patience more. He frequently checks to make sure I'm still around, and tests his limits more on the days I'm home. When I have to leave, he gets angry. "Mommy," he cries, "I don't want you to go to work. Can you please stay home?" It's amazing how he works out his frustration and sadness in his play. Jesse will say to me, "You be Jesse and I'll be Mommy. I am going to go to work so you cry. Now cry, Mommy. You need to cry!" My son knows himself well.

I'm grateful Jesse lets me knows how he feels so I can give him the reassurance he needs. I tell him when I'm going to work and when I'll be back. A stuffed animal and blanket that reminds him of me has also helped. When he misses me, he can cuddle with them to help ease his pain. A substitute to be held is important. That's why it means so much to me to know that we are all lambs of God. He holds us close to Him and reassures us that He is with us always.

▼ *Father, comfort our children just as You comfort us.*
Help them to feel safe and secure when we cannot be
with them.

LB

THE TEMPTATION TO SWING

"Watch and pray, lest you enter into temptation. The spirit indeed is willing, but the flesh is weak."
— MATT. 26:41

*I*n the privacy of my office, I have people tell me of the struggles they face as parents. At moments of true honesty, some parents tell of such intense frustration and anger that they feel like hitting their kids.

Imagine (maybe you don't have to imagine), a child who is continually disruptive. He talks loudly and incessantly. He has a million questions. You've had a hard day at work. The bills need to be paid. The clothes need to be washed, and the washing machine has just broken down. As soon as you get home, you are barraged by your child. He won't talk to you when you ask him questions, and he won't be quiet when you need silence.

In a moment of weakness, you might be likely to strike your child out of anger or frustration. Be strong! Take time out to cool down. Let your family know what your needs are. Never give consequences when you are angry. Admonishing spankings can easily turn to bruising and emotionally scarring blows.

 Dear God, when I'm tired and angry, help me not to sin. When I'm weak, fill me with Your strength.

GC

FAMILY HISTORIES

And Jacob begot Joseph the husband of Mary,
of whom was born Jesus who is called Christ.
—MATT. 1:16

*C*hildren are profoundly curious about themselves and their place in their families. They love to see their baby pictures and hear stories about times they acted cute or smart. They like hearing about the times they got in trouble because it reminds them that they are loved, even when they were not at their best.

Children also want to know about their grandparents, aunts, uncles, and cousins and about milestones in the family's life. When we share these memories with our children, they begin to see how they fit into the family and the rest of the world. And they gain a sense of belonging and identity.

The Bible records family histories, starting with the lives of Adam and Eve. From these stories, we learn our identity—who we are as God's children—and how God loves us, even when we make mistakes. When we know where we came from, we see how we fit in the world, and we have more choices about where we are headed.

▼ *Lord, remind me to take time to share our family history and the family histories of the Bible with my children.*

JS

TUMMYACHES

For He established a testimony in Jacob, . . .
That they may set their hope in God,
And not forget . . . His commandments.
—PS. 78:5, 7

Three-year-old Raymond cries, "Mommy, my tummy hurts," every time she comes home from work. Fourteen-year-old David says his head, his back, and his stomach hurt—all at once. Eileen, age six, complains, "My legs hurt; I can't walk."

Many times children and adults have a lot of physical ailments. Though the pain is real, it may or may not have a true medical cause. These *somatic* complaints, as they are called, are most commonly of headaches, stomachaches, and backaches. Rather than actually being physical illnesses, these pains are the result of emotional problems.

It's essential to check out problems with a doctor, but don't give in to physical complaints that may not be real. Find out what really is bothering them by asking questions. You might ask Raymond, "I hear your tummy hurts. I *think* you're saying, 'Hold me. I've missed you, Mommy.' Can you ask for what you want?" Listen for emotional pain that has been turned into physical pain—as was the case with David—and consider counseling. Or hear when your children, like Eileen, simply need attention—as do we all from God.

▼ *Lord, help us and our kids to express our feelings.*
LB

GRIEVING

"My spirit is broken,
My days are extinguished,
The grave is ready for me."
—JOB 17:1

I met a young man who had a tragic story to tell. He had recently lost his entire family in a car accident. He was angry at God, sad about such a great loss, and fearful of an uncertain future.

He continued to ask, "Why should I go on living?" I didn't answer at first. I only wanted to be with him—to acknowledge his pain. As we met over the next few weeks, he become emotionally stronger. He began to grieve. We talked about his reasons to live when he felt the waves of despair. Here are a few he listed for me that he often hung on to in his darkest moments.

God has a purpose for me.

I have an identity in Christ.

I have unique abilities.

I am loved and I can love.

There is hope and help available.

I think these are truths we should instill in our children from the very beginning. Life is a gift from God. It is precious. We should consider it such. He is our reason to live. He is the basis upon which life has true meaning.

▼ *Dear God, the reality of Your love is reason enough to live.*

GC

TEACH THEM TO READ

So they read distinctly from the book, in the Law of God; and they gave the sense, and helped them to understand the reading.
—NEH. 8:8

*T*he ability to read is one of the most valuable tools we can give our children. It gives us access to information in the Bible and other books that helps us live our lives.

Reading is taught in the first grade of school, and is necessary for every study throughout our education—math, physics, even sports. But a child doesn't start learning to read in the first grade. He begins when he first notices that you enjoy books.

Your children sense what your personal values are and incorporate them into their own lives. So if you enjoy reading, your children will learn to enjoy it as well.

Reading to your children is one way you can ensure their reading ability. And your warm cozy lap is the best place for them to curl up and begin hearing about the uncertain world outside. With those secure memories, the challenge of picking up a book and figuring out the words and their meanings will be an adventure.

▼ *God, let me instill in my children a desire to read, and let them be inspired to read Your Holy Book.*

JS

FACING THE TRUTH

*"The father shall make known Your truth to
the children."* —ISA. 38:19

*H*ow many times have you said something like this to
yourself? *I thought my dad was perfect, that he could do
no wrong.* Or, *I thought my mom was the neatest lady.
Then it all came crashing down when I faced the truth.*
Children tend to believe their parents are flawless. The
reality that parents aren't perfect can be hard to face.

Children of divorce are especially apt to feel false
guilt. Since it's too hard to accept that their parents
could have made mistakes, they blame themselves. A
child might say, "My mommy and daddy broke up because my sister and I fight too much." Or, "I didn't
have a good report card so my daddy left." Sadly, children take the blame that doesn't belong to them. We
need to help them see the truth—to see that they are not
responsible for the mistakes we make. We are not perfect.

Does God want us to be perfect? If He did, then why
did Jesus die for us on the cross? We are sinners and
need all the help we can get. God would have never sent
His Son if He thought we could be made perfect any
other way. God believes in grace.

▼ *Father, we praise You so much for Your grace and
for Your forgiveness of our sins. Help us to show our
children that we, too, are sinners. We are not perfect, but we are forgiven.*

LB

OVERCOMERS

"He who overcomes shall inherit all things, and I will be his God and he shall be My son."
—REV. 21:7

*H*e was an orphan. He was small and weak and ill most of his early years. He spent his childhood in one foster home after another. Much of his time he spent reading and dreaming about the future. The big business and better life he dreamed about seemed so far away.

Life was not easy. He learned by his failures—by his unpreparedness and by his trust in the wrong things and wrong people. But he studied and worked hard. He determined not to make the same mistake twice.

He invested what little he had and lost it all—several times. But he never gave up on his dream.

Today he owns his own multimillion dollar business and has realized many of his dreams. Will his "better life" last? Perhaps not. But he still walks and talks in confidence because he has learned to overcome many obstacles. Even if his fortune disappears, he knows he is a true success. He is a son of the heavenly Father.

Our children need to know that they can be overcomers. As a child of the living God there are no obstacles too great to defeat them.

▼ *Dear Lord, please help me to encourage my children to be dreamers and to put their trust in You.*

GC

FITTING IN

*And they continued steadfastly in the
apostles' doctrine and fellowship, in the
breaking of bread, and in prayers.*
—ACTS 2:42

*W*hen Susan was in the seventh grade, it was time to join the youth group at her church. Her first night, she bravely approached a few people but quickly recoiled when she wasn't greeted with opened arms. As the group left to go to the skating rink, Susan jumped into her mother's car, crying, and said she wasn't going.

Against Susan's protests, her mother took her to the skating rink, pressed a coin into her hand, and told her to call in thirty minutes if she wasn't having fun. Her mother wondered if she was being cruel, but the telephone call never came. And that night Susan found her niche in the group. The gamble paid off.

Fitting in is the primary goal for adolescents. When they don't feel they fit, they are miserable. We can help them by teaching them to take appropriate risks, pursuing new opportunities and people. With our assurance that they can handle the risks and survive, even if things don't work out as they hope, our children will learn balance and find their place.

 God, help us to find out where we fit in Your plan.
JS

INHIBITING ANGER

Fathers, do not provoke your children to wrath, but bring them up in the training and admonition of the Lord. —EPH. 6:4

*J*ohnny's mother was appalled. "My son got angry today and told me so. He said that he couldn't forgive me. I was shocked! He shouldn't get angry—especially at me. If he is, he should keep it to himself."

So many parents have difficulty in letting their children be angry. They think it's disrespectful and wrong. But how did God feel about His Son expressing His feelings? Did Jesus ever become angry? Yes, and He showed it too. In the temple His people were buying and selling goods as though it were a market. He let them know how He felt and showed it, too, by knocking tables down. He was angry for a just cause. Anger is a normal feeling. It needs to be expressed or we will become psychologically sick. It's *not* okay for your child to curse at you, but it is important that he be able to tell you that he's angry with you, and if possible, why. A child needs to learn the skills of working anger out, like hitting a doll, yelling in his room, or beating on a pillow. Can we accept our children's anger?

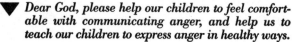 *Dear God, please help our children to feel comfortable with communicating anger, and help us to teach our children to express anger in healthy ways.*

LB

RIGHTS AND RESPONSIBILITIES

You therefore, beloved, since you know these things beforehand, beware lest you also fall from your own steadfastness, being led away with the error of the wicked.
—2 PETER 3:17

*Y*ou have heard the saying, "The Devil made me do it." Sometimes our kids say the same thing in a different way. "My friends made me do it." There are times when parents would prefer to blame other children than their own. Regardless of how we avoid or deny, our children do have rights and responsibilities to uphold.

Teach your children that they have a right to say no to drugs, alcohol, or anything that makes them feel uncomfortable. They have a right to be treated with respect, and the responsibility to treat others with respect. They also have the right to their own opinions, beliefs, and feelings.

Ronnie felt pressured into drugs when he was eleven years old. Carol felt she had to consent to sexual acts since she was five. Reggie thought . . . The stories are countless. Perhaps many could have been prevented if they had been taught their rights and responsibilities.

Take time to instruct your children about their personal rights and responsibilities.

▼ *Dear God, may my will be guided by Your gentle, firm hand.*

GC

DENYING FEELINGS

"Most assuredly, I say to you that you will weep and lament, but the world will rejoice; and you will be sorrowful, but your sorrow will be turned into joy." —JOHN 16:20

*Y*ou shouldn't feel that way." That's an easy response to quell a child's angry outburst. But it doesn't matter whether he *should* feel that way or not. The fact is he does.

Anger does not cease to exist when it is denied. Rather, it goes underground and is later expressed in unexpected ways such as depression, sarcasm, acting out, rage, physical illness. These are much more difficult to handle than is the simple expression of anger when it first comes up and everyone knows what it is about.

It is easy to accept and feel free to express our positive feelings. However, the negative emotions are just as real. God created all of our emotions. And when we refuse to accept and express the negative ones, we are denying part of His creation. The key is recognizing our feelings and responding appropriately.

You can help your child be "angry and sin not" by helping him take responsibility for his anger. Help him recognize it, talk about it, and then find an appropriate way to express it.

▼ *Father, help me to be honest about my anger and to teach my children acceptable ways to express anger.*

JS

STEPPARENTS AND STEPCHILDREN

Love suffers long and is kind.
—1 COR. 13:4

$\mathscr{B}$ill is almost twelve years old. He is living with his father and stepmother. In talking with me, he said, "My stepmother is okay, but she really overdoes it. She's always kissing or hugging me and telling me she loves me. Maybe she does, but I've only been with her for six months. I don't mind my mom hugging and kissing me, but I'm uncomfortable when my stepmom does it."

Being a stepparent or stepchild is hard. There are a lot of expectations on you that feel phony. If you don't perform, you're set up to feel guilty. But you need not to push or rush it. Love takes time to mature and grow. If you push, the other usually pushes away. Talk about it. Admit how you feel. Ask how you can both work on becoming closer.

Frequently a child may be jealous of the stepparent taking his parent's time. *If you weren't here, my real parent would be,* he is likely to think. The new stepparent may want to focus on the new relationship with his or her spouse instead of becoming an instant mom or dad. It is going to take time but love can grow if we're patient.

▼ *Father, it's hard to have a blended family and to be a new stepparent. Help us learn to love each other, to tear down the walls, and to heal the wounds.*

LB

SUICIDE

"Therefore now, O LORD, please take my life from me, for it is better for me to die than to live!"
—JONAH 4:3

$\mathcal{H}$ave you ever thought about just giving up on life? Oftentimes the stress we experience becomes unmanageable. It may lead to distress and then clinical depression. It should not be surprising to know that our children may become clinically depressed too. They also may have thoughts of giving up on life.

Never consider any suspicion that your child may be considering suicide as unimportant. Don't be afraid to talk about it. Openly discuss their thoughts and feelings. Ask them if they have a specific plan. Tell them of your concerns for their safety.

Look for signs: Feelings of hopelessness, intense emotional pain or anxiety, continual fatigue, loss of appetite, and lack of interest in activities. Also look for preoccupation with death, giving things away, or saying goodbye. Finally be sensitive to specific circumstances that may have occurred—the loss of a friend or relative, or failures in important events such as sports or grades.

The vast majority of those who attempt suicide do not want to die. They are crying for help. They only want to stop the pain.

▼ *Dear God, help me to understand and to be aware of my children's pain.*

GC

THE PINEWOOD DERBY

He fashions their hearts individually;
He considers all their works.
—PS. 33:15

$\mathscr{B}$en and his father were preparing for the annual Pinewood Derby. The Derby was a contest in which Cub Scouts and their fathers designed small wooden race cars from kits, following special rules. The purpose of the event was to provide quality time for fathers and sons. Everyone would win a ribbon or a prize.

Ben and his father enthusiastically talked about their plans, then started building. Ben sanded the car as his dad read the rules for the contest. After a few minutes, his dad remarked that he was using the wrong sandpaper. When Ben started to whittle the wood to make the car, his father said he might split the wood so he took over. Soon, building the car had become Ben's dad's project, and Ben sat on the sidelines, watching. Ben's dad even chose the color to paint the car, overruling Ben's choice of green for a shiny black.

Ben's dad had a great time and was excited when the car won a blue ribbon. Ben wasn't sure he even wanted to go to the race.

Parent-child projects are really relationship projects. If you involve yourself in the building of a relationship, the finished project will always be worth a blue ribbon.

▼ *Dear Lord, let me focus on building relationships with my children and family.*

JS

DOES THE CRYING EVER STOP?

*The LORD is my rock and my
fortress and my deliverer;
My God, my strength, in
whom I will trust.*
—PS. 18:2

If you ask the mother of an infant or a toddler, she will probably tell you, "No, the crying never seems to stop." From my own experience, I feel like someone is crying most all the time! If it's not my infant, it's my toddler. Cry, cry, cry! At times, I can hear crying when there is none. Then I tease myself about hearing things!

Tonight was especially hard because both children were crying at the same time. First I went to comfort one. I got him quieted and then went to the other one. After a few minutes, the first one started up again. Soon I was bouncing around like a ping-pong ball in a small room. Before it was over, I felt like sitting down on the floor and crying myself!

God is with each of us when we're crying, and I know He doesn't feel like a ping-pong ball. He will hear us when we say, "Father, please comfort my children and me as well. This has got to stop!"

▼ *Father, we praise You so much for being there for us, for hearing our every cry. Give us Your strength so we can comfort our children when they cry.*

LB

SENSITIVITY

The words of a talebearer are like
tasty trifles,
And they go down into the inmost body.
—PROV. 18:8

The mother was a social butterfly. She attended the bridge group, the women's prayer breakfast, Bible studies, and volunteered at the hospital.

Her daughter was asked out for a date. What happens to so many girls happened to her. Her face broke out! It was devastating to her, but comical to her mother. After all, she had gone through the same thing. It was easy to laugh about it now. She was sure her daughter would laugh when she looked back.

But what about *now?* It really was not a laughing matter. Unfortunately the mother was not sensitive to her daughter's feelings. The ladies at the bridge club giggled. So did her volunteer friend. The ladies at the Bible study prayed for her daughter's integrity.

Too bad the daughter overheard her mother relate the incident to someone over the phone. She was mortified. Her trust in her mother was destroyed.

We need to be careful to take to heart what teenagers say and go through in their lives. Be sensitive to their feelings, and careful not to add to their embarrassment by talking about them.

▼ *Lord, please help me to be sensitive to my children's*
feelings.

GC

SPRINGTIME

That they may see and know,
And consider and understand together,
That the hand of the LORD has done this.
—ISA. 41:20

*B*uddy was the member of a teenage gang involved in vandalism and petty theft. He was arrested several times. Finally, his older brother moved him to another town and influenced him to change his life. Buddy started school and carefully picked his friends. Today, he is a policeman. He is married and has three children and is a responsible member of his community.

We worry when our children falter and make mistakes—sometimes they are very serious mistakes. But the hand of God works in both our lives and the lives of our children in ways we can never see. The branches of our children's lives may seem bare, empty, even broken. But when they finally grow up, it is as if springtime has come. They begin to show generosity and care and responsibility, and only a few months before it seemed they would never bear such fruit.

Our hope is the promise that God will continue to love us and change us until His work has been completed.

▼ *Thank You, heavenly Father, for the promise of springtime.*

JS

WHY GOD?

*"The LORD gave, and the LORD
has taken away;
Blessed be the name of the
LORD."* —JOB 1:21

$\mathcal{A}$s a former pediatric nurse, I know many sad stories of children dying. One I remember very clearly. She was only five years old. Since birth she had been fighting cystic fibrosis. I cared for her several times. I put IV's in her thin, scarred arms, and then gave her strong antibiotics through already sore veins. One night I was called at midnight and told she was dying. Her mother wanted me there. I remember holding her as she gasped for air, still fighting to breathe. Her mother could only watch with tears, saying, "Let go. It's okay to let go, dear." I prayed God would take her soon so her suffering would stop. Mercifully He did.

In my heart, I questioned why God would let a small child even have such an evil disease. "Why, Father? Why do our children suffer?" I know the Enemy is responsible for much of the suffering, but still that doesn't take the pain away. The "why" probably will not be answered until we meet the Lord face to face. For now all we can do is trust Him and ask Him for the strength we need for every inch.

▼ *Father, it is hard to understand why evil things sometimes happen to our children. Please help us to cope. Be with us, Father, and keep our hearts from being embittered. Help us to trust in You always.*

LB

DEPRESSION

Hope deferred makes the heart sick,
But when the desire comes,
it is a tree of life.

—PROV. 13:12

*C*ould your child be depressed?

"Not my child!" you may think. But think again. We know that significant depression exists in about 5% of children and adolescents in the general population. Don't fool yourself. Young children can experience sad feelings just like we do. Watch for these signs.

When a child begins to act out, they may be attempting to deal with some emotional pain they are experiencing. They may be angry and explosive, skip school, or begin to experiment with drugs. Once compliant and pleasant to parents, a youngster may be suddenly and inexplicably defiant. Watch for physical complaints, changes in eating and sleeping patterns, or persistent boredom.

Young children are not immune to "sick hearts." Losses and hurtful events occur as soon as our children enter the world. Fortunately, God gives us wisdom to understand the hearts of children.

▼ *Dear God, help me to understand the heart that You have created. Help me to know my child.*

GC

ALL THINGS GREAT AND SMALL

"But seek the kingdom of God, and all these things shall be added." —LUKE 12:31

The first afternoon my fourteen-year-old daughter came home with her new contact lens, we spent on the floor looking for one she had dropped. Everyone panicked, thinking it was lost forever. And we've all panicked each time one has been dropped since then.

One day as we searched desperately for the lens, I prayed, "Lord, you know we don't have the money to replace these, so please help us find them." I had never before asked God's help for a thing like this, but we were wonderfully surprised to find God cares about contact lens, worried teenagers and their distraught mothers. We found the lens.

Now, our first line of attack is always to pray, then search. We've found the lens every time—the night they were dropped in tall grass; the time they were in a glass in a dishwasher after it had been through the wash cycle. Besides saving us a lot of money, the answered prayers have given my daughter a tangible way to tell others about God's love. And they've taught us all that God really loves us and cares about everything in our lives—small and great.

▼ *Why do we trust God with only the big things in our lives when He is there for the little ones too?*

JS

OBEY YOUR FATHER

Hear, my children,
the instruction of a father,
And give attention to know
understanding.
—PROV. 4:1

A father came to me once and said, "He is my son, and he will do as I say because I am his father." The son looked at his father and nodded his head, but I could see his anger and the way he drew back from his father. The son later told me that he did not respect his father anymore. He said his father was no longer obeying *his* heavenly Father. He was drinking and sleeping with other women. His disobedience to God's law caused the father to lose his son's respect.

Yes, our children are to listen to and follow their parents' instruction. However, we are not only to teach them the way of the Lord, we also are to live as the Lord commands. If your child does not respect you, he will not obey you or even want to obey you. He will despise you instead.

If we want our children to follow us in obedience and love, then we need to be careful to follow our heavenly Father's instructions. When we walk in obedience to our Father, our children are more likely to follow in our steps.

 Father God, show us the path that You want us to follow. Convict our consciences when we sin, and help us to repent and turn away from that sin. Enable us to be good examples in our children's eyes.

LB

FALSE GUILT

*For if our heart condemns us, God is greater
than our heart, and knows all things.*
—1 JOHN 3:20

*A*licia had overcontrolling parents. She often attempted to exert her independence but to no avail. Finally she found a sure way to rid herself of this burdensome umbrella. She became pregnant by her boyfriend of several months. They married, although both sets of parents gave their consent reluctantly. Instant independence. Mission accomplished.

The baby was born prematurely with congenital heart disease. Alicia was devastated. Still troubled by her "sinful act" to gain independence, her guilt was compounded by her sense that God had punished her by inflicting an illness on her baby.

It took much work on Alicia's part to deal with her tremendous sense of guilt. Through the years she began to see God for who He really is—a loving and just God, not a God who inflicts punishment. She saw her baby's condition for what it was. She found a support group and dealt assertively with her baby's illness.

Be careful not to let your heart condemn you.

If your child is ill or handicapped, take care not to carry false guilt that will weigh down your heart. Know that God is greater than any burden you may carry.

▼ *Dear God, please show me someone who can help to carry the burdens of my heavy heart.*

GC

CHANGE OF PLANS

A soft answer turns away wrath,
But a harsh word stirs up anger.
—PROV. 15:1

*P*aul wanted to go to the show with his friends, but it conflicted with a family visit to his grandparents. When his parents told him he couldn't go, he was extremely angry and quite vocal about it. Rather than tell Paul to be quiet and to go to his room, his father responded empathetically.

"I can understand your anger, Paul," his father said, "because you like to spend time with your friends. But you are important to your family and to your grandparents. So your Mom and I want you to be with the family today. You can be with your friends another day."

Paul's dad allowed him to continue talking about his anger, but the heat was gone from the argument.

People can accept their plans being thwarted but not their feelings. The most expeditious way to handle and defuse anger is to recognize and accept it. When children's (and adults') anger is validated, the anger and disappointment are more bearable.

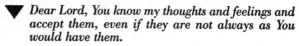 *Dear Lord, You know my thoughts and feelings and accept them, even if they are not always as You would have them.*

JS

PRAISE HIM

*Behold, children are a heritage
from the LORD,
The fruit of the womb is His reward.*
—PS. 127:3

The Lord has given you a marvelous seed to cultivate, fertilize, water, shelter, and expose to sunshine. As with all precious plants, you need to prune it as it gets out of hand, and trim it to grow into a mature and beautiful creation. That seed is your child. But remember that this child is not your possession. He belongs to the Lord. We are only His "gardeners."

Praise God for choosing us to be caretakers of a heritage so great! Praise Him for the privilege of being able to raise a child. Ask Him to guide you every step of the way, for these are His children. We need His wisdom at all times to raise them up exactly as our Father would like for us to.

▼ *Dear Father, we need guidance at every step on the journey on how to raise our children. Please guide us with Your hand.*

LB

DON'T BLAME YOURSELF

And He said, "Who told you that you were naked? Have you eaten from the tree of which I commanded you that you should not eat?"
—GEN. 3:11

*H*ow many times have you wanted boastfully to take credit for your children's accomplishments and then cowardly wondered why they would do something irresponsible or disgraceful? Have you ever said to your spouse, "I can't believe what *your* child has done."

All parents struggle with the issue of responsibility for the behavior and outcome of their children. This is no less a concern when children behave in incorrigible ways.

Resist feeling that you are a failure as a parent. For some children, you could do everything perfect (you have permission to laugh) and still they would make bad decisions, run away, or break the law. There are simply too many things that affect our children—disposition, peers, society, Satan himself!

Consider the actions of Adam and Eve. Didn't they have a perfect Parent? Yet they still disobeyed. Don't necessarily blame yourself for your child's actions. Don't forget to live under God's grace in your own life.

▼ *Dear God, help me to understand my limitations as a parent. Help me to know my responsibilities.*

GC

JUST LIKE DAD

Imitate me, just as I also imitate Christ.
—1 COR. 11:1

$\mathscr{H}$ave you ever noticed how children resemble their parents? Sometimes there are distinct physical resemblances. But even when there aren't, children take on an appearance like their parents. This results from watching and imitating the subtle characteristics of their parents. They may emulate their fathers' gaits or the way their mothers wrinkle their noses when they are thinking.

Jason was adopted as an infant. But by the time he became a teenager, he so resembled his father few people could believe he had been adopted. Jason walked like his dad and had many of the same facial expressions and figures of speech. If you looked carefully, Jason and his father were quite different physically, but over the years the influence of his adopted father transformed even his physical appearance.

When we are adopted into the family of God, we change, as Jason did, to become like our heavenly Father. If we keep our eyes on God and imitate Jesus, we will gradually become more like Him.

▼ *Dear Lord, help me to keep my eyes on Jesus and to become a good model for my child to imitate.*

JS

INVISIBLE FRIENDS

*All your children shall be taught
  by the LORD,
And great shall be the peace of
  your children.*

—ISA. 54:13

*E*ven before my first son was born, I asked God to help me to raise him. I especially prayed that He would help me to teach my child about Jesus, and that one day my child would accept Jesus as his Savior.

I continue to pray for my son, asking God to help him grow in the Spirit and to develop a deep love for Jesus. I also ask the Lord to help Jesse to learn to lean on Jesus not only in need, but also as a friend. It's exciting to see the way my prayers are being answered. Jesse is coming to know Jesus. He often talks about Him as though Jesus were his invisible friend.

At this age, invisible friends are common. You see young children talking with them, nurturing them, and even arguing with them. It's neat to know Jesse has chosen Jesus to be his friend. I, too, have chosen Jesus to be my invisible friend. Even though I can't see Him, He is still very real to me. Jesse and I both believe He is there all the time listening to us. And so we talk to Him often.

 Father, we praise You so much for Jesus. We thank You that He is a friend we can count on.

LB

TESTING THE LIMITS

What shall we say then? Shall we continue in sin that grace may abound? Certainly not! How shall we who died to sin live any longer in it?
—ROM. 6:1

*W*e know we should never test God by taking advantage of His grace. How foolish that would be. Yet have you ever felt your child is testing you? I'm sure there have been many times when grace did not abound and you felt at your wit's end. Why is it children tend to test the limits?

Children have an especially strong need to be protected. They need a sense of security from a scary world that they learn more about each day. They need a sense of security concerning themselves too. As children grow and change they do not automatically trust themselves or have complete control of their behavior and impulses. They can be uncertain about their abilities and need much reassurance that they will not be allowed to get out of control. As a result, there may be times when they act out of control to see if the limits are really there.

Another reason children test limits is to be reassured that they are still attached to us as parents. Do you still care? Are you paying attention to me? For some children these questions can only be answered when they act out. They may "sin" in order to experience your "grace."

▼ *Dear God, Your grace is sufficient. May my grace for my children be experienced as sufficient for them.*

GC

CONTROLLING STRESS

He makes me to lie down in green pastures;
He leads me beside the still waters.

—PS. 23:2

*L*anny was a somewhat uncertain first grader, experiencing his first learning difficulties. He felt frustrated, and showed some signs of depression and lowering self-esteem. His parents were having some serious marital problems that were also affecting his security and self-worth.

In the middle of this stressful time, the dentist recommended that Lanny get a dental appliance. It affected his speech and his ability to eat. Lanny felt self-conscious, uncomfortable, and out of control, which added to his feelings of stress.

Parents need to attend to their children's physical problems. But they need to consider all the stressors in their child's life before they make any decisions that will significantly change their child's appearance or ability to carry out daily functions. It takes wisdom to know when to say, "No. We need to wait awhile until family life is calmer."

▼ *Father God, please give me wisdom to know how to*
handle the stress in my life and in my child's life.

JS

BETWEEN VISITS

I have taught you in the way of wisdom.
—PROV. 4:11

$\mathcal{A}$lice's parents recently separated and she now lives with her mother. Her father has moved to another state several hundred miles away. One day Alice was at the airport on her way to visit her father. She felt very scared and clung to her mother. She wondered if her father had changed. What would his house be like? Where would she sleep? She also wondered if Mommy would be scared and lonely. Would Mommy even be here when she came back?

A child who has to travel back and forth between parents may have many fears. She may need a lot of extra reassurance. Her fears might seem irrational, but they are not irrational to her. It's important to comfort her, and to reassure her that you will be there waiting for her at the place where she said goodbye. Tell her it's okay to enjoy herself and to have a good time with the other parent.

If you are the parent who is being visited, make sure your child has someplace in the house that is her own space—if possible her own room where she can keep her things. Make her feel welcome and loved, but not guilty when she has to say goodbye.

▼ *Dear Father, You know how difficult it is for children whose parents do not live together. Please help them to cope with this change, and help both of their parents to assist them through the transition.*

LB

PLAY

*The LORD is my strength and my
shield;
My heart trusted in Him,
and I am helped;
Therefore my heart greatly rejoices,
And with my song I will praise Him.*
—PS. 28:7

Sometimes when I sing I am worshipping the Father.
Other times I catch myself singing just to sing. I feel
safe and I have no worries or cares. It's as if my heart is
at play—free to enjoy the moment. As adults, it is hard
to play, but it is still a necessary part of life.

Children accomplish many important things through
playing. It allows them to be children and not grow up
too fast. It prepares them to mature when the time is
right for them. It builds confidence and feelings of em-
powerment. Playing helps children to understand who
they are and to develop good social skills.

Play is also an excellent means for children to express and understand their emotions. They can release
fear, anger, and stress while drawing, building blocks,
or playing good guys and bad guys. They also may deal
with their emotions by playacting the outcomes they
wish would happen. It is interesting to notice how children will only play when they feel completely at ease—
when they feel safe and secure. It is our job as parents
to provide a world in which our children are free to play.

▼ *Dear God, help me to allow my children to play and
teach me the importance of play in my own life.*

GC

CAUSE AND AFFECT

Do not be deceived, God is not mocked; for whatever a man sows, that he will also reap.
—GAL. 6:7

$\mathcal{I}$ was tired of school and decided I needed a day off. I told my mother I felt terrible with a headache and sore throat, neither of which was disputable. She agreed I should stay home. What a glorious day! I got to do all the things I wanted to do, and I felt good enough to enjoy them. I even got special attention from my mother. When school was out, my friends started knocking on the door for me to come out to play. I was devastated when I heard my mother tell them I was too sick to play. It was miserable to hear them having fun. Never again did I try that tactic. I learned more from the natural consequences than all the lectures I could have heard.

Discipline is a hard taskmaster. Parents feel it is something they have to do to their child, but discipline really works better if it is something the child does to himself. Instead of rescuing or lecturing our children, we need to allow them to experience the consequences of their behavior. Natural consequences make an impact that we could never make.

▼ *Dear Father, cause and effect is an important principle. Don't let me get in the way of that lesson.*

JS

MONSTERS IN THE CLOSETS

" 'Fear not, for I am with you;
Be not dismayed, for I am your God.
I will strengthen you,
Yes, I will help you,
I will uphold you with My righteous
*   right hand.' "*
—ISA. 41:10

*R*emember at night when you used to check under the bed, behind the drapes, and then in the closet for those boogie monsters the older kids told you about? Then when the lights went out, every shadow looked like a person or monster. To a young child, those shadows look very real. He may really believe that there are monsters in his closet or under his bed. He may be truly terrified.

If your child is afraid of monsters, let him know you are nearby and will be there if needed. But it's more important to help the child believe in his own abilities. He can learn that he is more powerful than the monster and that he can overcome it. Teach him to use his imagination in a positive way to overcome his fear and gain control. Have him pretend he is a superhero, conquering the monsters. Or, even better, have him picture Jesus there with him, protecting him from the monsters. Then, teach him to pray for God's protection from all the monsters of life.

▼ *Father, help me to teach my children that You are their Rock—that with You they do not have to be afraid.*

LB

A GOOD FOUNDATION

Rejoice, O young man, in your youth, . . .
Walk in the ways of your heart,
And in the sight of your eyes;
But know that for all these
God will bring you into judgment.
                                        —ECCL. 11:9

John sat in my office and reflected on his childhood. He had many pleasant memories. He told of fishing trips with his father, riding his bike during long summer days, of laughing with his brother after playing a joke on dear Mom. His childhood was predominantly a positive one—unlike the childhoods of many who meet with me.

John was thankful for his parents and the home they had provided for him. Yet most of all John was thankful for how his parents presented Jesus to him. They never preached to him or pressured him. They loved him and treated him with respect. As a result he had come to know God not only as an all-loving, caring Father, but as One to be revered and viewed with awe.

John shared that he became a Christian early in his life but his older brother came to know Him much later. In comparing how he and his brother got through their teenage years, he expressed hope that his own children would know the Savior in their youth.

Create positive memories and Christian experiences for your children as they grow. They will never be children again.

▼ *Dear God, teach me what it means to come to You as a child.*

BUILDING ON ROCK

"He is like a man building a house, who dug deep and laid the foundation on the rock."
—LUKE 6:48

*W*hen my son was sixteen, he was six feet tall and towered over me. I remember one time I told him he could not use the car to go out. He chose to obey me.

I was very much aware that had he decided to be rebellious, there was no way I could have kept him from taking the keys and using the car. The only tool I had was the relationship we had built on love and respect. That started when he was two years of age or even earlier.

When a child turns thirteen, it's too late to start building a relationship with him and hoping to gain his respect. You need to begin much earlier. When he becomes a teenager, that relationship will pay off if it has been established. Your teen still may not always do what you say, but at least the relationship he has with you will impact his behavior to some degree. In reality, your past relationship probably will have more bearing than the present circumstances. The foundation you have laid will set the stage for the teen years and the future.

▼ *Dear Lord, I want to lay good foundations—with You and with my children. Please help me.*

JS

STORYTELLING

Then He spoke many things to them in parables, saying: "Behold, a sower went out to sow."
—MATT. 13:3

Sandra is five years old. She is very afraid of going to her father's house this summer because her parents have just been divorced. She wonders if her mother will be at home when she returns or if her mother will have left her. She wonders if she will have friends to play with at her father's.

Sandra's grandmother was visiting one day and picked up on Sandra's fears. She began to help Sandra by telling her a story about a little girl just like Sandra who was going on a trip to a far-away place. The child in her story learned how to cope with everything new as gifts from God. And so did Sandra through this great example.

Storytelling is an excellent way to help a child work through anxiety and fear. Remember Jesus' example. He taught in parables, knowing that we learn and understand better through stories.

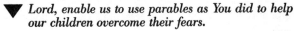 *Lord, enable us to use parables as You did to help our children overcome their fears.*

LB

TAKING CHARGE

> *"They should repent, turn to God, and do*
> *works befitting repentance."*
>
> —ACTS 26:20

*E*ric was an attractive young boy. He could have been a child model—selling cereal or maybe a children's cough medicine. He just had that certain look about him. Very irresistible, innocent, and endearing. It was obvious he knew it too!

Eric would often get into some kind of trouble and be caught red-handed. But somehow when people saw that "I didn't mean to!" look on his face, he would be completely absolved.

When his parents realized the manipulative nature of this scenario, they quickly changed a few things. They followed through with consequences. They held Eric responsible for all his actions—cute face or not!

At first Eric fought the drastic change, but soon he learned there were real consequences to his behavior. His troublemaking behavior was soon significantly curtailed.

Today, Eric is a young man. He is still attractive in appearance, but now he is attractive on the inside as well.

 Dear God, help me understand the true meaning of repentance. Help me teach my children, even through my own example.

GC

EVERYBODY'S DOING IT

But the excellence of knowledge
is that wisdom gives life
to those who have it.
—ECCL. 7:12

*E*verybody's doing it." Don't believe it for a moment. Yes, some people are doing it, but is that what you want for your teenagers? Is that even what your teenagers want for themselves?

Before you can come up with the answer, you need to understand the question and its ramifications. You need to have a listening conversation with your teen. Assess the situation to learn how important it is to your teen, to understand his feelings, and to clarify what he is really asking.

One time my teen asked to go out with a group. He was really insistent. The more I pressed for information, the more obvious it became that alcohol was involved in the outing. Finally I took a hard line and said absolutely no. To my surprise, there was an immediate sigh of relief, and that was the end of it. It's much easier for the parent to be the bad guy. Parents are the ones who are not "cool"—not the teen.

The point is to know what your teen needs and expects from you. The main thing they need is firm guidance and a genuine interest in their best interest.

▼ *Dear heavenly Father, being a parent demands great wisdom. The only place I can get that is from You.*

JS

COPING WITH PAIN

Trust in the LORD forever,
For in YAH, the LORD,
is everlasting strength.
—ISA. 26:4

$\mathcal{I}$t was time for seven-year-old Jeff's yearly flu shot. He came running home after school in tears. "Mommy, Mommy, I don't want a shot. I'm scared it will hurt!"

Mom said to Jeff, "Together we can work on it hurting less. It will still hurt some, but not as bad as you fear." She reminded him of the time he fell off his bike. "Remember how you got right back on it because you were racing against Pete. Later you saw all that blood and hadn't even noticed it hurting?"

"I remember," Jeff replied.

"Well, the reason you feel pain, Jeff, is because it goes to your brain. If you block it out, the pain will decrease."

"How do I do that?" Jeff asked.

"You can try to think of something else," mother said. "How about when you get the shot, you daydream about how your favorite chocolate chip ice cream tastes. And you also can ask God to help you block out the pain." Children have great imaginations. With practice they can learn techniques to tolerate painful things like shots and the dentist.

▼ *Dear God, we praise You for our imaginations and for the ability to relax and let go of pain.*

LB

UNHEALTHY DEPENDENCIES

"As the Father loved Me, I also have loved you; abide in My love." —JOHN 15:9

$\mathcal{A}$t first appearance, Vicki was the quintessential mother. She was always energetic, always caring, and always sacrificing. But on closer inspection, one could see trouble brewing.

Vicki had grown up in an unaffectionate family. There were few "I love you's," few physical touches, and many double messages about her parents' commitment to their daughter.

Through therapy, Vicki uncovered her strong fear of rejection and abandonment but only as it related to her own childhood. She could not see how it was affecting the parenting of her own children.

Vicki feared the rejection of her children. She was dependent on them for her own security. As a result, she became a slave to their every whim or dissatisfaction. When they wanted it, she got it. When they needed it, she sacrificed. This was the beginning of many difficulties for Vicki, not to mention her children.

Low self-worth and depression followed before Vicki was able to address honestly the true source of her insecurity. She eventually found the security she lacked in the one true God.

▼ *Dear God, help me to understand the difference between true love and unhealthy dependency.*

GC

CHAOS AND STABILITY

Jesus Christ is the same yesterday, today, and forever.
                                        —HEB. 13:8

*M*y fifteen-year-old daughter sat at the kitchen table for a long time discussing the upcoming presidential elections. She knew the platforms for both candidates and how labor and farm lobbies stood. She asked my opinion and gave her own. I must say I enjoyed our conversation. *This is what it is all about,* I thought to myself. *She has grown into adulthood and can carry on meaningful, thought provoking discussions.* As I patted myself on the back, she walked straight into the living room and started a fight with her little sister over a piece of candy.

Dealing with an adult one minute and a child the next is extremely confusing. You never know which you are dealing with because they change so fast. The one thing they need during this time is a solid foundation. Just as God promised to be the same yesterday, today, and forever, the basic structure of the family needs to be solid and consistent because everything else in the lives of teenagers is in chaos. Flexibility can be helpful, but only when it doesn't erode the basic principles of the family. Both parents and teens need to find the strength and stability only God can provide.

▼ *Dear God, give me the strength to stand firm for my adolescent in the midst of chaos.*

JS

"Which of you by worrying can add one cubit to his stature?" —MATT. 6:27

*J*onathan's fear was crippling him. He was afraid of being around certain things and people—a condition known as agoraphobia. He no longer went with his parents to restaurants, and now he was beginning to avoid going to school. He was worried and obsessed about everything. But Jonathan was especially worried about losing his mother. He learned how to overcome his fear as he and his mother learned to talk.

The Lord Jesus tells us not to worry. But how do we do it? God teaches us by asking us to trust in Him, even in situations we cannot control. We learn how to let go and believe He will care for us.

Ask yourself, *Whom do I trust?* It doesn't help to say, "Don't worry, be happy!" That's like saying, "Don't think of pink elephants." You automatically do, don't you? We need to confirm what and whom we trust in our rational thought process.

Sometimes like us adults, children may have irrational thoughts. With a lot of talking about what we fear, we can help them change irrational worries to rational truth. God tells us to stop our irrational worrying and cast our eyes on Him.

▼ *Dear God, help me to cast all my cares upon You.*

LB

PRIDE

*"And whoever exalts himself will be abased,
and he who humbles himself will be exalted."*
—MATT. 23:12

$\mathcal{G}$reg complained of feeling distant from his children. "They never come to me with their problems." Randy had a similar charge. "They never tell me what's going on." Lee's concern appeared somewhat different but was really the same. "We just can't seem to have fun with each other." What these three gentlemen had in common was a tremendous sense of pride.

Pride is one thing teens can sense a mile a way. It is too threatening and too phony. They won't tolerate it in a relationship with anyone—much less their parents.

Unfortunately many parents, especially men, have grown up with much insecurity in their lives. To cover their fears and feelings of low self-worth, they have developed a prideful arrogance. They especially feel the pressure to be someone they are not, and in fact can never be—a perfect parent. I'm sorry, that animal just doesn't exist.

Of course, we all want our children to respect us. But we should want them to relate to us first. Don't be a towering genius with all the right answers. Be a tender grown-up with all the time and patience.

▼ *Dear God, help me to stay close to my children when they need me and grow apart in a healthy way at the right time.*

GC

THAT'S THE BOOK FOR ME

"Now, O Israel, listen to the statutes and the judgments which I teach you to observe, that you may live, and go in and possess the land which the LORD God of your fathers is giving you."
—DEUT. 4:1

Reading the Bible is not something children automatically enjoy. The language of the Bible is hard to understand, and the Bible doesn't usually have pictures. Dr. Seuss catches their attention more readily. But the Bible contains the information they need to know about life and how to live it.

As a child, I remember sitting on my dad's lap as he read the Bible to me. He read so fast I could hardly understand what it meant. Then he would explain it to me. Bible reading became very important to me. I realized the Bible was very important to my dad, and he wanted to share it with me. It served as a precious time between us. As I got older, I knew where to look for answers to the questions I faced. I also always remembered curling up on my dad's lap.

We teach our children by how we live our lives. What better way to learn about our heavenly Father than reading His Word on our father's lap. Relationships speak louder than all the words.

▼ *Please help me, Lord, to teach Your truths to my children through the love You impart to me.*

JS

SLEEP DEPRIVATION

*"The LORD grant that you may find rest,
each in the house of her husband."*
—RUTH 1:9

*C*onnie said to her friend, "I don't seem to get much sleep anymore. My four kids are driving me crazy. My husband doesn't understand and is rarely home to help me. I feel so depressed. I feel like giving up and running away."

Many moms and dads feel like this—tired and worn-out, unsupported, and very unhappy. One of the major causes is sleep deprivation. If you have an infant or younger children, you simply may not be getting the sleep you need. As a result you find yourself exhausted and very irritable with everyone. One friend often reminds me that concentration camps and cults use sleep deprivation as a tool to control a person's mind. No wonder we are wiped out and delusional at times!

God never meant for us not to get enough sleep. He encourages us to take good care of our physical body—the temple in which the Holy Spirit lives. Sleep is not a luxury, but a necessity. So when slumber seems like an impossible dream and you wonder who will relieve you so you can sleep, ask God to provide that relief. God will relieve us usually through someone we know to take care of the kids so we can rest.

▼ *Father, I know I need to take care of my children. But while I do that, will You please take care of me?*
LB

AVOIDING CONFLICT

Let us search out and
examine our ways,
And turn back to the LORD.
—LAM. 3:40

A sure way to create a dysfunctional family is to pro-mote denial. Jack and Cathy did so for years, although it was not so obvious. While they were engaged, they seemed to be the perfect couple. They never argued or had any type of conflict. When they married, they wanted the perfect marriage—so much so, that they avoided all conflict.

Over the years they became experts at avoiding con-flicts and denying feelings. They never discussed feel-ings about big issues like budgeting, nor did they talk about their feelings when it came to the little things like dirty towels on the bathroom floor. All the while, every-one seemed happy—or at least so it appeared.

When problems are not addressed and feelings are not expressed, resentment builds. As denial continues, unresolved resentment becomes depression. The tragic result is that true intimacy with your spouse and your children becomes difficult, if not impossible.

Fortunately Jack and Cathy sought help. Will you seek help if you need it?

▼ *Lord, help me not to deny feelings or conflicts in my home. Show me what I can do to promote intimacy, not avoidance.*

GC

CAMPING TRIPS

According to the command of the LORD they would remain encamped, and according to the command of the LORD they would journey.
—NUM. 9:20

*C*amping is a great way for families to relate to each other. For a short time it puts parents and children on the same footing with few of the normal life stresses. It also gives the family an opportunity to figure out how to do things and solve problems together.

I overheard a conversation about a camping trip to the beach. One person said she had never been camping. The only time she went to the beach the wind blew hard, the tent filled up with sand, and the mosquitos almost carried them away. Their food was sandy and they got sunburned. Her friend responded, "You *did* go camping. That is exactly what happens on camping trips." The unexpected often happens on camping trips. Sometimes it rains. Other times the tent may collapse. But that doesn't make it an unsuccessful experience. In fact, those are the memories you will talk about. Everything does not have to be perfect to have a wonderful time.

 Dear Lord, prepare me for the unexpected things in life and help me to use them to build positive memories.

JS

SIBLING ABUSE

"He may command his children and his household after him, that they keep the way of the LORD, to do righteousness and justice."
—GEN. 18:19

$\mathcal{I}$t is one of the toughest realities to face—older siblings can emotionally and physically abuse a younger child. If this happens and is not corrected, the younger sibling may later feel very inferior and insecure. Kids are cruel to each other, but the degree depends on what is happening in the family.

I remember an older child who was very cruel to my son. I thought this was strange because my son was so much smaller. As I began to talk with this boy, he shared with me that his older brother did the same thing to him. So I talked to his older brother and found out that the father does the same thing to him. Now it makes sense. It comes from somewhere. Children are very impressionable. So who needs therapy in this family? The whole family does. The two brothers, the father, and the mother who is equally involved even if she is quiet.

▼ *God, help us to be healthy models for our children, and help us not to sin against them.*

LB

INTENTIONAL PARENTING

Therefore let us not sleep, as others do, but let us watch and be sober.
—1 THESS. 5:6

Stephen and Cindy had two great kids. Both teens, they were leaders in their high school. Kind and respectful, disciplined and fun loving, they were well liked by adults and their peers. The daughter was headed for college and a later degree in law. Their son was planning on college and seminary.

Even before their first born, Stephen and Cindy decided to be intentional in their parenting. They decided they would be involved parents. They attended open houses, PTA meetings, and school plays. Stephen even made it a point to attend all his son's football games. They planned family activities and made sure they were fun. They shared in their children's lives at church, school, and at home. In a phrase, they walked and talked with their children as they grew into adults.

Stephen and Cindy also attended workshops, lectures, and read loads of books. They learned how to relate to and respect their kids. They also learned the importance of watching their children mature at a distance. Every parent needs to be of a sober mind and watch their children. We need to pay attention to our children so they won't have to go to extremes to get it.

▼ *Dear God, thank You for the privilege of watching my children grow.*

GC

TEXAS SNOWFALLS

He gives snow like wool;
He scatters the frost like ashes.
—PS. 147:16

*L*iving in Texas makes snow a glorious event. The world is covered with a blanket of white. Quietness prevails. It's a time of giggles and snuggles. Boots and mittens are resurrected, and the dryer hums all the time to keep everything dry. Dry mittens get everyone ready for another bout in the snow.

The best thing is that the hectic pace comes to a complete standstill. In Texas people do not know how to drive in snow. Schools and businesses close, and everyone has a forced mini-vacation. Even though the adults complain, everyone really looks forward to at least one snowfall a year.

We need to stop and recharge. What better way than to have a snowfall? It provides time to laugh and to giggle, to build a snowman, and to improvise a sled. It is interesting that snow can turn serious adults into giddy children who are always ready for a snowball fight. God does know our needs and provides unique ways to meet them.

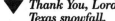 *Thank You, Lord, for the quietness and beauty of a Texas snowfall.*

JS

PARENTS AND IN-LAWS

*"Can a woman forget her nursing child,
And not have compassion on the son of
her womb?"*
—ISA. 49:15

*W*endy's two boys are a bit rambunctious and a handful to keep up with. She feels her parents make her job harder with their messages that the children have to be "gotten under control." A two-year-old and a three-year-old "under control"? Right! Children are children. They're acting their age. Wendy didn't feel much support from her in-laws either.

When Wendy took the children to visit her in-laws, they communicated loud and clear that she could do nothing right. She let them get away with too much or too little. She gave them too much or too little. She disciplined them too much or too little. What is a parent to do?

At times we all feel as if we are being persecuted by Pharisees. They thought Jesus was all wrong and constantly abused Him. Our Lord understands when we need a break. We can go to Him for refuge and support.

Despite other "expert" opinions on how to raise our children, God is the best expert. He loves us and gives us direction; He doesn't criticize. He helps us every step of the way, even with our own parents!

▼ *Father, thank You for being a refuge and a counselor as we raise our children.*

LB

OTHER BOOKS IN
THE MINIRTH-MEIER SERIES

Passages of Marriage Study Guide Series
New Love Study Guide
Realistic Love Study Guide
Steadfast Love Study Guide
Renewing Love Study Guide
Transcendent Love Study Guide
    Dr. Frank and Mary Alice Minirth, Drs. Brian and Deborah Newman,
    Dr. Robert and Susan Hemfelt

The Path to Serenity
    Dr. Robert Hemfelt, Dr. Frank Minirth, Dr. Richard Fowler,
Dr. Paul Meier

Please Let Me Know You, God
    Dr. Larry Stephens

The Quest
    Kevin J. Brown, Ray Mitsch

Steps to a New Beginning
    Sam Shoemaker, Dr. Frank Minirth, Dr. Richard Fowler,
    Dr. Brian Newman, Dave Carder

The Thin Disguise
    Pam Vredevelt, Dr. Deborah Newman, Harry Beverly,
Dr. Frank Minirth

Thngs That Go Bump in the Night
    Dr. Paul Warren, Dr. Frank Minirth

The Truths We Must Believe
    Dr. Chris Thurman

Together on a Tightrope
    Dr. Richard Fowler, Rita Schweitz

Hope for the Perfectionist
    Dr. David Stoop

For general information about other Minirth-Meier Clinic branch offices, counseling services, educational resources and hospital programs, call toll-free 1-800-545-1819. National Headquarters: (214) 669-1733 (800) 229-3000.

About the Authors

Guy Chandler leads family counseling sessions in the inpatient and outpatient facilities at the Minirth-Meier Clinic in Richardson, Texas.

Laura A. Brown is a hospital therapist and outpatient counselor at the Minirth-Meier Clinic in Richardson, Texas.

Jane Swindell maintains an active counseling practice at the Minirth-Meier Clinic and the Minirth-Meier Day Hospital.